GW00725432

# SOUTHERN AFRICA
# ACTIVITY ATLAS

FIRST EDITION PUBLISHED IN 2004 BY
MAP STUDIO

WWW.MAPSTUDIO.CO.ZA
0860 10 50 50

**HEAD OFFICE**
Cornelis Struik House
80 McKenzie Street
Cape Town
Tel: 021 462 4360

PO Box 1144
Cape Town, 8000

**SALES OFFICES**
Map Studio Johannesburg
7 Wessel Road, Rivonia
Tel: 011 807 2292

Map Studio Cape Town
Unit 7, M5 Freeway Park
Maitland
Tel: 021 510 4311

Map Studio Durban
Shop 3A, 47 Intersite Avenue
Umgeni Park
Tel: 031 263 1203

ISBN: 1 86809 758 7
10 9 8 7 6 5 4 3 2 1

Printed in Singapore by
Tien Wah Press (Pte) Ltd.

Copyright © 2004 in text: Map Studio
Copyright © 2004 in maps: Map Studio
Copyright © 2004 in photographs:
Photographers as credited
  (see Contact Details, spread 96)
Copyright © 2004 Map Studio

All rights reserved. No part of this publica-
tion may be reproduced, stored in a retrieval
system or transmitted, in any form or by any
means, electronic, mechanical, photocopying,
recording or otherwise, without the permission of the publishers and copyright holders.

Although every effort has been made to
ensure that this guide is up to date and current at time of going to print, the publisher
accepts no responsibility or liability for any
loss, injury or inconvenience incurred by
readers or travellers using this guide.

**MAP STUDIO TOURIST TEAM**
Dénielle Lategan
Edward Hill
Elaine Fick
John Loubser
Lois O'Brien
Maryna Beukes
Myrna Collins
Ryan Africa
Simon Lewis
Broderick Kupka (Sales: Johannesburg)
Gina Moniz (Sales: Cape Town / Durban)

Special thanks to Marielle Rènssen,
Sean Fraser and Fiona McIntosh for
their contributions.

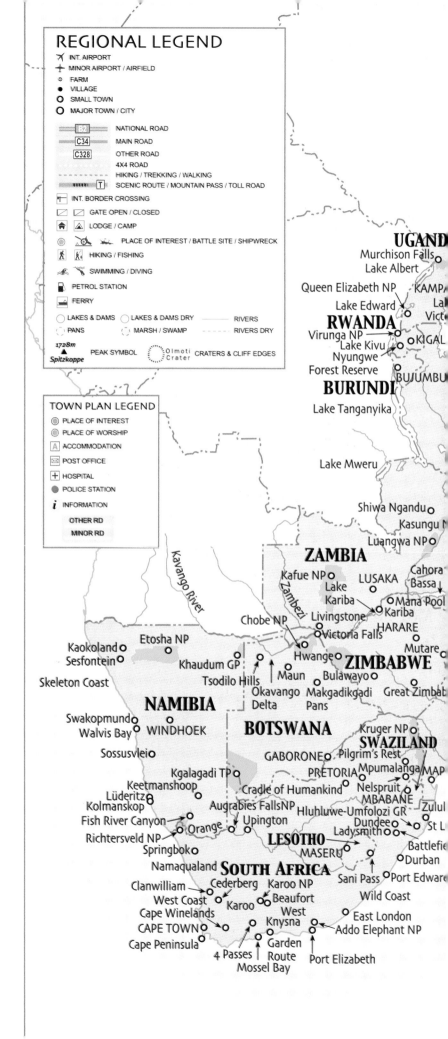

## REGIONAL LEGEND

- ✈ INT. AIRPORT
- ✈ MINOR AIRPORT / AIRFIELD
- ○ FARM
- ● VILLAGE
- ◎ SMALL TOWN
- ◎ MAJOR TOWN / CITY

- NATIONAL ROAD
- C34 MAIN ROAD
- C328 OTHER ROAD
- 4X4 ROAD
- HIKING / TREKKING / WALKING
- T SCENIC ROUTE / MOUNTAIN PASS / TOLL ROAD

- INT. BORDER CROSSING
- GATE OPEN / CLOSED
- LODGE / CAMP
- PLACE OF INTEREST / BATTLE SITE / SHIPWRECK
- HIKING / FISHING
- SWIMMING / DIVING
- PETROL STATION
- FERRY

- LAKES & DAMS   LAKES & DAMS DRY   RIVERS
- PANS   MARSH / SWAMP   RIVERS DRY

- 1728m ▲ Spitzkoppe   PEAK SYMBOL   Olmoti Crater   CRATERS & CLIFF EDGES

## TOWN PLAN LEGEND

- ◎ PLACE OF INTEREST
- ◎ PLACE OF WORSHIP
- A ACCOMMODATION
- ✉ POST OFFICE
- + HOSPITAL
- ● POLICE STATION
- i INFORMATION
- OTHER RD
- MINOR RD

Lake
Turkana

**KENYA**
Marsabit NR
Aberdare Losai NR
NP
Masai Buffalo Springs NR
Mara NP Mt Kenya NP
NAIROBI
engeti Nairobi NP
Tsavo NP Lamu
rongoro Amboseli NP
rater Malindi
angire NP Kilimanjaro Mombasa
Arusha NP Pemba Island
DOMA Zanzibar
**ANZANIA** DAR ES SALAAM
Mafia Island
Selous GR
**SEYCHELLES**
Praslin Island
**COMOROS** Mahé Island
Aldabra Islands
Montagne d'Ambre NP
Ankarana SR
yika NP
Lake Malawi
LONGWE
Monkey Bay Mozambique Island
Liwonde NP
**MALAWI**
**MOZAMBIQUE** Analamazaotra
(Périnet SR) **MAURITIUS**
ANTANANARIVO Rodrigues Island
rongosa NP
eira **MADAGASCAR**
**RÉUNION**
Bazaruto Archipelago **(FRANCE)**
nhambane

COUNTRIES COVERED BY THIS ATLAS

O    CITIES, TOWNS, REGIONS & SITES

# CONTENTS

# Southern African History

**BOTSWANA**
Believed to have been occupied by the ancient San people for over 30,000 years.

**COMOROS**
Shiraz Arab royal clans arrived from the 1600s onwards and built mosques and an infrastructure; French mercenary Bob Denard put down rebellions and coups in the 1970s.

**KENYA**
Footprints on Kenyan soil date back to 2000BC, while the bloody Mau Mau rebellion of the 1950s left over 13,500 dead in a failed attempt at driving white settlers out of the land.

**LESOTHO**
Moshoeshoe the Great established territory in the 1820s through to the 1840s with a bit of help from the British.

**MADAGASCAR**
The British attacked and briefly colonised Madagascar during WWII to prevent the Japanese from taking the country, thus establishing a major Indian Ocean powerbase.

**MALAWI**
Intrepid explorer David Livingstone was reportedly the first white man to lay eyes on Lake Malawi – he named the great water mass Lake Nyasa.

**MAURITIUS**
Frequented by Arab traders for more than a thousand years, it was once known as Ile de France after the Dutch had given up their claims to it (along with killing off the dodo).

**MOZAMBIQUE**
The MLF (aka Frelimo) waged a 10-year war of liberation which they won in the mid-1970s. The immediate withdrawal of the Portuguese left the country in economic turmoil.

**SUDAN**
**(ANGLO-EGYPTIA**
**SUDAN)**

**UGAND**

**RWANDA**
**(GERMAN EAST AFRICA)**
RUANDA-URUNDI
(BELGIUM)

**DEMOCRATIC**
**REPUBLIC**
**OF THE CONGO**
**(BELGIAN CONGO)**

**BURUNDI**
**(GERMAN EAST AFRICA)**
*Lake*
*Tanganyika*

La
Victo

Suku

Nyamwe

**ANGOLA**

Barotseland

**MALAWI**
**(NYASALAN**
Bemba

**ZAMBIA**
**(NORTHERN RHODESIA)**

*Lake*
*Kariba*

Mar

*Zambezi*

**HARARE**
(Salisbury)
○

Sho

**ZIMBABWE**
**(RHODESIA)**
Matabeleland

**NAMIBIA**
**(SOUTH WEST**
**AFRICA)**

Herero

Hereroland

Khoisan

*Orange*

**BOTSWANA**
**(BECHUANALAND)**
Tswana

Ndebele

Nguni

**SWAZILAND**
Boers ○ MAP

Tswana

**LESOTHO**
**(BASUTOLAND)**
Sotho

Boers

**SOUTH AFRICA**
**(UNION OF SOUTH AFRICA)**
Khoisan

Zulu

CAPE TOWN ○ Cape Colony
(Cape of Good Hope,
Dutch Settlement 1652)

(British)

DIAS 1487 to 1488
Reaches the Great Fish River

SOME FAMOUS MOMENTS IN THE HISTORY OF SOUTHERN AFRICA

| 1498 | Da Gama brings 'Portugal' to Mozambique | 1652 | Jan van Riebeeck estab- lishes a base at Cape Town | 1800 | 80–100,000 Africans are sold into slav- ery annually | 1820 | British se start tar SA's c and int |

← SPANISH MOROCCO
MOROCCO

RIO DE ORO

FRENCH WEST AFRICA

EGYPT

ERITREA
FRENCH
SOMALILAND
BRITISH
SOMALILAND

ANGLO
EGYPTIAN
SUDAN

ETHIOPIA

FRENCH EQUATORIAL AFRICA

BELGIAN
CONGO

ITALIAN
SOMALILAND

KENYA
BRITISH EAST
AFRICA)
Masai
Kikuyu

SOMALIA
(ITALIAN
SOMALILAND)

ANGOLA

MOMBASA
(Dutch port in the 1600s)

ZANZIBAR
(Portuguese port in the 1600s)

ANGANYIKA
(BRITISH)

TANZANIA
(GERMAN EAST
AFRICA)

COLONIAL RULE 1913
BRITISH
GERMAN
FRENCH
PORTUGUESE
BELGIAN
ITALIAN
SPANISH

DA GAMA 1497 to 1499
Uses Dias' route to reach India

COMOROS

SEYCHELLES

MOZAMBIQUE
(Mozambique, Portuguese
port in the 1600s)

Yao

MOZAMBIQUE
(PORTUGUESE
EAST AFRICA)

MAURITIUS
(ILE DE FRANCE)

MADAGASCAR

RÉUNION

OFALA
ofala, Portuguese port
the 1600s)

Opposite page: statue of David
Livingstone in Zimbabwe.
Right: statue of Cecil John Rhodes
in Cape Town, South Africa.

urenço Marques & Delagoa Bay)

DISCOVERIES TRACING EARLY MAN
MAJOR VOYAGES OF DISCOVERY
Khoisan          1600-1800 PEOPLE / REGIONS
Ndebele          1800-1880 PEOPLE / REGIONS
NYASALAND)       1913 COUNTRY NAMES
RUANDA-URUNDI     1939 COUNTRY NAMES
(BELGIUM)
ZAMBIA           2004 COUNTRY NAMES

PREVIOUSLY KNOWN AS
BOTSWANA      Bechuanaland
KENYA         British East Africa
LESOTHO       Basutoland
MALAWI        Nyasaland
MOZAMBIQUE    Portuguese East Africa
NAMIBIA       South West Africa
MAURITIUS     Ile de France
ZAMBIA        Northern Rhodesia
ZIMBABWE      Rhodesia

## NAMIBIA
Ignored by colonial powers for its harsh and desolate nature, the country was largely a set of coastal hotspots for trading and refreshments … until diamonds were discovered in the early 1900s.

## RÉUNION (FRANCE)
Traded back and forth by colonial powers, the British introduced sugar crops which became one of the island's great cash cows.

## SEYCHELLES
Originally used as a base for Caribbean pirates in search of fresh waters and treasures in the Indian Ocean. South African mercenaries led a failed coup here in the 1980s.

## SOUTH AFRICA
Many territorial wars were fought between the British, Boers and Zulus in Natal. The voortrekkers dragged their wagons into the interior in a monumental effort at establishing towns throughout the interior.

## SWAZILAND
A magnet for the great white hunters, traders and missionaries, by 1968 the country was largely-Swazi controlled and run by a succession of Zulu kings.

## TANZANIA
Journalist Henry Stanley finally tracked down the missing explorer David Livingstone on the banks of Lake Tanganyika, reportedly bursting forth with his timeless (and often repeated) quote: "Dr Livingstone, I presume."

## ZAMBIA
Livingstone wandered around Zambia in the 1850s, ploughing the Zambezi River in search of a route to the interior on his mission to bring christianity and 'civilisation' to the people.

## ZIMBABWE
The ruins at Great Zimbabwe hide a mystery of a thriving and affluent agricultural and trading society dating back to the 11th century.

04 | Namibia's Herero and Nama rebellion is crushed | 1967 | Botswana's fortunes change as diamonds are discovered | 1980 | Robert Mugabe wins control of Zimbabwe | 1994 | South Africa holds its first democratic elections

**BOTSWANA**
Traditional Tswana food and home-baked bread (*Shakawe*); Sir Seretse Khama, Mpule Kwelagobe (Miss Universe 1999).

**COMOROS**
Comorian cuisine; Ali Soilih (the leader of a successful coup, he was later shot dead by Bob Denard's mercenaries).

**KENYA**
Carved gourds, beads, makonde (ebony) wood carvings; authors Kuki Galman and Ngugi wa Thiong'o, World Cup cricket captain Steve Tikolo, President Daniel Arap Moi.

**LESOTHO**
Basotho grass hats, carpets and woven jerseys from Teyateyaneng ('the place of quick sands'); author Thomas Mofolo.

**MADAGASCAR**
Local wine, a ticket to a *hira gasy* performance; author Michèle Rakotoson.

**MALAWI**
Roasted locusts in Lilongwe; author Paul Tiyambe Zeleza, former president Hastings Banda.

**MAURITIUS**
A T-shirt with a dodo on it; author Edouard J Maunick.

**MOZAMBIQUE**
Donations to the landmine clearing fund, leatherwork; Joaquim Chissano & Samora Michel, author Mia Couto.

**HIGHEST HUMAN DENSITY
294 PER KM²**

+7 MILLION
**RWANDA**
3%   KIGALI

BUJUMBURA
+6,5 MILLION
2% **BURUNDI**

*Lake Tanganyika*

+10 MILLION
**ZAMBIA**
3%   LUSAKA
*Lake Kariba*

*Zambezi*

HARARE

+12 MILLION
**ZIMBABWE**
3%

+1,5 MILLION
**NAMIBIA**
3%
WINDHOEK

+1,5 MILLION
**BOTSWANA**
3%

GABORONE
+1 MILLION
**SWAZILAND**
PRETORIA
MBABANE

+2 MILLION
**LESOTHO**
BLOEMFONTEIN
MASERU

+43.5 MILLION
**SOUTH AFRICA**
3%

CAPE TOWN
+2.3 MILLION

*Orange*

Left: Maputo skyline at sunrise.
Opposite page: downtown Nairobi (Kenya), and Tanzania's Maasai women in traditional clothing.

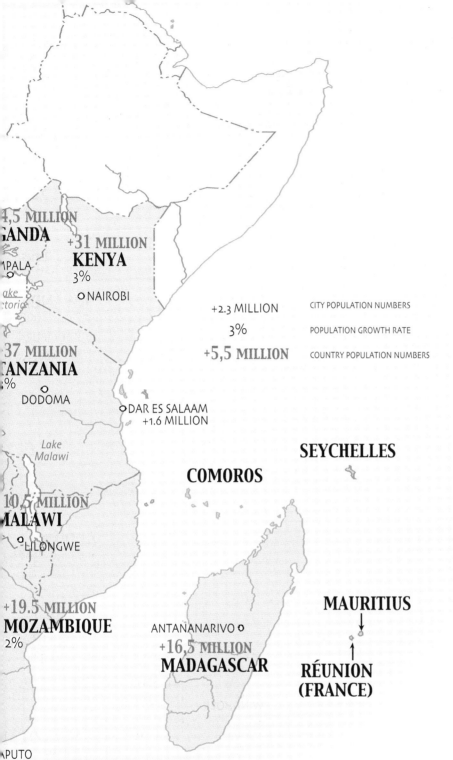

+4,5 MILLION
**GANDA**
KAMPALA
3%
Lake Victoria
o NAIROBI

+31 MILLION
**KENYA**
3%

+37 MILLION
**TANZANIA**
3%
DODOMA

o DAR ES SALAAM
+1.6 MILLION

Lake Malawi

+10,5 MILLION
**MALAWI**
o LILONGWE

+19,5 MILLION
**MOZAMBIQUE**
2%

**COMOROS**

**SEYCHELLES**

ANTANANARIVO o
+16,5 MILLION
**MADAGASCAR**

**MAURITIUS**
↓
↑
**RÉUNION
(FRANCE)**

+2.3 MILLION — CITY POPULATION NUMBERS

3% — POPULATION GROWTH RATE

+5,5 MILLION — COUNTRY POPULATION NUMBERS

MAPUTO

**NAMIBIA**
Local 'German' beer, woodcarvings and baskets; athlete Frank Fredericks, Michelle McLean (former Miss Universe).

**RÉUNION (FRANCE)**
Creole meals; poet and painter Léon Dierx.

**SEYCHELLES**
A coco de mer nut; artist Michael Adams, Esmeralda (the island's 150-year-old tortoise).

**SOUTH AFRICA**
Decorated ostrich eggs; human rights icon and former president Nelson Mandela, author Wilbur Smith, former rugby captain Francois Pienaar.

**SWAZILAND**
Local craftwork; King Sobhuza II.

**TANZANIA**
Makonde (ebony) carvings; the late Freddie Mercury (lead singer of rock group *Queen*).

**ZAMBIA**
Reed and papyrus mats, semi-precious stones, *chitenjes* cloth, wooden carvings, basketwork; statesman Cecil John Rhodes, journalist and poet Gideon Nyirendra, singer Samantha Mumba.

**ZIMBABWE**
Handicrafts, pottery, woven goods, soapstone and wood carvings, African carved faces (wood or stone); controversial president Robert Mugabe, cricket stars Henry Olonga and Andy Flower, author/activist/former Zimbabwe Liberation Army member, Freedom Nyamubuya.

# The Natural Wonders of Southern Africa

**BOTSWANA**
The majestic wetlands of the Okavango Delta; San rock art (Tsodilo Hills); *mokoro* (dugout canoe) and elephant-back rides.

**COMOROS**
Empty yet glorious beaches; endangered green turtles laying their eggs.

**KENYA**
Wildebeest migrations of the Masai Mara; the endangered black rhino in Amboseli NP; Lake Turkana.

**LESOTHO**
Thabana Ntlenyana's views and the stony slopes of the mountain peak; pony trekking throughout the rugged mountain kingdom.

**MADAGASCAR**
Fianarantsoa to Manakara by train; Périnet's endemic wildlife; the rainforest inhabitants of Analamazaotra (Périnet) Special Reserve.

**MALAWI**
Liwonde's wildlife & scenery; boating on the water world of Lake Malawi.

**MAURITIUS**
Sir Seewoosagur Ramgoolam Botanical Gardens; numerous stunning beaches and abundant water activities; the rugged terrain of Black River Gorges National Park.

**MOZAMBIQUE**
Mozambique Island's WHS buildings; Maputo nightlife; the diving splendour of the Bazaruto Archipelago.

**NAMIBIA**
Fish River Canyon; rock engravings; the petrified forest; Kolmanskop's ghost town; the stark beauty of the treacherous Skeleton Coast.

**RÉUNION (FRANCE)**
Gorgeous tropical scenery; Cilaos' hot springs; the dramatic volcanic landscape of the cirques.

**SEYCHELLES**
Exotic vegetation & wildlife; the beaches and watery playgrounds.

**SOUTH AFRICA**
Table Mountain; the Cango Caves; the Drakensberg mountain range; the Namaqualand in full bloom; the wildlife spectacle of the Kruger National Park; St Lucia's amazing wetland reserve.

**SWAZILAND**
Walking Hlane Royal National Park; white-water rafting; the gentle grandeur of Mkhaya Nature Reserve.

**TANZANIA**
Olduvai Gorge, the site of presumed evolution of early humans; the legendary savannas of the Serengeti; Ngorongoro Crater.

**ZAMBIA**
Thrilling game park night drives; the untamed valley of the mighty Zambezi River.

**ZIMBABWE**
Watching someone else (!) bungee-jump off the Zambezi Bridge; the breathtaking Zimbabwe ruins; the San rock paintings at Matobo Hills; the awesome giant cascades of Victoria Falls.

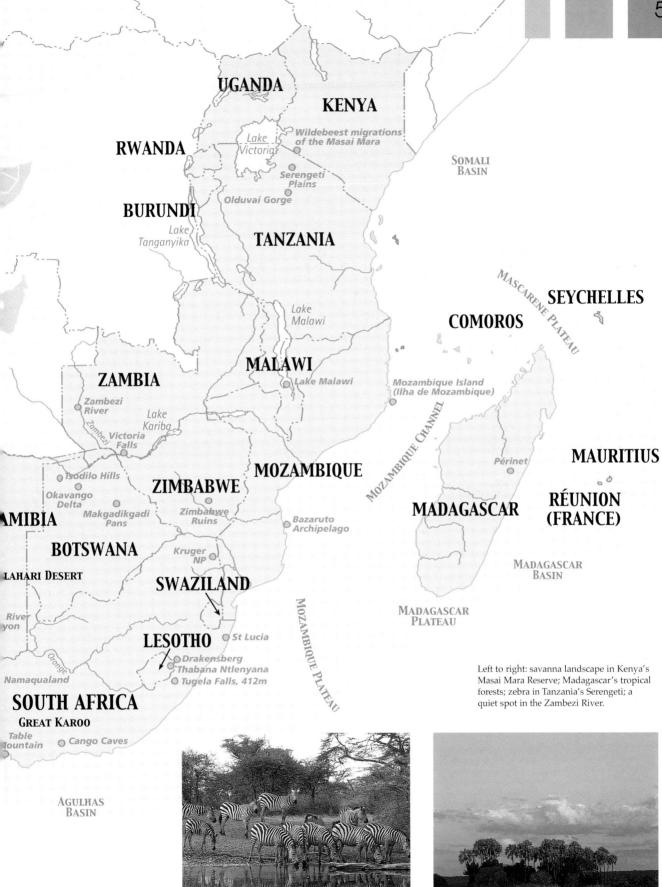

UGANDA

KENYA

RWANDA

*Lake Victoria*

*Wildebeest migrations of the Masai Mara*

SOMALI BASIN

BURUNDI

*Serengeti Plains*

*Olduvai Gorge*

*Lake Tanganyika*

TANZANIA

*Lake Malawi*

MASCARENE PLATEAU

SEYCHELLES

COMOROS

MALAWI

*Lake Malawi*

*Mozambique Island (Ilha de Moçambique)*

ZAMBIA

*Zambezi River*

*Lake Kariba*

*Zambezi Victoria Falls*

MOZAMBIQUE CHANNEL

MADAGASCAR

*Périnet*

MAURITIUS

RÉUNION (FRANCE)

*Tsodilo Hills*

ZIMBABWE

*Zimbabwe Ruins*

*Bazaruto Archipelago*

MADAGASCAR BASIN

*Okavango Delta*

ΑMIBIA

*Makgadikgadi Pans*

BOTSWANA

*Kruger NP*

MADAGASCAR PLATEAU

LAHARI DESERT

SWAZILAND

MOZAMBIQUE PLATEAU

*River yon*

LESOTHO

*St Lucia*

*Orange*

*Drakensberg*
*Thabana Ntlenyana*
*Tugela Falls, 412m*

*Namaqualand*

SOUTH AFRICA

GREAT KAROO

*Table Mountain*

*Cango Caves*

AGULHAS BASIN

Left to right: savanna landscape in Kenya's Masai Mara Reserve; Madagascar's tropical forests; zebra in Tanzania's Serengeti; a quiet spot in the Zambezi River.

# Animals & Plants of Southern Africa

**BOTSWANA**
Elephant, rhino, buffalo, wildebeest, zebra, giraffe, hippo, kudu, puku; savanna grassland, mopane trees, sausage tree.

**KENYA**
Wildebeest, black rhino, reticulated giraffe, beisa oryx; flamingoes.

**LESOTHO**
Rhebok, baboon, rhebok, reedbuck; black eagle, bearded vulture; spiral aloe.

**MADAGASCAR**
Lemur (such as indri and sifaka), fossa; chameleons; baobab, traveller's palm.

**MALAWI**
Hippo, crocodile, elephant, kudu, impala, bushbuck; cichlid fish; mopane trees, sausage trees.

**MAURITIUS**
Telfair skink; Mauritius fruit bat; Mauritius fody; Mauritius kestrel, pink pigeon.

**MOZAMBIQUE**
Elephant, buffalo, zebra; Tongaland squirrel, Three toed elephant shrew; loggerhead and leatherback turtles (amongst others), seacows, marlin; Cape vulture, wattled crane, pink throated longclaw, Zululand Cycad.

**NAMIBIA**
Desert rhino, elephant, gemsbok, Hartmann's mountain zebra, desert hyena; Cape fur seals; jackass penguins, Damara tern; toktokkie beetle; welwitschia, baobab, quiver tree and abundant species of lichen.

**SEYCHELLES**
Giant tortoises, turtles, dolphins, whales and manta rays; fairy tern, long-tailed Seychelles black paradise flycacther, Seychelles kestrel, blue pigeon; coco de mer palms.

**SOUTH AFRICA**
Lion, leopard, cheetah, buffalo, elephant, hippo, rhino, giraffe, honey badger, crocodile; ostrich, kori bustard, fish eagle; *halfmens* tree, fynbos (including proteas, heaths & ericas).

**SWAZILAND**
White rhino, elephant, lion, zebra, warthog, mongoose, crocodile; free-tailed bat; rich in flora.

**TANZANIA**
Lion, leopard, cheetah, rhino, elephant, wild dog, chimpanzee.

**ZAMBIA**
Lion, leopard, elephant, buffalo, Thornicroft's giraffe, zebra, puku, sitatunga.

**ZIMBABWE**
Elephant, giraffe, buffalo, sable, kudu.

Etosha National Park

Skeleton Coast Park

**NAMIBIA**

Namib-Naukluft Park

Kgalaga Transfron Park

**Ai-Ais / Richtersveld Transfrontier Park**

Orange

Left to right: four of Africa's mighty Big Five … buffalo, leopard, lion, elephant.

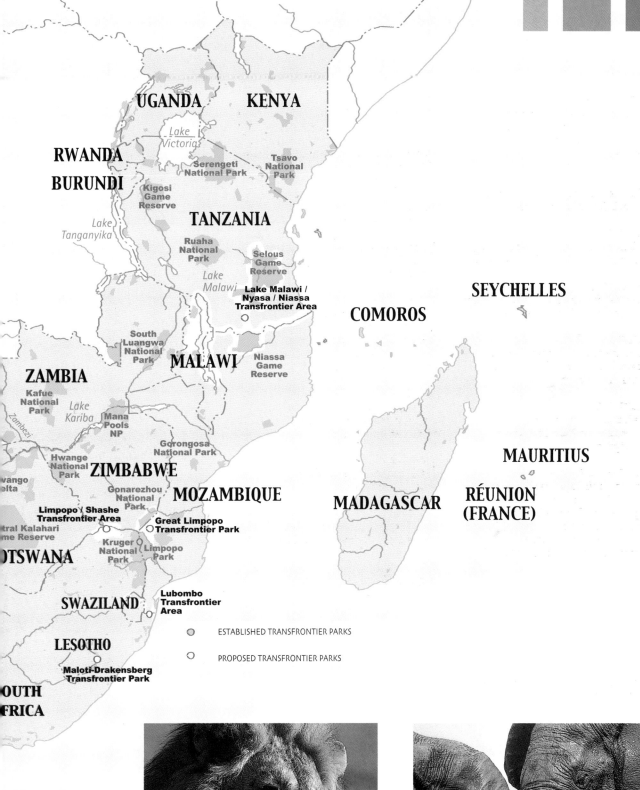

UGANDA

KENYA

RWANDA

BURUNDI

*Lake Victoria*

Serengeti National Park

Tsavo National Park

Kigosi Game Reserve

*Lake Tanganyika*

TANZANIA

Ruaha National Park

Selous Game Reserve

*Lake Malawi*

Lake Malawi / Nyasa / Niassa Transfrontier Area

SEYCHELLES

COMOROS

South Luangwa National Park

MALAWI

Niassa Game Reserve

ZAMBIA

Kafue National Park

*Lake Kariba*

Mana Pools NP

*Zambezi*

Gorongosa National Park

MOZAMBIQUE

MAURITIUS

Hwange National Park

ZIMBABWE

MADAGASCAR

RÉUNION (FRANCE)

vango elta

Gonarezhou National Park

Limpopo / Shashe Transfrontier Area

Great Limpopo Transfrontier Park

tral Kalahari me Reserve

Kruger National Park

Limpopo Park

OTSWANA

SWAZILAND

Lubombo Transfrontier Area

LESOTHO

○ ESTABLISHED TRANSFRONTIER PARKS

○ PROPOSED TRANSFRONTIER PARKS

Maloti-Drakensberg Transfrontier Park

OUTH FRICA

## TRAIN JOURNEYS

Travelling Africa's rugged terrain is most memorable when enjoyed from the rhythmic motion of a train steaming across the seemingly endless countryside. The continent boasts a number of these journeys, from the rudimentary comforts of the journey from Wadi Halfa to Khartoum in Sudan and the Red Lizard Train Journey in Tunisia to the ultimate luxury of South Africa's Blue Train or the Pride of Africa rail trip between Kenya and South Africa. To experience 'Real Africa', take the Tazara Express between Zambia and Tanzania.

## ELEPHANTBACK SAFARIS

Elephants are an integral part of the African landscape, and apart from the famed Dumbo Trek in Nigeria, a number of African nations (especially in the south) offer wildlife safaris from the backs of these great beasts. The most popular are those around Zimbabwe's Victoria Falls and through the floodplains of Botswana's Okavango Delta.

## WHALE WATCHING

Whales are popular visitors to Africa's coast, with many of the southern species such as the Southern Right making their way from the cold Antarctic waters to the warmer climes further north during southern winters. They mate and calve here before returning to their home territories. South Africa and most of the Indian Ocean Islands are much-favoured stopovers for these giants of the ocean, with plenty of land-based viewing points from which to watch them.

## SHARK DIVING

A number of prominent stretches of the African coastline are bathed by warm waters (particularly those of the Indian Ocean) which makes for ideal shark conditions. Many of these form natural breeding grounds for seals and an abundance of seabirds, and (because of the plentiful prey) are the hunting ground of the Great White and other sharks. Although it is always advisable to be on the lookout for these much-feared and often-seen predators, relatively few attacks have been reported in recent years and a number of private operators (most notably in South Africa, a much-favoured haunt of great whites) offer excursions to view sharks and even dive to see them up close … protected by reinforced metal cages, naturally!

## FERRY TRIPS

Much of Africa's coastline is serviced by ferries, carrying passengers and transporting goods across the massive lakes, meandering rivers and from the mainland to offshore islands. Although most cater largely for the day-to-day needs of locals, facilities are generally very basic and offer few luxuries, although they do offer a unique opportunity to experience Africa at its most rustic. One of the most inspiring trips is on the famed lake steamer *MV Liemba* on Tanzania's Lake Tanganyika (in the Great Lakes region of East Africa).

## KAYAKING

Watersports are probably some of the most popular leisure activities on the continent, especially considering that Africa boasts some of the world's largest lakes and a coastline that stretches some 30,500km (19,000 miles), with conditions varying from gentle to choppy right up to downright hazardous. Although sometimes icy cold, sometimes wonderfully tepid and, on occasion, disturbingly turbulent, the waters of Morocco's Mediterranean coast, Egypt's Red Sea, Malawi's Lake Malawi, and the Indian Ocean off Tanzania's Zanzibar Island have become the favourite playground of kayakers and other watersport enthusiasts. And the warm waters off the Cape Garden Route on the east coast of South Africa are a particular delight.

Kunene River

Kaokoland

**NAMIBI**

Skeleton Coast

Swakopmund

WINDHO

Sossusvl

Orange River
& Richtersveld

West Coast

CAPE TOW

**UGANDA**
KAMPALA
Lake Turkana

**KENYA**
Mt Kenya
NAIROBI

**RWANDA**
Rainforests
KIGALI
BUJUMBURA
Serengeti
Kilimanjaro
Luvironza River
Mombasa

**BURUNDI**
**TANZANIA**
Lake Tanganyika
DODOMA
Zanzibar
DAR ES SALAAM
Lake Victoria

**SEYCHELLES**

**COMOROS**

Lake Malawi

**MALAWI**
LILONGWE
Lake Malawi
Mozambique Island

**ZAMBIA**
LUSAKA
Lake Kariba
Zambezi River
Mt Mulanje
Victoria Falls

**MAURITIUS**

HARARE
Chobe
Hwange

**ZIMBABWE**
**MOZAMBIQUE**
Bazaruto Archipelago

**MADAGASCAR**
ANTANANARIVO

**RÉUNION (FRANCE)**

Okavango Delta
Makgadikgadi Pans
Tuli Block

**BOTSWANA**
GABORONE
Kruger NP

**SWAZILAND**
PRETORIA
MAPUTO
Maputo Province
MBABANE

BLOEMFONTEIN
**LESOTHO**
St Lucia
MASERU
Drakensberg
Maluti Mountains

**SOUTH AFRICA**
Wild Coast

Garden Route

ACTIVITY REGIONS, CITIES & TOWNS

NO MALARIA RISK

**MALARIA AREAS**
Malaria is a major problem in Africa for locals as well as tourists. It is always advisable to take the necessary medication and injections prior to departure, as prevention is better than cure.

**KILLING KILI'S ICE FIELDS**
According to environmental activists affiliated to Greenpeace, dramatic changes in latter-day climate may mean that towering Mount Kilimanjaro's ice field could retreat to such a degree that it may be lost entirely by the year 2015. Some 80 per cent of the ice – situated virtually on the equator – has already been lost since the area was first mapped almost 100 years ago.

**AFRICAN ADVENTURE CAPITALS**
It is a misconception that locals walk barefoot and communication is restricted to antiquated telephone systems. Africa's capitals are remarkably developed and boast a surprisingly sophisticated infrastructure. Adventurers should enjoy success with most of their information needs, particularly in the more popular travel destinations, as indicated on the map. These destinations are the main adventure activity hotspots or serve as the best point of entry to specific adventure regions.

**A LIFE-GIVING RIVER**
The Orange River (also known as the Gariep River) forms a natural border between South Africa and Namibia. Originating in the high mountain slopes of the Drakensberg on the eastern coast of southern Africa, the Orange empties into the Atlantic, stretching some 2,200km (1,367mi) across what is mostly dry, arid and inhospitable terrain.

Opposite, left to right: whale watching in Hermanus; mountainbiking in the forests around Stellenbosch.

# South Africa

## ADVENTURING THROUGH SOUTH AFRICA (See Contact Details 92-95)

## ON LAND

**ABSEILING / RAPP JUMPING**
Table Mountain, Western Cape
Knysna Heads and Robberg Peninsula, Western Cape
Bergwoning, Free State
Howick Falls, KwaZulu-Natal

**ROCK CLIMBING & MOUNTAINEERING**
Table Mountain and Cederberg, Western Cape
Clarens, Free State
Waterval-Boven, Mpumalanga
Drakensberg, KwaZulu-Natal

**KLOOFING**
Stormsriver Mouth, Eastern Cape
Sabie, Mpumalanga

**HIKING**
Graskop, Mpumalanga
Cape of Good Hope and Hoerikwaggo Trails, SANParks
Whale trail, De Hoop Reserve
Oystercatcher Trail, Mossel Bay
Wild Coast, Eastern Cape
Dolphin Trail, Tsitsikamma
Stormsriver Adventures
Amatola Trail, Eastern Cape

**HORSERIDING**
Waterberg, North West
Bokpoort Horseback Adventures and Game Ranch, Free State
Maputaland Horse Safaris, KZN
Spier Horse Trails, Western Cape

Wine Valley Horse Trails
Hawane Horse Trails, Swaziland

**CAMEL RIDING**
Cape Camel Rides, Cape Town

**CAVING**
Cango Caves, Western Cape

**SANDBOARDING**
Jeffreys Bay, Eastern Cape
Downhill Adventures, Cape Town

**SNOW SKIING / SNOW BOARDING**
Rhodes, Eastern Cape
Tiffindell Ski and Alpine Resort

**GAME VIEWING**
SANParks (Kruger NP, etc)
Shamwari Game Reserve

## IN THE AIR

**BUNGEE JUMPING**
Bloukrans, Eastern Cape
Gouritz, Western Cape

**FLYING**
Garden Route

**BRIDGE SWING**
Gouritz, Western Cape
Graskop, Mpumalanga
Tsitsikamma, Eastern Cape
Stormsriver Adventures

**BALLOONING**
Wineland Ballooning, Western Cape
Balloon Drifters, Garden Route
Balloons Over Africa, Mpumalanga

**SKYDIVING**
EP Skydive, Eastern Cape
Skydive Citrusdal, Western Cape
Outeniqua Skydivers, Garden Route

## ON WHEELS

**4X4 TRAILS**
Continental Off-Road Academy
Four Wheel Drive Club Of SA
Bass Lake Adventures, Gauteng
African Ivory Route, Limpopo
Off Road Adventures, Eastern Cape
Cederberg Guided 4x4, Western Cape
Kalahari 4x4 Adventures, Northern Cape
Khamkirri, Northern Cape
Sani Pass, Lesotho

**TRAIN RIDES**
Outeniqua Choo-Tjoe, Garden Route

**MTB**
Knysna Cycleworks, Garden Route
Kalahari Adventure Centre, N. Cape

**QUAD BIKING**
Adventure Village, Western Cape
Bush Bandits, Gauteng
Four Rivers Rafting and Adventures, KwaZulu-Natal

## ON (OR IN) WATER

**SCUBA & WRECK DIVING**
Cape Peninsula, Western Cape
Sodwana Bay, KwaZulu-Natal
Aliwal Shoal, KwaZulu-Natal

**SHARK CAGE DIVING**
Gansbaai, Western Cape
False Bay, Western Cape

**SARDINE RUN**
Wild Coast & KZN South Coast

**INLAND DIVING**
Komati Springs, Mpumalanga

**SEA KAYAKING**
Berg River, Western Cape
Plettenberg Bay, Garden Route
Seal Island, Mossel Bay
St Lucia, KwaZulu-Natal

**WHITEWATER RAFTING**
Tugela River, KwaZulu-Natal

Orange River, Northern Cape
Great Usutu River, Swaziland

**WHALE / DOLPHIN WATCHING**
Garden Route
Dyer Island, Gansbaai

**FISHING**
Dullstroom, Mpumalanga

**WINDSURFING**
Langebaan, Western Cape

Rie

Augra
Falls
Aug
River
Rafting

Richtersveld
NP

Alexander
Bay
Viooldrif
Pofadd

N7
Goegap
NR
N14

Port Nolloth

Springbok

Namaqua
NP
Bra

Rock Paintings

ATLANTIC
OCEAN
Loeriesfontein
Nuwerus
Calvini

Vanrhynsdorp

Lambert's Bay
Clanwilliam

St Helena
Bay
Doring
N7

Saldanha
Moorreesburg
West Coast
NP
Touws R

Wellington
Wor

Table
Bay
Stellenbosc
CAPE TOWN
Table Mt
Somerset
West
Caled
NP

Agulha

L'A

**SOUTH AFRICA**
**Capitals:** Pretoria (administrative),
 Cape Town (legislative) and Bloemfontein (judicial)
**Area:** 1,221,040 km² / 471,446mi²
**Population:** 43.6 million
**Main ethnic groups:** • Black (75%) • White (14%)
• Coloured (mixed race) (9%) • Asian (2%)
**Main languages:** • 11 official languages, including
 nine indigenous black languages, English and Afrikaans
**Main religions:** • Protestant (55%)
• Catholic (9%) • Hindu (1%) • Muslim (1%)
• Other (including traditional spiritual beliefs) (34%)
**Currency:** Rand (100 cents)

Reptile Footprints
Musina
N1
Tom Burke
Louis Trichardt
Thohoyandou
N11
Giyani
Lephalale
Tzaneen
Mineral Springs
Makopane
Polokwane
Kruger NP
Crocodile
Echo Caves
Madikwe GR
N1
Geological Exposure
Pilanesberg GR
Bela-Bela
Sudwala Caves
Sun City/ Lost City
N11
Lydenburg
Temba
Bray
Ramatlhabama
N4
Rustenburg
PRETORIA
N4
Komatipoort
Mafikeng/Mmabatho
Middelburg
Lichtenburg
JOHANNESBURG
N12
Soweto
Germiston
N17
MBABANE
Heidelberg
N17
Ermelo
SWAZILAND
Vryburg
Klerksdorp
Sasolburg
N11
N2
Tembe Elephant GR
N14
Vaal
Piet Retief
Golela
Kuruman
Bloemhof
N1
Volksrust
Pongolo
Sodwana Bay
Eye of Kuruman
Kroonstad
Newcastle
Blood River
Vryheid
Mkuzi GR
Sishen
Wilge
N3
St Lucia Marine Sanctuary
ington
Postmasburg
Welkom
Golden Gate Highlands NP
Harrismith
Dundee
Prince Imperial 1879 Monument
Lake St Lucia
Groblershoop
Warrenton
N5
N3
Dingaan's Kraal
Greater St Lucia Wetland Park
'Big Hole' Old Mine
Kimberley
Modder
Ladysmith
Empangeni
St Lucia
Kenhardt
Butha Buthe
N2
Estcourt
Richards Bay
First Diamond Discovered 1866
N8
BLOEMFONTEIN
Rock Paintings
MASERU
Katse Dam
Tugela
Valley of 1000 Hills
Prieska
Hopetown
LESOTHO
Natal Drakensberg Park
Stanger
neuk Pan
Orange
N1
Caledon
Pietermaritzburg
N10
Gariep NR
Durban
Bushman Drawings
Britstown
Gariep Dam
Kokstad
Oribi Gorge NR
De Aar
Aliwal North
N2
Port Shepstone
Carnarvon
Colesberg
N9
Mkambati NR
Port Edward
illiston
Hanover
N6
Maclear
Middelburg
Umtata
Rock of Execution
Three Sisters
Karoo NP
Graaff-Reinet
Cradock
Queenstown
Idutywa
Hole-in-the-Wall
vatory
Karoo NR
N10
rland
Beaufort West
Aberdeen
Mountain Zebra NP
N9
King William's Town
N1
Cango Caves
Baviaanskloof Wilderness Area
Addo Elephant NP
Grahamstown
East london
gsburg
Oudtshoorn
Uniondale
Uitenhage
N2
Port Alfred
George
Tsitsikamma NP
Knysna
Algoa Bay
Port Elizabeth
dam
Mossel Bay
INDIAN OCEAN
oop

---

**12 GREAT ADVENTURES**
1. Bungee jumping
2. Shark cage diving
3. Hiking
4. Horseriding
5. Fishing
6. 4x4 trails
7. Kitesurfing
8. Sea kayaking
9. Skydiving
10. Canoeing / whitewater rafting
11. Game viewing
12. Sardine run

# West Coast & Namaqualand

FLOWER ROUTE

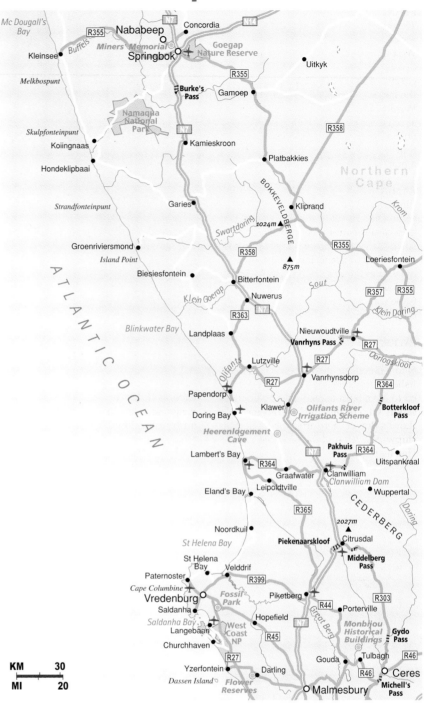

## THE FLOWER ROUTE

Every year between August and October, Spring puts on her prettiest bloom-bedecked frock. The official flower route covers vast distances (from the Tienie Versveld Reserve in Darling to the Orange River in the north) and can take up to three days to cover fully. The arid, stony, scrubby Namaqualand region has different climatic zones, with flower species (4000 at the last count) ranging from neon daisies, gazanias and mesembryanthemums, to hardy fleshy succulents to geophytes (bulbs, corms and tubers) like irises and bulbinellas. Visitors often need travel no further than the Postberg Nature Reserve on Langebaan Lagoon (an hour's drive) to enjoy a mesmerising magic-carpet ride. Flowers open with the sun, so cloudy days are no good for viewing. Blooms are best between 11:00 and 16:00; ensure that you drive facing the opened petals, and with the sun behind you.

## THE WEST COAST

It's perhaps a combination of the cold upwelling of the Benguela Current (nourishing the dark kelp forests that sway lazily in the wind-blown, big-waved seas) and the stark and rocky coastal landscapes that give the West Coast its wild air. This, coupled with the barren, almost desert-like conditions inland where rain is scarce and summers are ferocious, creates a sometimes-forbidding picture. But that's not taking into account two major rivers: the Orange in the far north and the Olifants, snaking from its mouth to the north of Lambert's Bay into Clanwilliam Dam and through Citrusdal. Both rivers have been harnessed to irrigate vast citrus orchards, wheatfields and vineyards. At Clanwilliam the Olifants is backed by the craggy, contorted Cederberg mountains. The N7 highway forges a route up the West Coast and connects Malmesbury (centre of the region's wheat industry and proud home of SA's largest flour mills) with Citrusdal, Clanwilliam and Vanrhynsdorp's spectacular spring-flower displays.

## LANGEBAAN

The lagoon is what draws the crowds to the sleepy town of Langebaan: hobie sailers, windsurfers and parasailers fill the horizon! Part of the West Coast National Park, and an important wetland for birdlife, the lagoon's 16km (10-mile) expanse turns a delicate shade of pink at times of the year as masses of crimson-winged flamingoes descend on its waters. Hartlaub's Gulls, ibis, herons, white pelicans and curlews also get a look-in, while Cape Cormorants hang out their wings to dry.

## ELAND'S BAY

This coastline is an extension of the rocky, turquoise-dyed, crayfish-creviced West Coast. Eland's Bay is mobbed by divers and their extended families in crayfish season, when the long arm of the law is lifted from December to April. Permits are your ticket to that tender, succulent, sweet-meat. On dry land, the terrain makes great offroad territory, and tourist information will supply you with a map of the best 4x4 trails.

## LAMBERT'S BAY

Bird Island is what makes Lambert's Bay somewhat different. Accessed via a breakwater-cum-harbour wall, you'll smell the guano before you get to see the birds on their island breeding ground. Massed in their thousands are African (Jackass) Penguins, cormorants and Cape Gannets, all of whom you can spy on from a viewing tower.

## PATERNOSTER & ST HELENA BAY

Paternoster's village shows off traditional low-slung, small-windowed, thatched fishermen's cottages. The town is reputed to have been named after Portuguese sailors who recited the Paternoster (Lord's Prayer) here after surviving a shipwreck. Around the promontory, St Helena Bay is another fishing village

perched at the edge of a pretty bay. The waters off this coast have a particularly turquoise hue while the chilling cold nurtures healthy crayfish (Cape lobster), which in turn draws scuba divers by the bucketload.

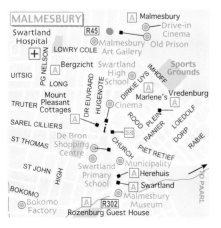

## MALMESBURY HISTORIC WALK

The local tourist bureau's 'historic route' brochure will guide you through the wide range of architectural styles gracing the town centre. There's Gothic Revival style, Georgian, Edwardian, Victorian and also the eclectic twin shops in Piet Retief Street (1880).

Top to bottom: fishing boats in Paternoster; Cape Gannets on Bird Island; Namaqualand.

# Cederberg Region

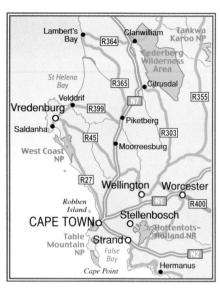

## CEDERBERG HIKING

The Cederberg range is part of the Cape Folded Mountains, its ingredients being sandstone, shale and quartzite, each being open to erosion to varying degrees. The result – powerful biting winds, dissolving rain and abrasion have nimbly and artfully sculpted a moonscape peopled by rocky gargoyles and goblins. No wonder walkers and overnight backpackers can't keep away from this place of bizarre and other-worldly 'creatures'. The 20m-high (65ft) Maltese Cross is a day-hike from Dwarsrivier, the impressive stone 30m (98ft) Wolfberg Arch is less than a half-day away, and the Wolfberg Cracks are closer still, although it takes some squeezing, slithering and pushing from the rear to get there. Not for the half-hearted! Views from all the sites are quite stupendous. The monoliths of Tafelberg and Sneeuberg can also be climbed. The Snow Protea (*Protea cryophila*) – meaning 'fond of the cold'! – grows on Sneeuberg. Over countless centuries wind and water have carved the Cederberg into its fairytale land-scape of pinnacles, arches and bold fis-sures. Don't miss out on the San paint-ings in their natural surreal settings which have names like the Amphitheatre and Stadsaal (roughly translated as 'city hall') caves; the spirit of such places is awesome. Permits are required for visitors.

## CLANWILLIAM

Another spot on the map whose body of water is more famous than the town: the 18km (11-mile) stretch of lake at the foot of the gnarled, weather-eroded Ceder-berg mountain range is mini-heaven for boaters and waterskiers. In summer they emerge soon after sunrise from holiday cabins, or the idyllically placed campsite nudging the water's edge, to glide across the dam's mirror-smooth surfaces before the winds stir. The dam, fed by the Olifants River, irrigates the surroun-ding farmlands and water can often be seen bursting through its sluice gates. The Cederberg mountains and surroun-ding area are named after the Clan-william cedar, a protected species in the Cederberg Wilderness Area.

## CITRUSDAL

A great base for day trips into the Cederberg, Citrusdal has good informa-tion centres as well as a good many accommodation options (albeit mostly out of town). It has a great little museum which shows off the area's history, thick with the tradition of the early pioneering settlers and the local Khoisan, while the Signal Cannon is another little piece of history. It is the original cannon that used to signal the arrival of ships in Table Bay. Mountainbiking trips in the area are also popular, and the more free-spirited can take the world-famous plunge that kicks off on the Modderfon-tein farm (tandem, freefall and training for beginners). There's a whole lot more to do around Citrusdal, from bass fish-ing to freshwater angling (the Olifants River boasts the country's richest en-demic fish population), handfuls of hik-ing trails, 4x4 routes, scenic drives, sight-seeing (from rock art to wildflowers) and wine-tasting at Citrusdal Cellars.

## TANKWA KAROO NATIONAL PARK

More of a Scientific National Park than a tourist trap, the Tankwa Karoo is still in the development phases of re-establish-ing the original vegetation of the region. The 80,000 hectare (197,600 acre) park is one of the most arid regions of the Karoo. Tankwa's annual rainfall of just 80mm (3.1 inches) a year means that the gentlest downpour sends its landscape into a dazzling display of flowering suc-culents. The park does offer solitude, spectacular views and the occasional floral eruption.

## WHAT NOT TO DO IN THE 'BERG

- Please don't (PD) touch the rock art! Touching damages the paintings.
- PD damage rock surfaces.
- PD use rock-bolts when climbing.
- PD interfere with plants or wildlife.
- PD litter (this includes toilet paper!) and remember to take home all the litter you bring in or create.
- PD discard cigarette butts, as they can cause veld-fires and are unsightly.
- PD make open-fires away from the des-ignated areas.
- PD use soap or detergents in or near rivers and mountain streams.
- PD bring pets unless you check before-hand that they are allowed where you are staying.
- PD forget to get the necessary permits for outdoor recreational activities and attractions.
- PD damage the sensitive vegetation by walking off the hiking paths.
- PD remove or disturb any fossils – they are all protected as National Monuments.

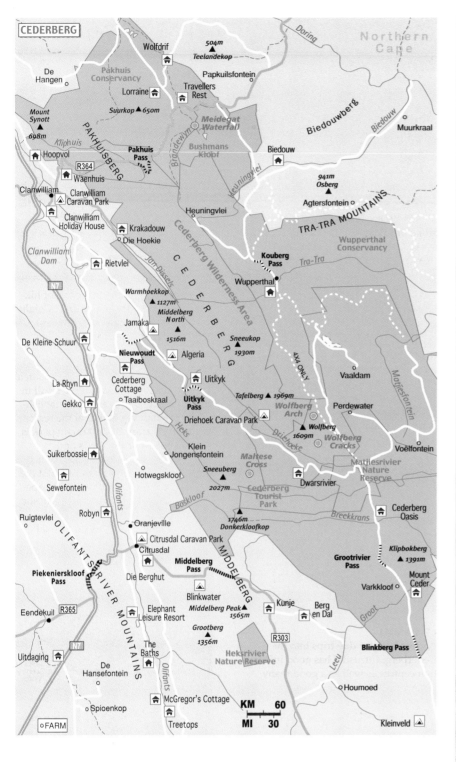

**CEDERBERG**

Northern Cape

Wolfdrif
504m ▲ Teelandekop
Papkuilsfontein
De Hangen
Pakhuis Conservancy
Lorraine
Travellers Rest
Biedouwberg
Biedouw
Muurkraal
Suurkop ▲ 650m
Mount Synott ▲ 698m
Meidegat Waterfall
Kliphuis
PAKHUISBERG
Bushmans kloof
Pakhuis Pass
Biedouw
Hoopvol
R364
941m Osberg
Waenhuis
Clanwilliam
Clanwilliam Caravan Park
Heuningvlei
Agtersfontein
Clanwilliam Holiday House
Krakadouw
Die Hoekie
TRA-TRA MOUNTAINS
Wupperthal Conservancy
Clanwilliam Dam
Rietvlei
N7
Kouberg Pass
Tra-Tra
Wupperthal
Warmhoekkop
▲ 1127m
Middelberg North
Jamaka
1516m
Sneeukop ▲ 1930m
De Kleine Schuur
Nieuwoudt Pass
Algeria
Cederberg Cottage
Uitkyk
Vaaldam
La Rhyn
Taaiboskraal
Tafelberg ▲ 1969m
Gekko
Uitkyk Pass
Driehoek Caravan Park
Wolfberg Arch
Perdewater
Heks
Wolfberg ▲ 1609m
Klein Jongensfontein
Wolfberg Cracks
Voëlfontein
Suikerbossie
Hotwegskloof
Sneeuberg ▲ 2027m
Maltese Cross
Matjiesrivier Nature Reserve
Sewefontein
Boskloof
Cederberg Tourist Park
Dwarsrivier
Breekkrans
Cederberg Oasis
Ruigtevlei
Olifants
Robyn
Oranjeville
1746m Donkerkloofkop
OLIFANTSRIVIER MOUNTAINS
Citrusdal Caravan Park
Citrusdal
Grootrivier Pass
Klipbokberg ▲ 1391m
Mount Ceder
Piekenierskloof Pass
Die Berghut
Middelberg Pass
MIDDELBERG
Varkkloof
Eendekuil
R365
Elephant Leisure Resort
Blinkwater
Middelberg Peak ▲ 1565m
Kunje
Berg en Dal
Uitdaging
N7
The Baths
Grootberg ▲ 1356m
Heksrivier Nature Reserve
R303
Blinkberg Pass
De Hansefontein
Olifants
Leeu
McGregor's Cottage
Spioenkop
Houmoed
FARM
Treetops
KM 60
MI 30
Kleinveld

**CEDERBERG IN A NUTSHELL**
Requirements: Permits are required for hiking and camping.
Risk factor: Wear proper hiking boots and thick socks to prevent insect and animal bites.
Facilities: There are a number of camp sites that cater for hikers and offer down-to-earth facilities.

Top to bottom: the Maltese Cross; Protea; a rock climber ascending Bukketraube.

# Cape Peninsula

Thermopylae 1899  Athens 1865
SA Seafarer 1966
Lighthouse
Three Anchor Bay
**Cape Town**
Noon gun
Victoria & Alfred
Waterfront
Canal Walk
M5
Cape Town
Convention
Centre
N1
R102
SA Astronomical
Observatory
Sea Point
Bantry Bay
Lion's
Head
Castle of
Good Hope
**Woodstock**
Clifton Bay
670
N2
Camps Bay
M6
**Camps Bay**
Rhodes
Memorial
Theatre on the Bay
TABLE MOUNTAIN
Devil's Peak ▲ 1001
**Athlone**
Het Huis te
Kraaiestein 1698
Orion's
Cave
M17
Bellsfontein
Kramat
Kirstenbosch
National
Botanical Garden
Boshof
Gateway
Antipolis 1977
Oudekraal
Van Riebeeck's
Hedge
**Claremont**
Kenilworth
Race course
M6
TWELVE APOSTLES
Table Mountain
National Park
M9
Llandudno Bay
Little
Lion's Head
Alphen
1714
Romelia 1977
M63
Maynardville
Open Air
Theatre
Sandy Bay
436
**Constantia**
CONSTANTIABERG
M41
Oude Schip
614
Suther Peak
World
of Birds
Groot
Constantia
1685
Maori 1909
Boss 400
**Hout Bay**
Mariner's
Wharf
The
Leopard
Constantiaberg
928
**Grassy Park**
M42
M41
M5
Karbonkelberg
Sanctuary Zone
Hout
Bay
Elephant's Eye
Cave
The Lonely
Bridge
Rondevlei
Zeekoevlei
Duiker Island West Fort
1781
Astor
M6
Spotty
Dog
Rondevlei
Bird Sanctuary
Vulcan Rock
Katzmaru 1970
Tokai
Forest
M4
M5
Die Josie
Chapman's Peak
592
Higher
Steenberg Peak
537
**Muizenberg**
R310
Chapman's Point
Silvermine
1687
Muizenberg
Cave
Noordhoek
Toll Booth
M6
Silvermine
Nature Reserve
Neptune's Corner
Chapman's Bay
Tunnel
Cave
Peer's
Cave
Rhodes Cottage
Kakapo 1900
Tidal
Lagoon
Kalk Bay
Cave
Klein Slangkop Point
**Fish Hoek**
False
Bay
Kommetjie Bay
M65
M65
Trappies
Caves
Slangkop Point
Clan
Munroe 1905
Slangkop
174
Rooikrans
364
Else
Peak
303
Fish Hoek Bay
Skeleton Rock
The Anchor
Hartenberg
circa 1730
Else Bay
M4
Clan Stuart 1914
M65
Die Eiland
Witsand
Bay
Table Mountain
National Park
Die Gebroeders
1792
Simon's Bay
Lighthouse
Phoenix 1829
Camel
Rock
Red Hill
256
Just Nuisance
Statue
Schuster's Bay
**Simon's Town**
Schusterskraal
Simonsberg ▲ 548
SWARTKOP MOUNTAINS
Bonteberg
227
M4
Dassiekop
314
Miller's Point
Lookout
Post
M65
Menskop Point
Olifantsbos Bay
Olifantsbos
Cottage
View Point
Smitswinkel Bay
Olifantsbos Point
Thomas T Tucker 1942
Judas Peak
319
Blaasbalk Cave
Nolloth 1965
Cape of Good Hope
Nature Reserve
Old
Cannon
Phyllisia 1968
Hoek van Bobbejaan
114
Dias
Monument
1488
Da Gama
Monument 1497
Bordjiesrif
Kommetjieberg
107
Tania 1972
Bloubergstrand
GROOT-BLOUBERG
Matrooskop
Platboom Bay
View Point
Rooikrans
View Point
Lighthouse
Cape of Good Hope
Shir-Yib
1970
Cape Point

KM 6
MI 3

## GETTING WRECKED

High winds and a wicked coastline play havoc to much of Southern Africa's coastline, but Cape Town is famous for its many shipwrecks. Many are still visible and provide excellent wreck diving opportunities.

- Kakapo (1900)
- Thomas T Tucker (1942)
- Athens (1865)
- Antipolis (1977)
- Romelia (1977)
- Nolloth (1965)
- Phyllisia (1968)
- Clan Stuart (1914)

TO BUFFELSFONTEIN
VISITORS CENTRE
**CAPE POINT**
N
Whale
Whatch
Point
False Bay
View
Point
Fishing
Rooikrans
Trappiesgrotte
266m
Plumpudding
Rock
Two Oceans
Restaurant
View
Point
Penguin
Rock
Cape
Point
Hiking
Trails
Vasco da
Gama
208m
Toilet
Lighthouse
View
Point
Shir-Yib
Beach
(1970)
Dias
Rocks
Neptune's
Dairy
Pappiesbank
Hiking
Trails
Dias
Beach
Cape Maclear
Maclear
Beach
View
Point
**ATLANTIC OCEAN**
Cape of Good Hope
Most south-westerly point of Africa

## BAD NEWS FOR SAILORS

Shipwrecks aren't the only reasons for a coastline to be described as treacherous … piracy and general warfare also cause ships to sink from trace. Lovers of shipwrecks will be magnetised to the following coastlines:

- Namibia's Skeleton Coast
- The Bay of Villefranche sur Mer (France)
- Argentina's Tierra del Fuega
- Mexico's Matagorda Bay
- Australia's Queensland and New South Wales
- The Caribbean
- The Spanish Azores
- The Red Sea

ATLANTIC OCEAN

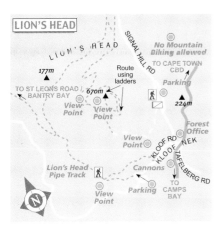

## TABLE MOUNTAIN
The greatest natural asset in the Cape Peninsula, Table Mountain was carved over hundreds of millions of years as a result of dramatic geological movements and climatic changes, varying from ice ages to periods of low sea level and even volcanic disturbances. It is South Africa's most recognisable icon, the most photogenic of structures, and without it Capetonians would be lost (they navigate around the city with the aid of the Mountain as a reference point).

## KRAMATS AND THE CIRCLE OF ISLAM
*Kramats* (*Mazaars*), the holy shrines of Islam, mark the graves of Holy Men of the Muslim faith who have died at the Cape. There are more than 20 recognized kramats in the Peninsula area, with at least another three in the outlying districts of Faure, Caledon, Rawsonville and Bain's Kloof. Locals and foreigners visit these special places to seek help with personal and physical problems as well as purely to practise their faith.

## KIRSTENBOSCH GARDEN
Many of South Africa's finest floral treasures are on display in the easily accessible Kirstenbosch National Botanical Garden, nestled under Table Mountain. Numerous art and craft exhibitions (as well as flower shows and sales) occur through the year, as do music concerts and the incredibly popular Carols by Candlelight over the Xmas period.

## CAPE POINT
Cape Point offers a varied experience of fynbos, topped off with rocky outcrops and intriguing stretches of beach. A nature reserve since 1938, its 7,750ha (19,150 acres) of rich and varied flora and fauna and 40 kilometres (24.8 miles) of coastline provide a fitting 'ending' for the African continent! The mythical Adamastor was said to be sent to the Point to guard sailors rounding the Peninsula.

## JUST A NUISANCE
Just Nuisance was a massive great dane that became a legend for looking after drunken sailors in WWII. Friendly, much loved and terribly spoiled, Nuisance became the first and only dog to be officially enlisted into the British Royal Navy. Born in 1937 (on April Fool's Day) a much-visited statue at Jubilee Square (Main Road, Simon's Town) commemorates this fine fellow's life.

## HOUT BAY AND CHAPMAN'S PEAK
On a big rock below the start of the recently revamped Chapman's Peak Drive (one of the world's most wanted views) is a statue of a leopard. The iron effigy is a lasting tribute to the wild animals that used to roam Hout Bay (leopards used to wander around the village!). Hout Bay is popular with arts and crafters, is a lovely family and walking beach, as well as being popular with surfers and kayakers. The nearby World of Birds Sanctuary is another popular diversion.

## SUPER SCUBA
Coastal conditions are generally good to accommodate diving (with a wetsuit!) year-round off the Cape Peninsula. The Peninsula offers fantastic kelp diving for all abilities in depths usually not greater than 15m, and you can embark on shore diving from just about anywhere on the coast. Not for the faint-hearted or inexperienced, boat diving provides as good a wreck and rock diving experience as you could wish for in the world.

## BOULDERS BEACH
Boulders Beach's spectacular rounded granite boulders offer unique, sheltered bathing coves. The boulders were shaped through a combination of fracturing, erosion, and sea-level fluctuation – they did NOT roll down the mountain! Boulders is a vital conservation ground for the African Penguin for future generations. There were just two breeding pairs of penguins in 1982, but 3,600 penguins currently waddle around Boulders. Boulders Beach was rated one of the five best beaches to visit before you die by none other than the BBC!

Opposite page: view of the city and Table Mountain from Signal Hill.
Top to bottom: Fourth Beach (Lion's Head in the background); the cablecar descending Table Mountain; the Thomas T Tucker shipwreck (1942) at Cape Point.

# Winelands

## THE TOP WINE COUNTRIES

| | Wine Producers | | Wine Drinkers |
|---|---|---|---|
| 1 | Italy | 1 | Luxembourg |
| 2 | France | 2 | France |
| 3 | Spain | 3 | Portugal |
| 4 | USA | 4 | Italy |
| 5 | Argentina | 5 | Switzerland |
| 6 | Germany | 6 | Argentina |
| 7 | South Africa | 7 | Greece |
| 8 | Australia | 8 | Spain |
| 9 | Chile | 9 | Uruguay |
| 10 | Romania | 10 | Austria |

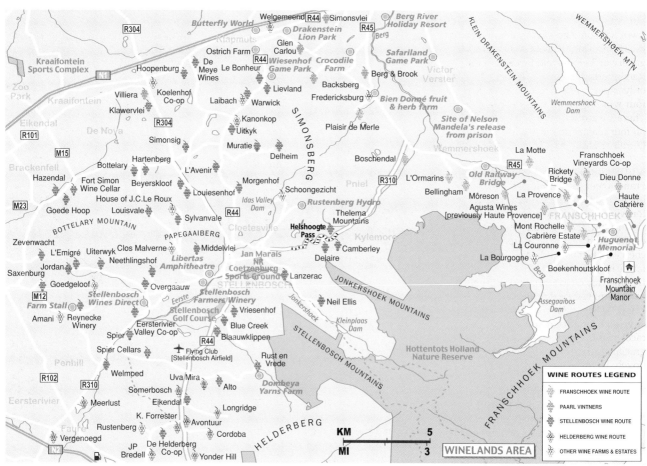

## THE CAPE WINELANDS

How do you compete with towering jagged mountains, one range giving way to another, and many carrying whimsical names like Hex ('witch'), Drakenstein ('dragon stone') and Riviersonderend ('river with no end')? At the foot of these great mountain ranges lie tightly manicured vine terraces, capped off with the eternally graceful curved and moulded gables of historical manor houses, a heritage left behind by early Dutch settlers. Passes forged through this mountain barrier to the east made it a gateway to the rest of the country. This region that was, early on, baptised the 'overberg', meaning 'over (or across) the mountains'. The Western Cape's winelands are the main reason for South Africa's plum position as seventh-largest wine producer in the world. A constantly mushrooming number of estates presently stands in the 90s; there are just fewer than 70 co-operatives and over 100 private cellars. The wineland areas are accessed via two major national routes, the N1 and N2, with multiple connecting and well-signposted principal roads.

## CONSTANTIA

The official Constantia Wine Route is limited to five estates, but dynamite comes in small packages! Leafy oaks, whitewashed gables, vine-terraces and soaring mountains create an amazing backdrop to some stunning wines. Buitenverwachting, Groot Constantia, Klein Constantia and Constantia Uitsig all once formed part of a farm granted to Simon van der Stel in 1685.

## DURBANVILLE WINE ROUTE

Settled into undulating hills and mountains, with the surrounding slopes decked in vines, Durbanville's vineyards are producing very respectable grapes that are being pressed into highly quaffable wines. Durbanville Hills winery waves its magic wand with some very fine lemon-butter chardonnays and grassy-nosed sauvignon blancs ('sav blanc' and 'chard' to the wine toff). The Diemersdal, Nitida, Meerendal and Altydgedacht estates don't do too badly either on all lip-smacking scores of both red and white wines.

## STELLENBOSCH

Its streets lined with leafy oaks, this pretty university town's buildings rub shoulders with historical cottages and restored Cape Dutch, Cape Georgian, Regency and Victorian houses. Dorp Street is a marvel for its meticulously preserved façades and most of them are historical monuments. Stellenbosch buys into café society, and there's a good selection of trendy coffee shops spilling out onto the pavement. The university town has some good art galleries and art museums: Dorp Street Gallery, the gallery at 34 Ryneveld Street and the Rembrandt van Rijn Art Gallery. You can only expect to successfully visit three or four wine cellars in a day, so plan well. There are around 30 cellars and co-ops on four major roads within a 12km (7-mile) radius from Cape Town.

## A CORNER OF FRANCE

Franschhoek is a den for hedonists; taking its cue from the French, it's a centre for wining and dining, festivals and fun. Year-round, the town stages festivals celebrating olives, cheese, grapes, with the cherry on top being Bastille Day. The top farms include the graciously gabled L'Ormarins, La Motte (its fawny wine barrels are visible through a wall of glass), Môreson (a working farm with a large airy restaurant and a pretty terrace), Haute Provence (superb wines in gracious surrounds) and La Petite Ferme (lovely lawns and a stupendous view).

## THE PEARL OF THE WINELANDS

The Main Street in Paarl, which tails the Berg River, runs an amazing 11km (7 miles) and boasts rows of 18th- and 19th-century Cape Dutch and Georgian houses. About one-fifth of the country's total wine production comes from Paarl, and the most striking symbol of its wine

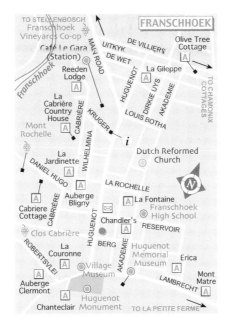

### GREAT WINE REGIONS
- Bordeaux — France
- Stellenbosch — South Africa
- Napa Valley — California, USA
- Alto Douro — Portugal
- Marlborough — New Zealand
- Porto — Portugal
- Sonoma Valley — California, USA
- Chianti — Tuscany, Italy
- Yarra Valley — Melbourne, Australia
- Florence — Tuscany, Italy
- Maipo Valley — Santiago, Chile
- Rhein-Mösel — Germany
- Bilbao-Rioja — Spain

history is La Concorde, a Neo-Classical building with a sculpted pediment, dating back to 1956. Watch Fairview Wine Estate's Saanen (Swiss) goats nimbly navigate a thin spiral ramp up a tall tower, and then test their milk cheeses! At Zanddrift you can taste wines in a stone chapel that was built in the early 1940s by Italian prisoners of war while world-famous Nederburg holds an annual wine auction. The swooping white spires on the hill are part of the Taal (or 'language') Monument, a tribute to the Afrikaans *taal*, it has three domes and three small pillars that vary in size and height. Nearby, Paarl Mountain can be climbed with the help of chain handholds. This granite outcrop, the world's second largest after Australia's Uluru, wears its age well – 500 million years and counting.

*Opposite page: Bergkelder tasting room.
Top to bottom: typical winelands landscape; wine barrels waiting in the winelands sunshine; grapes of the Carignon variety.*

# Garden Route & Route 62

### THE GARDEN ROUTE

The official start of the Garden Route, Mossel Bay is famous for its natural gas deposits, but the idiotically brave can enjoy shark cage dives which operate off the coast. The Dias Museum celebrates the 500th anniversary of Dias' historic arrival, while outside by the famous milkwood tree a stone boot acts as a mailbox for visitors' postcards, which are duly marked with a special stamp. The coastline is fed by countless rivers, drenching rains, and mists sweeping in from the sea, keeping it enduringly moist, fertile and green. This is punctuated by wave-lapped beaches, river mouths, lagoons and lakes, making it the natural playground for outdoor types – walkers and hikers, cyclists and mountain bikers, canoeists and board-sailors. The Wilderness Lakes (a loop of sinuous waterways, lakes, a lagoon and estuary) offer bird-watching trails guaranteed to get you close to the tweeters. Knysna's serene 17km-long (10,5-mile)

### GARDEN ROUTE IN A NUTSHELL

Climate: Conditions are generally good year-round, but winter rains can be bothersome. Summer is the peak holiday period and is really crowded.
Risk factor: Usually gentle, but the warm ocean can pose a shark risk.
Pack: Some sunscreen and waterproof clothing, but operators should provide the necessary equipment.
Facilities: Facilities offered by operators are generally good to very good, although the nature of the adventure means that participants should be prepared to get at least a little wet, with some discomfort in the cold winter.

lagoon is guarded at its sea entrance by two sandstone cliffs, the Knysna Heads. The quaint town is one of a number of beach and watersport havens that are packed during the holiday season. North of Knysna, Noetzie's stone castles line a stunning curve of beach which is accessible via steep stairs.

### KAYAKING THE GARDEN ROUTE

The more than 200km (125-mile) stretch of scenic coastline between Mossel Bay and the Storms River Mouth is remarkably undeveloped: craggy cliffs, soft beaches, gentle inland waters and endless ocean. Barricaded from the arid interior by the Outeniqua and Tsitsikamma mountains (both offer famed trails through rugged mountains and tangled forest), the Garden Route is a world of cliffs and coves, lakes and lagoons fed by the Indian Ocean, and a playground for the canoeist and kayaker. The wild ocean, placid inlets and lazy lagoons offer many watersports: surfing to sailing, waterskiing to angling and, most notably, kayaking and canoeing. The beaches and ocean, blessed with sunny summers and mostly temperate winters, are set against a verdant backdrop. Thousands of hectares of reserves and conservation areas, such as the Wilderness Lakes Area, lie along the beaches, but it is the salty sea air and gentle winds that lure kayakers. Operators are relatively few, but those who do work these shores are knowledgeable and helpful. The best times to take to the waters are at sunset, when dolphins cavort in the waves, seals ply the ocean and gentle 'white horses' ripple across the sea. Remember that the ocean is untamed, and beach-based lifesavers

KNYSNA LAGOON

and rescue units are not on duty in the off-season. It is not unheard of for kayaks to be surrounded by relatively harmless hammerhead sharks and even the occasional great white. The weather, although generally faultless, can be temperamental, waves unpredictable and sun harsh, but this is a small price to pay for superb kayaking conditions.

### OUTENIQUA CHOO-TJOE

Leaving from George at 08:10 and arriving in Knysna at 11:30, this narrow-gauge steam train huffs and puffs around precipitous cliffs, crossing bridges, hooting its way over lakes and chugging through gum and pine forests. The leisurely three-hour trip culminates in a crossing of the 2km (1 mile) bridge over the Knysna Lagoon, pulling into the station amid much noise and steam. The 7-day, 108km (67-mile) Outeniqua Hiking Trail is popular but tough, over mountains, along a rocky coastline and through heaving forests. Book ahead ... and get yourself fit before you start!

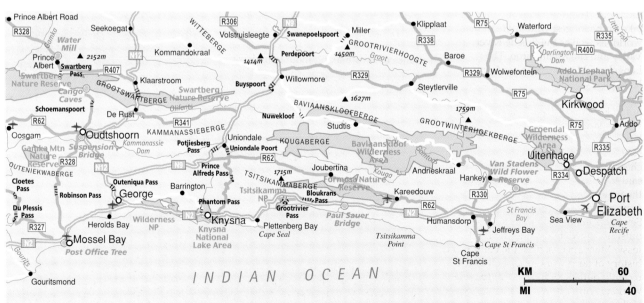

ROUTE 62

KNYSNA

MOSSEL BAY

## SURFING AT JEFFREYS BAY

Jeffreys Bay is a surfers haven: the air is alive with sea spray, the beach sand rich with mesmerizing collections of shells to enthrall conchologists, pods of dolphins to spot if you're lucky … and some of the finest surf you're likely to find on earth, according to the locals. 'J Bay' is proudly clinging to its laidback roots despite plenty of local development for the tourist industry.

## STORMS RIVER

Storms River is a hive of adventure activities, including black-water tubing, abseiling and snorkelling. The big daddy, however, is bungee jumping … and the Bloukrans River Bridge has the world's highest at a gut-wrenching 216m (708ft)! No-one will hear your screams from that height!

## ROUTE 62

Much like the famous Route 66 in the USA links the urban and rural communities of Chicago and Los Angeles, Route 62 links Cape Town and Port Elizabeth. The route allows travellers to take in the longest wine route in the world, as well as the Breede River Valley and the Klein Karoo. The Langeberg Mountains around Ashton have plenty of hiking routes and trails for the adventure seeker, while Soekershof in Robertson is home to one of the world's largest hedge-mazes – the Klaas Voogds Maze covers 13,870m$^2$ (149,241ft$^2$). Robertson is famous for its cheese, wine, roses and horses and is said to be the most hospitable towns in the region, but one of Route 62's most famous landmarks has to be Ronnie's Sex Shop, about 25 kilometres (15 miles) outside Barrydale. Bonnievale's Tokkelossie Museum describes the culture and history of farm workers as well as the recently outlawed dop system (paying workers with alcohol). The Breede River Valley is rich in diversity, with an abun-dance of breathtaking mountain views, sparkling streams, orchards, vineyards (the largest wine producing valley in the Western Cape) indigenous flora, springs and adventure. Montagu is the bed & breakfast capital of Route 62 and is a firm favourite as a 'weekend away' destination, and its hot springs are a great crowd-puller.

Top to bottom: Robberg Nature Reserve; the elusive Knysna loerie; the Dutch Reformed Church in Swellendam; Bloukrans Pass tree.

# Karoo

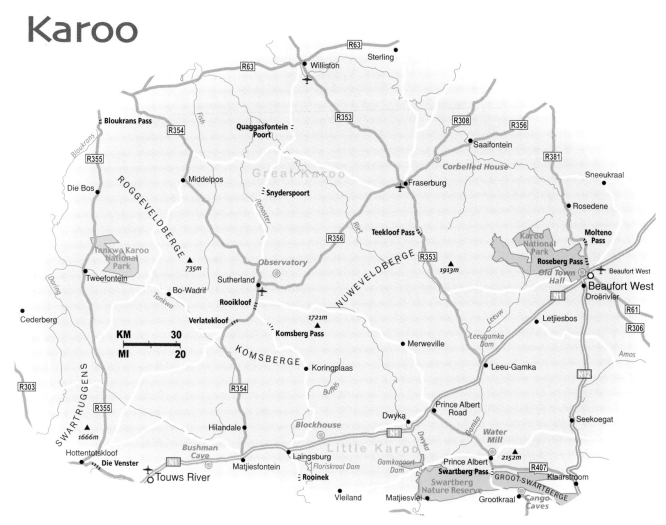

## THE TWO KAROOS

The Karoo is a vast, dry expanse of desert-like terrain that stretches across sections of the Western Cape and into the Northern Cape. It is divided into the Little and the Great Karoo, according to geological factors as well as topography, vegetation and climate. Its name comes from the indigenous Khoi people's description as the 'land of great thirst', yet the Karoo boasts the world's greatest amount of succulents (as well as some of the largest specimens), with more than 9,000 in the Beaufort West region. The scenery is flat, monotonous, and stretches to every horizon, but here and there pancake-layered outcrops reveal the typical Karoo shale and sandstone strata. Dolerite formations do break the monotony – here, the volcanic lava has thrust up through the earth, and over time been weathered into weird and wonderful shapes as the harder rock resisted the moulding and reshaping forces of wind and water. Some are highly distinctive, with names like the Three Sisters – three similarly shaped conical hills – north of Beaufort West. An enduring image of this slice of South African landscape is, here and there, a lone wind pump, like a sentinel in the crisp, eternally clear Karoo air.

## KAROO NATIONAL PARK

Just north of Beaufort West, the vast flat plains of the Karoo National Park are deceptive in the sweet green fodder they so obviously provide to kudu, hartebeest and springbok. Other wildlife has been re-introduced, 'big guns' such as black rhino, black wildebeest – 'gnu' is an apt name for a creature that looks like it's stepped out of *Jungle Book* – and Cape mountain zebra. Animal supreme is the gemsbok, with its rapier horns that seem to rip the air, and its ability to endure the tough, dry conditions. The park has a 4x4 trail, and the Fossil (geology) and Bossie (vegetation) walking trails.

## BEAUFORT WEST

The N1 is the Great North Road that connects Cape Town and Johannesburg by bisecting the Karoo. Beaufort West, the 'capital' of the Karoo region (or at least its largest town!) is located on the N1. The town has little to commend it, other than its role as a centre of civilisation in the flat, featureless middle of nowhere. Travellers can find a basic, clean place to stay overnight, fill travel-weary tums, refuel their equally travel-weary vehicles, and then cram it with lots of treats to stave off boredom from the many hours spent on the road.

## MATJIESFONTEIN

A turn-of-the-century town centering on the 1900 Lord Milner Hotel, Matjiesfontein is in its entirety a national monument. It was all started by Scotsman James Logan in 1883, when he established a dining place alongside the railway line in an age when trains had no dining coaches. Over time, this expanded to become a hotel and today, Lord Milner's decorative iron-lace verandahs and white-painted square turrets are reminiscent of that elegant time. Despite

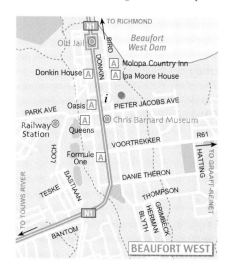

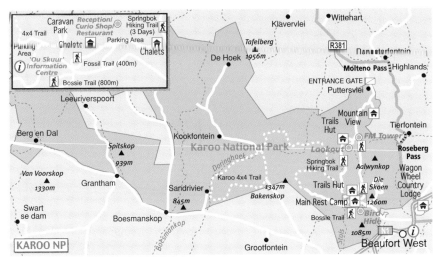

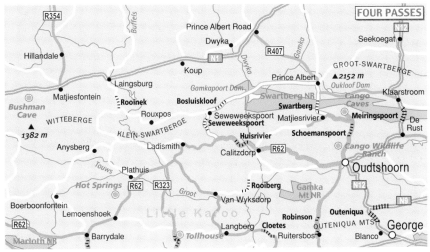

the lattice-fringed post office nearby, Matjiesfontein is, essentially, a charming hotel complex planted in the middle of the Little Karoo. The iron lace that prettifies South Africa's Victorian homes is locally termed 'broekie' lace – a reminder of the delicate lace edgings of a lady's bloomers! Matjiesfontein boasts some interesting museums (such as the Transport Museum and the Marie Rawdon Museum), while a trip around town on the local (yet authentic!) London double-decker bus is a must.

### OUDTSHOORN
The country's ostrich-farming capital has earned its reputation and status, boasting grandiose sandstone mansions (aka 'feather' palaces), with dyed feathers, ostrich leather handbags, belts, shoes and painted eggs for sale. Visitors can choose to sit on an ostrich, brave a canter or rather just sit and watch other people perched atop these giant – albeit

*Top to bottom: Swartberg pass; sand snake; ostriches; a lonely Karoo windmill and dam.*

flightless – birds. The Cango Wildlife Ranch has lion and cheetah to spy on (from the safety of an aerial walkway), and crocodiles and alligators that snap their ugly teeth at you. The Cango Caves offer a phantasmagorical display of limestone drip formations as well as hours of fun exploring the age-old caves.

### THE FOUR PASSES
Composed of rough-hewn rock and deep sky, the Four Passes has an amazing concentration of mountain landscapes, including the Swartberg, Langeberg and Outeniqua mountains. Pass builder Thomas Bain earned his spurs at the base of these rock barriers: Seweweekspoort rises to 2,325m (7,628ft), Schoemanspoort chisels through a 10km (6-mile) long narrow chasm, Swartberg winds on for 24km (15 miles) and Meiringspoort bares its cliffs in contorted, burnt-orange folds. According to legend, Seweweekspoort ('seven weeks pass') refers to the time it took the early brandy smugglers to cross this mountain barrier.

# Lesotho

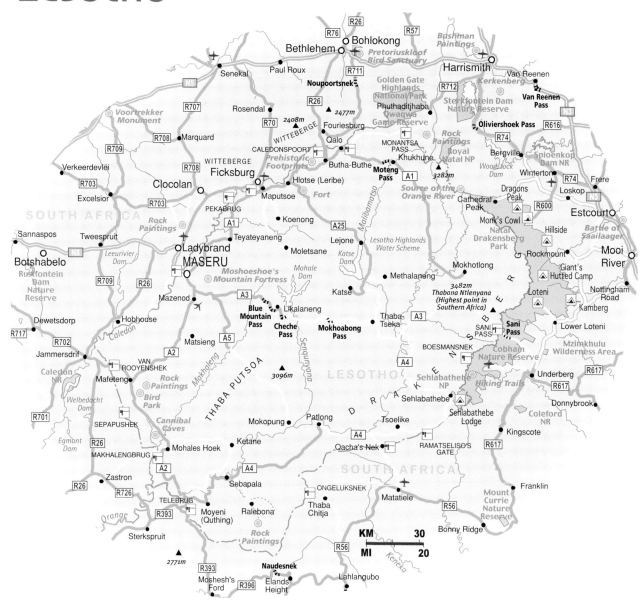

## PONY TREKKING IN THE MALUTIS

The landscape of the traditional home of the Basotho people is wild and rugged. Its open veld and golden grassland are skirted by rocky ridges, and much of the land is untamed and inaccessible, even on foot or by four-wheel-drive. The largely rural Basotho use horses and the sure-footed Basotho pony to navigate this terrain. These tough and hardy mounts are the most dependable way to traverse Lesotho, and an entire industry (albeit rather basic) has grown around the Basotho pony and its strengths. In the summer, the mountain is carpeted with indigenous plants, while winter brings snow to the mountain peaks that still shelter pastoral herdsmen wearing little more than the ornately decorated blankets for which the Basotho are renowned. Although the people of Lesotho are at home on horseback on these hilly plains, this does not mean that crossing the countryside is easy. The going is extremely tough in places. Despite this, you do not have to be a practised horseman to take advantage of the unspoiled wilderness, but familiarize yourself with some horseriding basics. The logistics of most pony trekking tours are carefully planned by operators based in Lesotho and South Africa. It is best to make use of their services rather than rely on your own abilities to interpret local conditions in a landscape that is both challenging and deceptive. Every care needs to be taken to avoid complications on a trip into such an isolated world, making trained guides your most vital 'accessory'. Amenities on the South African side are far more sophisticated, and the foothills of the Drakensberg are dotted with some fine lodges, private reserves and overnight facilities.

## THE MALUTI IN A NUTSHELL

Requirements: Border crossings can be problematic without the correct documentation. Plan carefully.

Climate: Winter temperatures can be icy, with a formidable wind-chill factor contributing to freezing conditions. Summers are moderate to hot.

Facilities: Facilities are virtually non-existent. Be prepared.

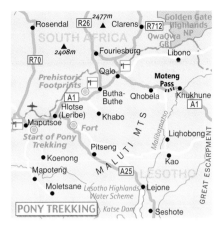

**SANI PASS IN A NUTSHELL**
Climate: Snowfalls in the icy winters and heavy downpours in the hot summers make spring (from August to November) the best bet.
Risk factor: Not for the uninitiated, anyone with less than impressive driving skills or with no head for heights. Pass is closed in bad weather.
Pack: Warm clothing during the freezing winter. Carry every conceivable necessary spare vehicle part.
Facilities: Comfortable overnight amenities in foothill towns.

## THABANA NTLENYANA

Part of the Drakensberg mountain range, which formed over 150 million years ago, Thabana Ntlenyana in the north-eastern corner of Lesotho is the highest peak in the southern subcontinent. Thabana Ntlenyana ironically means 'beautiful little mountain', yet it lies 3,482m (11,417ft) above sea level, offering spectacular views over some of southern Africa's most panoramic vistas. In winter, the snow-covered slopes are icy cold, a chilling wind whipping its way through every valley and down rock cliffs. In the balmy summer months, the rains bring with them a green blanket that clothes the rugged terrain. The hike to the top of Thabana Ntlenyana is along 25km (16 miles) of some of Lesotho's roughest terrain, rising to a height of 2,000m (6,562ft).

## SANI PASS

High above some of the tiny nation's most magnificent scenery stands Sani Top, an eerily windswept haven for hikers and adventurers – but the summit boasts some comfort with the highest pub in Africa! Sani Pass snakes through the Mkhomazana River Valley in the Drakensberg from just beyond the tiny village of Himeville up to Sani Top. Sani soars 1,000m (3,280ft) over a length of only 7km (4.3 miles). The route is demanding at best, perilous at worst. The broader region caters for hikers, trailists and 'pony trekkers', usually led by the blanket-clad local Basotho people.

## DRIVING SANI PASS

One of the most jaw-dropping mountain gateways in southern Africa, Sani Pass is the highest in the country and opens up unsurpassed views over vast tracts of South Africa. The world here is a lost one, whipped by winds that emit a ghostly wail as they batter the rugged slopes and pummel every nook and crevice. Extremes of weather and vegetation make the countryside all the more picturesque, and the long, winding Sani Pass is the lifeline of this remote expanse of the steep escarpment. The pass itself is a small but significant chink in the great mountain. Once little more than a rough bridle path crafted by man and beast, and mostly by blanketed Basotho horsemen and the occasional adventurer, Sani Pass is today the only road link between KwaZulu-Natal and the remote Lesotho highlands. Cut by breathtaking hairpin bends carved into the rocky slopes, even at its least trying the pass is an arduous and difficult climb, twisting and slicing its way along the steep inclines of the valley formed by the meandering Mkhomazana River. This is the simplest way to ascend the 2,875m (9,500ft) mountain face, and the vistas from even relatively low down on the pass will knock your breath away.

## DO NOT LOOK DOWN!

This is not a place for sufferers of even mild vertigo. The drops are long and hard. Plus the 6km (4-mile) route from the South African border post carries the traveller no less than 1,000m (3,280ft). Not surprising, then, that no standard sedan vehicle is permitted beyond that point: this is total 4x4 terrain, and every conceivable attribute of an offroad vehicle is put to the test. A few private individuals operate from the nearby hamlets of Underberg and Himeville. They offer the next best thing to negotiating yourself up the perilous pass to the mountainous heights of Lesotho. It is so precipitous that even the Basotho ponies struggle a little – especially when the rocky ground is covered by a soft mantle of snow. Although local townsfolk know the lie of the land well and are ready for most emergencies, winter snow can play havoc with even the most meticulously planned excursion.

Top to bottom: traditional hut door; shepherd in the Maluti mountains; Mafka Lisiu Pass.

# The Orange River Region

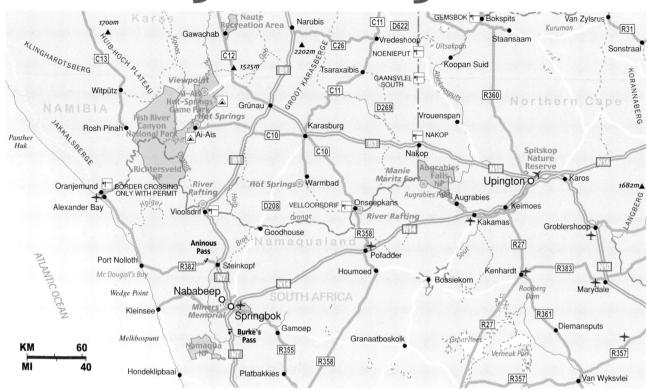

## RAFTING THE ORANGE RIVER

Slicing through an apparently lifeless landscape is the winding course of the mighty Orange, South Africa's greatest river and 'homeland' of its river-rafting adventures. It is the most revered by watersport enthusiasts and, with its succession of tortuous bends, raging waters and breathtaking rapids, is justifiably one of South Africa's premier adventure destinations. Time spent on the Orange is unmatched in high-pulse excitement and wonder at the scenic beauty of its banks. The often parched landscape is simply spectacular – and taking it all in from a canoe on the river makes it all the more memorable. Although known more for its turbulent white waters and

adrenaline-pumping rapids, canoe trails and circular routes including the impressive Augrabies Falls National Park, the Orange does have less demanding routes where little experience is required. This is one of the subcontinent's most powerful watercourses, so be sure to keep your wits about you, especially in the sections named

Rollercoaster, Crunch and Crusher. They will call on your strength, knowledge of the river and application of important pointers dispensed by the more experienced water guides and instructors in the introductory lecture offered by operators. Trips can stretch from one to five days (or longer), and while you aren't expected to have any rafting experience

## THE ORANGE IN A NUTSHELL

Climate: Best during the summer rains (November–January) when waters are high.

Risk factor: Moderate to challenging, but professional river guides provide valuable instruction and guidance.

Pack: Protective, waterproof clothing adds to your comfort levels; tour operators will provide most of your requirements. Sunscreen is essential.

Facilities: Facilities offered by operators are generally good to very good, although the nature of the adventure means that participants should be willing to rough it in the wilderness.

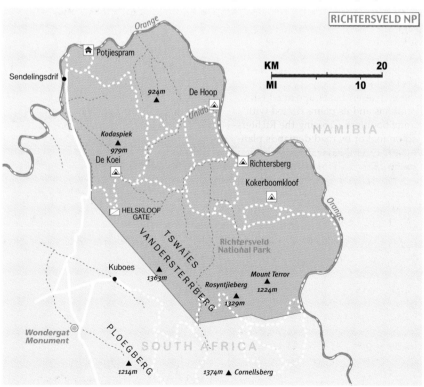

## RICHTERSVELD IN A NUTSHELL

**Requirements:** Permits for hiking, angling and 4x4 trails.

**Climate:** Winter (May–August) is best, as summer heat can be oppressive, with sandstorms and strong winds.

**Risk factor:** Moderate- to high-risk driving; easy to physically demanding hiking routes.

**Pack:** Sunscreen is essential, along with a high fluid intake. Strong winds and very basic facilities necessitate a tent that can be sealed.

**Facilities:** Amenities within the park vary from basic camp sites with no facilities at all to comfortable self-catering, fully equipped accommodation. Official routes and trails are clearly signposted.

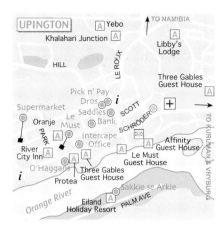

to tackle the Orange, novice canoeists should stick to routes and trips in keeping with their ability. It is all too easy for the fun of an exhilarating adventure to end in disaster if you take the river too lightly. Water levels fluctuate according to the season – the river floods in summer and the rocky river bed below the cascading waters presents dangers of its own. Sensible handling and the right equipment should ensure a safe and invigorating trip, though!

### CROSSING THE RICHTERSVELD

Although accessible from a number of points in South Africa and along the Namibian border, many roads leading to the 160,000ha (395,400 acre) Richtersveld National Park may not be numbered, while routes within the park can only accommodate high-clearance and 4x4 vehicles. Situated more than 200km (125 miles) from Springbok, the region is remote, a desert landscape lined with mountains and its plains dotted with granite boulders. Crossing the Richtersveld on foot or by road demands planning and careful navigation. Make good use, too, of the few existing facilities at the camp sites and overnight stopovers.

### THE ROADS LESS TRAVELLED

The 4x4 routes and hiking trails that crisscross the veld, compact sands and rocky passes vary in intensity – it is not for nothing that natural features such as Mount Terror have earned their fearful reputation! Although the rough, unsophisticated tracks and often unbearable heat have only served to add to its popularity as one of the region's most formidable wilderness areas. The national park that shares the name of the broader region was proclaimed in 1991 and, with its geological extremes and variety

of succulent vegetation, remains the traditional home of the pastoralist Nama. They still own the land and continue to farm with livestock, keeping alive some remnants of their customs. Many of the existing 4x4 trails are the legacy of early pioneers who left their tracks here during the prospecting days of the early 20th century. To preserve the delicate ecosystem, offroad driving is limited to these numbered tracks. Because the park's official routes are relatively new, the opportunity to explore some spectacularly unspoiled wilderness is unique and, to keep it that way, the number of vehicles is restricted to three, carrying no more than a dozen travellers at a time. The hiking routes are also limited to specially demarcated zones, and from April to October special guided hikes take parties of between five and 12 individuals on two- to five-day excursions.

Top to bottom: a weary *Halfmens* tree;
a klipspringer on rocky path; Augrabies Falls.

# Wild Coast
## Port Elizabeth to Port Edward

### PORT ELIZABETH

Alive with beaches, parks and historical architecture and monuments, PE (aka the Friendly City, as well as the Windy City) bears its colonial past throughout town, with statues of the like of Queen Victoria and the Horse Memorial, as well as structures such as the towering Campanile which commemorates the arrival of the 1820 Settlers. The Campanile offers a spiral staircase leading up the 52m (168 ft) tower with a super viewing platform to get a great perspective of the city and surrounds. Other sites worth visiting include the 54ha (133-acre) Settlers Park, the Port Elizabeth Museum, the snake park and aquarium, while townships tours take advantage of incorporating the many surrounding townships into the tourist's itinerary. Big favourites with locals and tourists are the coastline, with great beaches for hobie sailors and surfers, as well as scores of great diving sites. The 1799 Fort Frederick was the first stone building in the district and was built by the Brits to repel possible French invasion. The fort was never called upon to fire a shot in self-defence or in anger!

### SHIPWRECK COAST

A delightfully unspoilt stretch of coastline (formerly part of the Ciskei homeland) between Port Alfred and East London offers superb natural vegetation and sandy stretches of beach. This natural haven has seen the unhappy demise of countless ships, and the 64km (39-mile) Shipwreck Hiking Trail takes in some of the 'grave sites', from the Great Fish River through to the Ncera River. The trail offers a unique hiking and camping experience in South Africa, with greater freedom to camp and make fires where you please.

### WILD COAST HIKING HOTSPOTS
- Tsitsikamma Trail — 5 days
- Otter Trail — 5 days
- Shipwreck Hiking Trail — 3 days
- Strandloper Hiking Trail — 5 days
- Amatola Trail — 6 days
- Evelyn Valley Loop Trail — 2 days
- Zingcuka Loop Trail — 2 days
- Hogsback area — 1-3 days
- Wild Coast Hiking Trail — 1-14 days

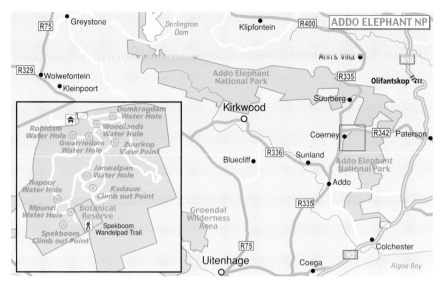

## ADDO ELEPHANT NATIONAL PARK

Lying just 72km (44 miles) north of PE is the 125,000 ha (309,000 acre) refuge for the remainder of the once prolific elephant population that called this area home. Visitors should be assured of seeing some of the 350-plus elephants in the park, along with almost 300 Cape buffalo, black rhino, numerous antelope and the unique flightless dung beetle. The park is being expanded into the 492,000 ha (1,2 million acre) "Greater Addo" park which will offer an increased natural diversity (five of SA's seven major vegetation biomes) as well as the Big 7 (Elephant, rhino, lion, buffalo, leopard, whales and great white sharks!) by incorporating part of the coastline into the park.

## EAST LONDON

A busy little port city, East London's excellent surfing conditions are a big hit with boarders young and old, notably at the famous Nahoon Beach. Holidays see the main beaches horribly overcrowded, so look to surf out of season or slightly further away from the madding crowd. The city offers a small aquarium, while the East London Museum has excellent displays of local Xhosa culture as well as two prize 'catches': a coelacanth and the world's only dodo egg.

## UMTATA

Founded on the Umtata River in 1871 by European settlers answering the call from the Thembu tribe to offer a barrier to invasions from the rival Pondo tribe. The small museum has interesting displays of beadwork and traditional costumes of the Xhosa people.

## WILD COAST NATURE RESERVES

The Wild Coast Hiking Trail is blessed with deliciously quiet evenings that send up sparkling explosions of stars, and hikers usually choose to do small sections of the 14-day route, which takes in a number of nature reserves. Mkambati Nature Reserve offers canoe trips up the Msikaba River as well as walking trails, Silaka NR throws up Cape clawless otters on the beach along with white-breasted cormorants, Hluleka NR is a beautifully scenic combination of sea, lagoon and forest from Port St Johns to Coffee Bay (reportedly so called due to a shipwrecked 'coffee carrier'!). Cwebe NR has great forests, beaches and trails, Cape clawless otters in the lagoon and the impressive Mbanyana Falls. Dwesa NR is thought by many to be one of South Africa's most beautiful reserves, with crocodile being reintroduced into the Kobole River and herds of eland that stroll down to the beach towards sunset, while the forest areas includes tree dassie, blue duiker and samango monkeys.

Opposite page: Addo Elephant Park.
Top to bottom: 'Hole in the Wall', Wild Coast;
Jacaranda wreck; Hobie pier, Port Elizabeth.

# East Coast
## St Lucia, Maputaland & Zululand

### ST LUCIA WETLAND PARK
A World Heritage Site, the park includes the St Lucia Game Reserve, False Bay National Park, St Lucia Marine Reserve, Sodwana Bay National Park, Maputaland Marine Reserve and Mkuzi Game Reserve. Nature lovers and eco-tourists will find bucketloads of Mother Nature's bounty with which to amuse and excite themselves in the wetlands. Mangroves, swamps, lagoons and five eco-systems form one of the world's most incredible eco-destinations: seashore and dune forest, fresh water lakes, wetlands, mangrove swamps, dry savannah and papyrus banks. This 32,800ha (81,016-acre) reserve includes a coastline stretching 280km (1,730 miles), while the Greater St Lucia Wetland Park on Lake St Lucia is one of Africa's largest estuaries. In addition to acting as a nursery for innumerable species of marine life it teems with 1,200 crocodile, 800 hippo and numerous bird species, including the famous family of fish eagles.

### ST LUCIA AND SURROUNDS
Part of the World Heritage Site, St Lucia offers magnificent views from the village, a wide range of arts and crafts and a Crocodile Centre that breeds the endangered dwarf and longsnout crocs. Around 15km (9.3 miles) north of St Lucia village is Mission Rock (a popular braai site), while the Grace Mission Station dates back to 1898.

### KOSI BAY AND SURROUNDS
Exploring Maputaland offers an insight into the Tsonga people who live in this region. They employ ingenious traditional fish traps positioned close to the mouth of the Kosi Estuary. The famous fish *kraals* are patrolled by the Tembe. This somewhat primitive (yet highly-effective) system of catching fish has provided a vital source of sustenance for their people for centuries. This is living history in its most pristine form!

### SODWANA BAY
One of the most popular family holiday destinations, Sodwana offers a variety of accommodation, from excellent hotels and lodges to self-catering chalets, caravan parks and tent sites located along many hectares of coastal forest. Fresh produce as well as local craftwork is sold at numerous roadside markets. Sodwana is a diving hotspot and is famous for its marine life.

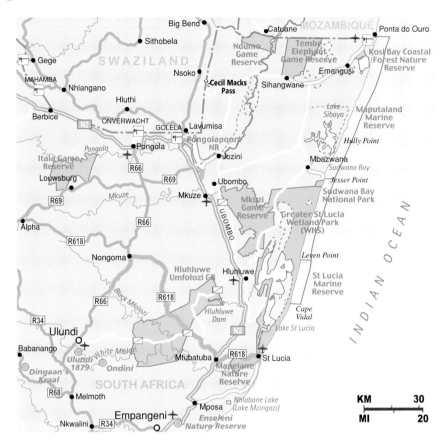

### CAPE VIDAL
Outdoor enthusiasts can sail, swim, snorkel and fish along this beautiful stretch of beach where record catches of marlin and barracuda have been notched up. Saltwater flyfishing addicts will really enjoy Mission Rocks.

### TEMBE NATIONAL PARK
Lying on the SA-Mozambique border, Tembe proclaims itself as the place of wild and untamed Africa. Boasting the world's largest elephants, it also offers great viewing for birders. Tongaland's nearby reefs are appreciated by scuba divers. The reserve protects the last of the Maputaland elephant population.

### HLUHLUWE-UMFOLOZI PARK
Established in 1895, these are Africa's oldest animal sanctuaries and their pride and joy is the success of Operation Rhino in the the 1960s, which saw white rhino relocated to places of safety in South Africa as well as overseas. Hluhluwe-Umfolozi has the Big Five on offer, along with an amazing diversity of wildlife to please the most hardened nature lovers. Visitors with time on their hands can meet a fifth of the world's population of black and white rhino.

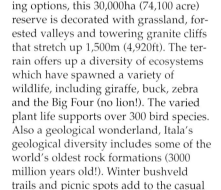

## PHINDA PRIVATE GAME RESERVE

Squeezed in between St Lucia and Mkuzi, Phinda has seven habitats that cater for the Big Five and 380 bird species. For an exhilarating walking adventure, Phinda's walking safaris take you through pristine wilderness: African wildlife doesn't come better!

## ITALA GAME RESERVE

Criss-crossed with rivers and many hiking options, this 30,000ha (74,100 acre) reserve is decorated with grassland, forested valleys and towering granite cliffs that stretch up 1,500m (4,920ft). The terrain offers up a diversity of ecosystems which have spawned a variety of wildlife, including giraffe, buck, zebra and the Big Four (no lion!). The varied plant life supports over 300 bird species. Also a geological wonderland, Itala's geological diversity includes some of the world's oldest rock formations (3000 million years old!). Winter bushveld trails and picnic spots add to the casual visitor's enjoyment and wildlife experience in what is now one of KZN's premier nature reserves.

## MKUZI GAME RESERVE, ZULULAND

Mkuzi is rich in animal life such as rhino, giraffe, zebra, kudu and impala, yet one of its more unique features is a rare forest of giant fig trees that reach up to 25m (82ft) in height. Nearly 400 species of bird enjoy the varied vegetation, and the excellent bird hide at Nsumo Pan take full advantage of this.

Top to bottom: coastal surfing; loggerhead hatchlings; fisherman at Banga Neck.

# Battlefields & the Drakensberg

### THE GRIM WEEPERS

For 80 years war raged through the KwaZulu-Natal countryside, bloody conflicts being waged between Boer, Brit and Zulu. The peace that currently drifts across this lush and rolling countryside belies the grim and brutal fighting that took place throughout most of the 1800s. The Battlefields Route takes visitors across hundreds of kilometres of road, so time can be spent indulging in the small, unusual or dramatic towns dotting the landscape, each with its own history, mystery and dramas to recount … as well as bed and breakfast spots, at the ready to serve you! So much desolate surrounding countryside allows you to let your mind wander, imagining what it must have been like to face an army of attacking Zulu warriors, sunburnt British soldiers, or crafty Boer horsemen.

### RORKE'S DRIFT

The Rorke's Drift Museum pays homage to a mighty British defence: 100 soldiers kept 4,000 Zulu warriors at bay for 12 of their soldiers.

### BLOOD RIVER

The life-size statues of a semi-circle of a wagon *laager* provide an awesome monument of this great battle. It saw so much loss of life, the victorious Boers proclaimed that the Ncome River ran red with Zulu blood.

### ISANDLWANA

In response to an invasion of their land (which was an attempt to conquer the mighty Zulu nation), 25,000 Zulu *impis* defeated the 24th Regiment on 22 January 1879. Their attack was delayed as they waited for the right phase of the moon under which to launch their offensive, at which point they unleashed their trademark pincer movement to overthrow the British.

### GETTING AROUND

The Battlefields Route Association has developed six self-drive sub-routes to assist tourists in planning their trips, each with its own theme.
- King Shaka's Way
- Remembrance Route
- Rifleman's Road
- Warrior's Trek
- Siege Salute
- Red Soldier's March

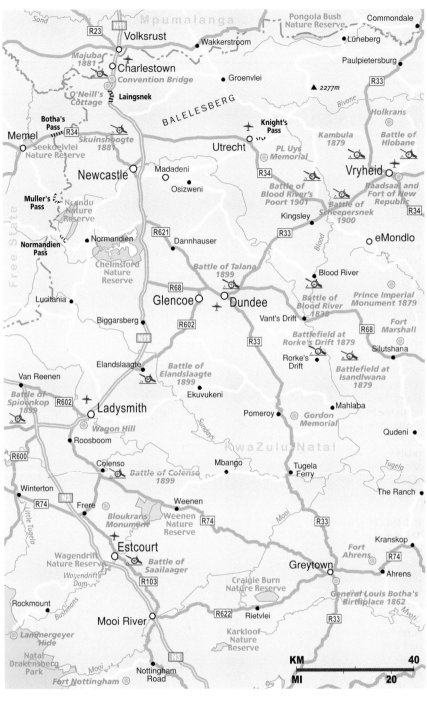

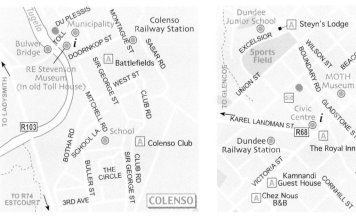

## DUNDEE
Close to many battlesites and the comprehensive Talana Museum, Dundee has plenty of historic buildings to visit and photograph, including the Cenotaph war memorial, a MOTH Museum with superb war artifacts, and plenty of historic churches. There are a host of country activities and adventures in the town's surrounds, such as horseriding and 4x4 and hiking trails.

## SPIOENKOP
Spioenkop has a battlefield, a dam and a nature reserve with a wealth of wildlife – to be viewed from the safety of your car – including zebra, rhino, giraffe and a handful of buck. The nearby Rangeworthy Cemetery is the resting place for victims at Spioenkop and Bastion Hill.

## NEWCASTLE
The mountains surrounding Newcastle are great hiking venues, and the peaks of Koningsberg and Kranskop both soaring to over 2,000m (6,560ft). Hilldrop House is a National Monument as is the former home of author, Rider Haggard. Haggard's life and work are documented in the museum at Fort Amiel (1876), built to stave off Zulu advances. Fort Terror is one of a number of signalling posts in the area, and another National Monument, St Dominics Pavilion (1916), was a social hub when originally built as a skating rink.

## HIKING THE DRAKENSBERG
The ridge of high peaks that forms the escarpment between South Africa's east coast and the mountainous hinterland is one of Africa's most remarkable, proudly displaying grand formations and extraordinary rock sculptures. The air here is soft, gentle and silent, while the earth beneath your hiking boots is studded with rocks, stones and plantlife that date back thousands of years. The steep ravines and rugged inclines of the Drakensberg remain one of Africa's most remarkable geological features. The environmental awareness of its custodians thankfully keeps it a pristine wilderness. This wild country is a hiker's dream, offering relatively undemanding walking trails, rolling hills and rugged cliffs that require some resilience. The most arduous climbs, on the other hand, require supreme fitness and commitment. High peaks and rocky routes take their toll, and even casual hikers are advised to familiarise themselves with some of the dangers of areas such as Mzimkhulu, Bushman's Nek, Giant's Castle and the state forests. Scenic

### DRAKENSBERG IN A NUTSHELL
Requirements: Valid passport only. Permits, where required, are available at the various park entrances. Booking is essential throughout the area.
Climate: Snowfalls in the icy winters and heavy downpours in the hot summer. Spring is best (Aug–Nov).
Pack: Camping equipment, comfortable and firm hiking boots, warm, protective clothing and sleeping bags for the freezing winters; or lightweight clothing and rain gear for the blistering summer days.
Facilities: Relatively sophisticated, varying from basic camp sites with ablutions to very comfortable overnight huts and private lodges. Many routes and trails are well signposted.

beauty abounds, but then so do precarious drops, steep slopes and the sheer isolation of many routes and trails. The foothills of the southern region, part of which borders Lesotho and its remarkable Sani Pass, provide a fractionally gentler alternative to the hikes of the northern Drakensberg. Nevertheless, they require diligence and an ability to navigate the rigorous inclines. There are a few short hikes and overnight walks, such as the Giant's Cup Hiking Trail which takes about five days, but even 'simple' routes have dangers. The 3,315m (11,000ft) peak of Giant's Castle, for example, requires a high level of fitness, endurance and experience. The rewards are unparalleled and the views that stretch forever are a short, sharp panacea.

Top to bottom: graves at Fort Pearson; Spioenkop Memorial; Tugela river.

# Swaziland

**A PROUD KINGDOM**

Swaziland is a small landlocked country bordered on three sides by South Africa, with Mozambique lying on its eastern side. The local people are friendly and have a good many traditions and customs, with traditional dances on display throughout the countryside. There is also a flourishing handicraft industry. Swaziland offers an extraordinary diversity of scenery and its excellent national parks and game drives are home to a wide diversity of game, notably the somewhat elusive rhino. The national bird is the purple-crested Loerie.

**TO DO IN SWAZILAND**

- River-rafting down the Great Usutu River.
- Trout fishing at Mhlambanyatsi ('waterplace of the buffaloes').
- Hiking in the Malolotja Nature Reserve (a walker's paradise offering some of the finest hiking trails in southern Africa).
- Horseriding and walking trails through wonderfully scenic locations such as Malolotja, Meikles Mount and Mlilwane.

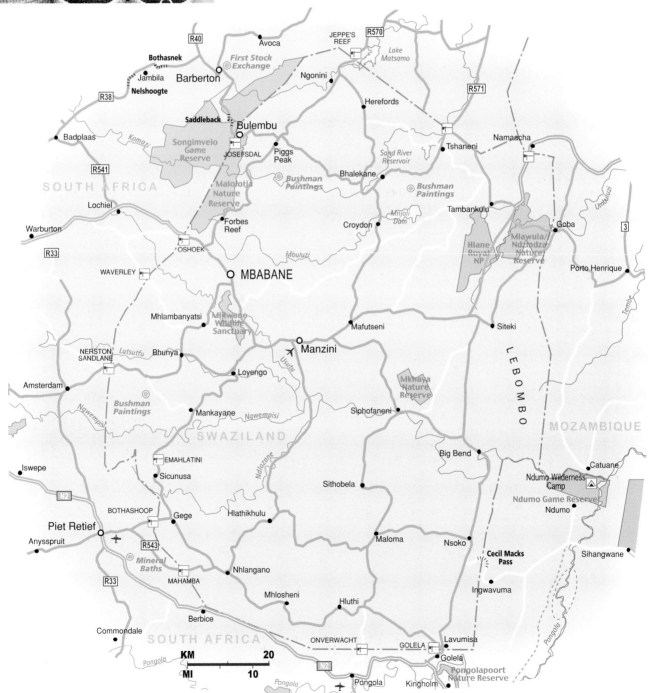

## MBABANE

The capital, Mbabane, boasts the Swazi Plaza – a large modern shopping complex which is a good landmark and houses the Tourist Office – and the interesting Indinglilizi Art Gallery, established in 1982 in order to showcase the work of the many talented local Swazi artists. The Siteki Inyanga Sangoma School trains traditional healers and diviners, while the Muti-Muti Nature Reserve is used by the school's trainers and students as a rich source of vital herbs which grow abundantly throughout the reserve.

## PIGGS PEAK

Located in the far north of Swaziland, Piggs Peak was once a gold mining centre named after an early prospector, William Pigg. Modern-day prospectors swarm to the new gambling centre in the hope of striking it rich, or simply just to enjoy a few hours of entertainment at a casino. Inside the Malolotja Reserve, just 40km (24 miles) south of Piggs Peak, is the old Forbes Reef Gold Mine. Visitors can safely explore the abandoned horizontal mine shafts with the visual aid of a torch.

## HIGHS AND LOWS

The smallest country in the southern Hemisphere, Swaziland's highest point is at Emlembem which is a popular point to climb at 1,862m (6,107ft) above sea level. The Sibebe Rock is the world's second-largest granite rock and is a good picnic spot near to Mbabane. The local Sibebe beer is named in honour of

the great rock. The Ngwenya Mine is one of the oldest known mines in the world and dates back to 41,000BC. You can get to the mine by car, while a visit to the Ngwenya Glass Factory (just west of Mbabane) will showcase some of the glasswork and art that the locals are famous for producing.

## CULTURE VULTURE

Ezulwini Valley (also near to Mbabane) has all the cultural attractions you could wish for and is, in addition, a relaxing place to unwind in – understandably, since locals call it 'the place of heaven'. Not to be missed is the Incwala ceremony and the Umhlanga dances, and Ezulwini is the nation's entertainment centre and the valley is home to the Mlilwane Wildlife Sanctuary. Lobamba is the royal family residence and the Royal Kraal, Somhlolo National Stadium and the National Museum are all interesting cultural hotspots. The national museum offers displays on Swazi origin, tradition, dress and lifestyle. Next to the museum are the parliament buildings as well as the King Sobhuze II Memorial.

## NOT VERY RESERVED

Mkhaya Nature Reserve is the kingdom's VIP destination and is a refuge for endangered species – this 6,200 hectares (15,314-acre) birdwatchers paradise is particularly memorable if you are interested in raptors. Mlilwane is a private reserve dominated by the striking Nyonyane (Little Bird) Peak and boasting a good collection of wildlife, including hippo and black eagles means 'little fire', named after the many fires started by lightning strikes in the region. Hlane National Park has very good accommodation and offers visitors some of the best game viewing in Swaziland, with up to 10,000 animals gathering here during the dry season. Mantenga is a small protected area of 725ha (1,790 acres) in a corner of the Ezulwini Valley and is bordered by the little Usutu River in the south and Mlilwane to the north and west. Possibly the reserve's most famous attraction is the Mantenga Falls, the largest in Swaziland in terms of water. Birdlife here is abundant and includes the endangered bald ibis.

Opposite page: a woman weaving baskets.
Top to bottom: a Swazi homestead; horseback safari in the Mlilwane Wildlife Sanctuary; Phophonyane Falls.

# Cradle of Humankind

## SIMILAR WORLD HERITAGE SITES

The Sangiran Early Man Site    Java, Indonesia
The Peking Man Site    Zhoukoudian, People's Republic of China
Australian Fossil Mammal Sites    Riversleigh/Narcoote, Australia
The Lower Valley of the Awash    Ethiopia
The Lower Valley of the Omo    Ethiopia

SITE OF Sts 5 CRANIUM OF AUSTRALOPITHECUS AFRICANUS (PLESIANTHROPUS) "MRS. PLES." DISCOVERED 18 APRIL 1947 BY DR. ROBERT BROOM AND MR. JOHN T. ROBINSON.

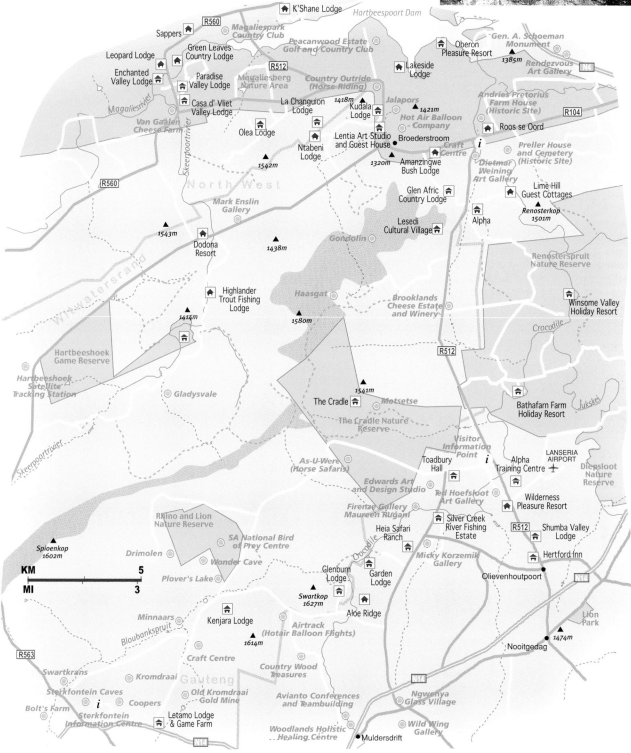

## THE CRADLE OF HUMANKIND

Located around 45 minutes away from South Africa's famous goldfields, and lying across the North West and Gauteng provinces, the Cradle of Humankind is one of the world's richest areas of prehistoric findings. It is a truly unique location. This quiet and peaceful valley kept its human origins secret for millions of years until the first fossilised discoveries in the late 1890s. The Cradle of Humankind is a listed World Heritage Site, and holds some of the most significant and plentiful archaeological finds known to man. The site is very important for Africa; it serves as evidence that humankind probably began in these humble hills, bestowed with such gentle beauty and glorious solitude.

## FROM THE CRADLE TO THE GRAVE

The official name for The Cradle is the much more wordy Sterkfontein, Swartkrans, Kromdraai and Environs World Heritage Site – lacking the romance and passion of its more commonly used name. Ironically, the remains of this supposed birthplace of humankind are now made up solely of deliberate or accidental graves, as well as artefacts and dwellings scattering the landscape. For fossil-finders there are 12 major sites to visit as well as scores of smaller sites. Of course, it's highly protected and a great deal of relic-hunting has already gone on, so don't expect to fill your bucket (but there's always the chance of a lucky discovery). Bear in mind, though, that amateur picking of fossil treasures could detract from new knowledge of our forefathers and our shared education. In the meanwhile, there are plenty of sites to explore and learn from.

## SKULLS AND CROSSBONES

Some of the more famous discoveries include the skull of Mrs Ples (although recent research suggests it was in fact a

### ICONS OF THE NORTH WEST
- Hartbeespoort Dam
- The Magaliesberg mountain range
- Madikwe Game Reserve
- Mafikeng
- The Pilanesberg National Park
- Sun City
- The Palace of the Lost City
- The Vredefort Dome and Dome Conservancy
- The Taung Heritage Site

Mr Ples!) and the amazing Little Foot (a 3.3 million-year-old skeletal remains believed to be the key to linking the family tree of humans and apes). The Sterkfontein Valley boasts numerous sites that helped scientists in piecing together the jigsaw puzzle of humankind's long history. Some of the most famous of these palaeo-anthropological sites include Sterkfontein (identified as having the oldest stone tools in southern Africa), Swartkrans, Kromdraai, Coopers B, Wonder Cave, Drimolen, Gladysvale, Gondolin, Plover's Lake, Haasgat, Bolt's Farm and Minnaars Caves. Bolt's Farm is credited with the discovery of microfauna that scientists believe to be around 4,5 million years old.

## HARTBEESPOORT DAM

A popular weekend getaway spot surrounded by the majestic Magaliesberg mountain range, Hartbeespoort Dam is a favourite destination for day trips and adventure thrills. Watersports abound, with parasailing, windsurfing, water- and jetskiing to excite both locals and tourists. The more adventurous can take to the skies, their adrenaline pumping to the thrill of paragliding, hang-gliding or hot-air ballooning.

Opposite page: Mrs Ples's discovery site.
Top to bottom: the Twins rock formation; Sterkfontein caves; hikers in Retief Kloof.

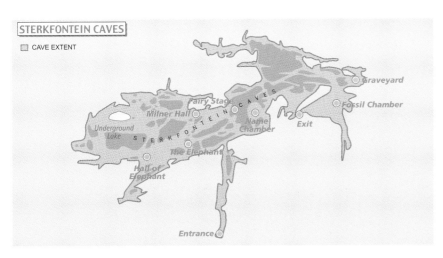

### STERKFONTEIN CAVES
☐ CAVE EXTENT

Graveyard
Fairy Stage
Fossil Chamber
Milner Hall
STERKFONTEIN CAVES
Underground Lake
Name Chamber
Exit
The Elephant
Hall of Elephant
Entrance

# Kruger National Park

### AS OLD AS THE HILLS

In Kruger's northern region you can take a drive to Baobab Hill to see the majestic solitary baobab tree that has been there for centuries. This northern area may be remote, but it's definitely an area worth visiting, what with the baobabs, amongst numerous other tree species that can be seen across the plains. Trees are an important food source for several animals, notably elephants, who find them irresistible, stripping them of their bark to satisfy their considerable appetite.

### THE LION THING

King of the animal world, the lion tops the wish list of most visitors when it comes to Things To See In Kruger. Many animals will make a noise if a lion is nearby but you should also watch the skyline for giraffes: they often stare fixedly in the direction of any danger (aka lions!).

### A BIG SIX

There is such an abundance of birds compared with mammals, it's understandable that the compilers of the 'must-see' bird list couldn't agree on just five, hence the Birding Big Six: Ground Hornbill, Kori Bustard, Lappetfaced Vulture, Martial Eagle, Pel's Fishing Owl and the Saddle-bill

### THE FAMOUS FIVE

Africa's BIG FIVE are handsomely on display in Kruger, but you dare not forget who's IN the five: Buffalo, Rhino, Elephant, Lion and Leopard … BRELL! Not as well known, the LITTLE FIVE is a play on words, affording some lesser known (and infinitely less-feared) animals a shot at fame: Buffalo Weaver, Rhino Beetle, Elephant Shrew, Ant Lion and Leopard Tortoise. The Little Five might not be the stuff of major advertising campaigns, but it's fun to include them in your animal checklist.

Stork. Kruger has many superb bird hides which offer plenty of excellent 'twitching' opportunities.

### ONE, TWO, TREE

Of course trees had to get in on the act as well. The five tree species experts advise you to seek out for your checklist are: Baobab, Fever Tree, Knob Thorn, Marula and Mopane. Baobabs are the great-great-grandpapa of the floral world, mopane are amongst the most abundant in Kruger, while the marula is surely the tastiest (when transformed into the delectable liqueur, that is!).

### A LOT OF LOGS IN ONE RIVER

It's something of an irony that Kruger has a Crocodile River and an Olifants (elephants) River … and yet the Olifants River is the one which boasts one of the highest densities of crocodile in all of Africa!

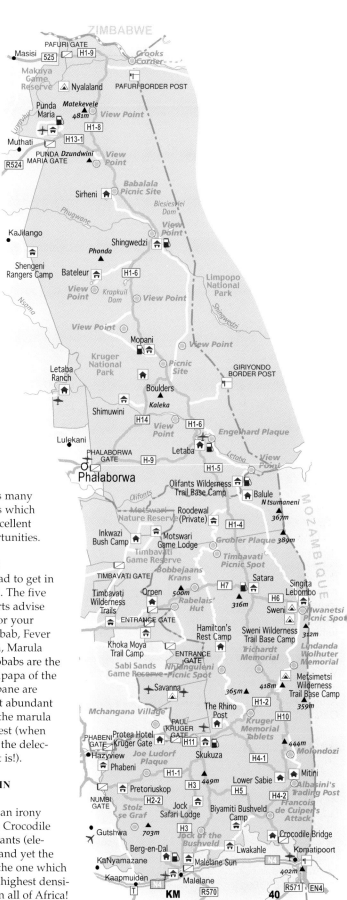

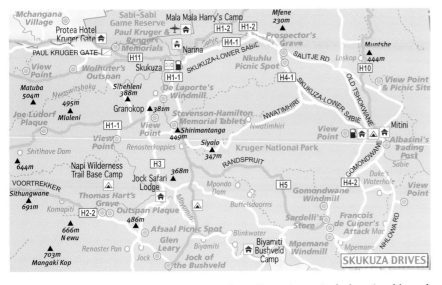

SKUKUZA DRIVES

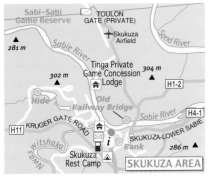

SKUKUZA AREA

## JOCK OF THE BUSHVELD

Dogs provide game rangers with companionship and protection, during which time strong bonds develop. Hence the dog's graveyard where 'fallen friends' are buried. The most famous dog to have trodden Kruger's soil was Jock, immortalised in Percy Fitzpatrick's book, *Jock of the Bushveld*. Jock Safari Lodge was named in honour of that brave *staffie*, a statue commemorates his famous duel with a sable antelope, and other tributes to him can be seen in the park.

## DRIVING TRIPS FURTHER AFIELD

You can't go wrong spending three days driving around the central region of Kruger, which is between the Sabie and Olifants rivers. The Satara / Timbavati River Route is particularly enjoyable and should offer sightings of elephant and giraffe, but the Nwanetsi River to Lindanda Route is not to be missed, with magnificent scenery and multiple animals to be seen. The Sabie River drive will excite kids of all ages as it covers the famous 'lion route' through lush riverside vegetation packed with wildlife. The Kanniedood Dam drive is a spectacle on which to train your binoculars: marvellous scenery, mischievous monkeys, stately elephants and lazy crocodiles. The birding is super. Night drives dish up some of the best wildlife spotting opportunities as many animals are livelier in the cooler evenings, a fact which draws out a lot of predators.

## THE SOUTHERN KRUGER LOOP TRIP

A big favourite with tourists for the abundant wildlife, varied landscapes and diverse vegetation. Driving around the southern parts of Kruger leads visitors to numerous animal-friendly waterholes, as well as great picnic spots, viewpoints and memorials. Using Skukuza as your base, you have numerous choices and options, depending on the time available and your interests. The routes also link-up with two exit gates, making the trips ideal as a final excursion on your way out of the park.

## BEST GAME VIEWING IN AFRICA
- Mombo Camp
  Moremi NP, Botswana
- Il Moran Camp – Governors Camp
  Masai Mara NP, Kenya
- Ngorongoro Crater Lodge
  Ngorongoro Crater NP, Tanzania
- Migration Camp
  Serengeti NP, Tanzania
- Singita
  Sabi Sands GR, South Africa

Opposite page: a herd of zebra grazing.
Top to bottom: baobabs at sunrise; a giraffe grazing on the treetops; steenbok mother and young; tawny eagle.

# Mpumalanga

## PILGRIM'S REST

Visitors to this former mining town are prone to falling in love with its charm and beauty, and many speak of it with a glint in the eye for years to come. The town sprang up as a result of the 1873 gold rush, with almost 1,500 prospectors massing to the area within the year to seek their fortune. The gold held out for more than a hundred years! The beautifully restored town is now a national monument and visitors can explore the Old Print House, Miner's House, St Mary's Anglican Church, Joubert Bridge, the cemetery (with its infamous Robber's Grave) and Dredzen & Co's general dealer store. To get a taste of life as a Pilgrim's Rest prospector, try out panning for gold at the Diggings Site on the banks of Pilgrim's Creek. There are gold-panning demonstrations to watch first if you don't want to risk throwing your name (or a 'valuable' nugget) away. If you take to panning like a duck to water, then stick around till November for the annual National Gold Panning Championships, a fun festival spread over five days. Each competitor receives a bucket of sand and a regulation gold pan. Only the officials know how many nuggets are in the buckets – contestants are penalised for nuggets missed. The 'prospector' who pans out the most nuggets in the shortest time is the winner.

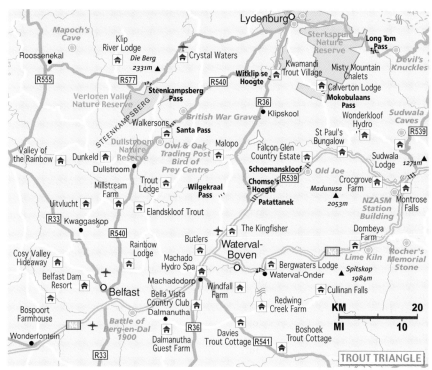

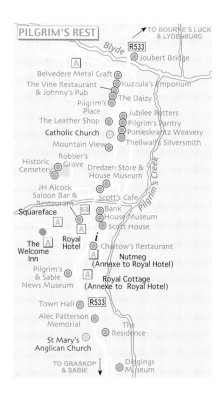

## THE TROUT TRIANGLE

The legendary Trout Triangle is made up of the towns of Belfast, Machadodorp, Dullstroom, Waterval-Boven, and Lydenburg. This area is a mecca for fly-fishing and, as a result, facilities are well developed for tourists and locals. Sabie and Pilgrim's Rest are two other prime fishing sites. Trout are not indigenous to the area and, as legend has it (told in the light of a camp fire), the fish were introduced into the dams and rivers around Dullstroom some 80 years ago by the local postmaster (Mr Gurr) and a watchmaker (Mr Braun). These trout-rich waters now allow for dam and river angling to satisfy the fussiest (some call it being a perfectionist!) of anglers.

Hatcheries in Mpumalanga produce 60 percent of South Africa's trout for the retail market. These hatcheries also ensure that dams and rivers remain well stocked. They provide stock for the European export market, too. Rainbow and Brown Trout are found happily gliding through the water in most dams and rivers. These are definite highlights on the flyfishing calendar! Apart from fishing guides and trips, you can arrange for one-on-one lessons or even group and corporate fishing lessons as well as advice sessions.

**BLYDE RVER CANYON**

R531 Mariepsig Rondavels
Marepe Lodge
Mariepskop
Aventura Swadini Resort
Kaya Bokmakierie
Mariepskop
Blydepoort Dam
▲1944m
R532
World's End
Aventura Blydepoort Resort
Three Rondavels
Denys Reitz' Grave
Blyde River Canyon Nature Reserve
Three Sisters 1704m
Groendak House
Op-de-Berg
The Devil's Window 1771m
Bourke's Luck Potholes
Muilhuis
New Chum Falls
Oswald Pirow's Grave
Mapasebone 1857m
Caspersnek
Sacramento
Maragise 1611m
R532
The Peak 1832m
Crystal Springs Mountain Resort
Themeda Hill Mountain Lodge
Lisbon Hideaway
Marite
Clearstream
R533
Alanglade House Museum
R534
Wonder View
God's Window
Jock of the Bushveld 1885
Pilgrim's Rest
Natural Rock Bridge
The Pinnacle
Mount Sheba
Mac-Mac
Graskop
R533
Kowyn Pass
R535
Mount Sheba Nature Reserve
Trout Hideaway
Jock of the Bushveld Trek 1885
R532
Mac-Mac Falls

**SUDWALA CAVES**

**MUST SEE & DO IN MPUMALANGA**
- Lure trout and spot the Big Five.
- Spot a Barberton Daisy.
- Admire the ancient cycads.
- Taste the delicious local fruit.
- Hike the Blyde River Canyon.
- Walk over Bourke's Luck Potholes.
- Navigate Sudwala Caves.
- Picnic under the many waterfalls.
- Stare in awe at The Pinnacle.
- Repeat yourself in the Echo Caves.
- Peer through God's Window.
- Pat the cheetahs at Hoedspruit.
- Solve a 'murder' in Dullstroom (murder mystery evenings are held at the old railway station!).
- Rest up at one of the many stunning waterfalls in the region.

**BLYDE RIVER CANYON**

The majestic and immense 20km-long (12.4-mile) Blyde River Canyon reaches depths of 700m (2,296ft) in places, its dramatic cliffs and slopes of the ravine covered by bush and forest. Antelope, small mammals, the full range of Southern Africa's primate family and a variety of birds live in the reserve, along with an abundance of flowering plants, orchids, lichens, mosses and montane forest. The much-photographed Three Rondavels are a trio of rocky outcrops that have eroded in the shape of traditional round Zulu or Xhosa tribal huts. Two other favourite visual feasts for visitors to indulge in from the road running above the canyon are World's End and Lowveld View. Popular activities include the circular drive, short hikes and overnight trails, *kloofing*, microlighting and leisurely boat trips that take in the wide array of wildlife within the Canyon, as well as some of the best whitewater in South Africa.

**BOURKE'S LUCK**

Looking down from the bridge across the potholes (sunken circular wells, to be more specific), you will stare in awe at the amazing cylindrical holes scooped out of the yellow dolomite rock floor. Swirling pebbles and gushing water from the Blyde and Treur rivers over millions of years created these dramatic natural 'rock carvings'.

**ECHO CAVES**

The Echo Caves are a sprawling mass of dolomite cut out by an underground river. Legend has it that the Sotho hid here from Swazi warriors and used the cave's stalactites to make spears, which is why so many of them are broken.

**SUDWALA CAVES**

The Sudwala Caves are the world's oldest dolomite caves and have a floor surface of 14,000m² (45,920 sq. miles) and feature weird and wonderful dripstone formations. The caves contain stalagmites, stalactites, and the fossilized remains of 'collenia' (a form of algae believed to be the very origins of life on earth). Many of the rock formations in the caves have biblical names, such as Devil's Workshop, Samson's Pillar and the Weeping Madonna. A five-hour tour of the Crystal Chambers can be organised. Outside the caves is a timeline of humankind as well as a 'dinosaur' park: life-size models of prehistoric wildlife that lived here 100 million years ago are set amidst cycad and palm species.

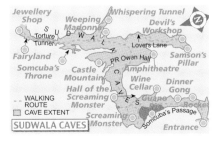

Jewellery Shop
Whispering Tunnel
Weeping Madonna
Devil's Workshop
Torture Tunnel
SUDWALA
Lovers Lane
Fairyland
PR Owan Hall
Samson's Pillar
Somcuba's Throne
Castle Mountain
Amphitheatre
Wine Cellar
Dinner Gong
Hall of the Screaming Monster
CAVES
Guano
Rocket
WALKING ROUTE
☐ CAVE EXTENT
Screaming Monster
Somcuba's Passage
Entrance
**SUDWALA CAVES**

Opposite page: hiking in the Blyde River Canyon.
Top to bottom: flyfishing in comfort; the Three Rondavels; the Berlin Falls.

# Namibia

## ADVENTURING THROUGH NAMIBIA
### (See Contact Details 92-95)

**NAMIBIA**
Capital: Windhoek
Area: 824,290 km² / 318,260mi²
Population: 1.8 million
Main ethnic groups:
• Ovambo (50%)
• Kavango (9%)
• Herero (7%)
• Damara (7%)
• White (6%)
Main languages:
• English
• Afrikaans
• Ovambo
• Kavango
• German
Main religion: Christian and Lutheran (90%)
Currency: Namibian dollar (100 cents)

## ON (OR IN) WATER

**ANGLING**

| | |
|---|---|
| Swakopmund | Laramon Tours |
| | Henry's Fishing |
| | Ocean Adventures & Angling Tours |
| | Sunrise Fishing |
| Upper Zambezi River and Caprivi Strip | Kalizo Lodge |

**SEAL AND DOLPHIN CRUISES**

| | |
|---|---|
| Swakopmund | Mola Mola |
| | Levo Tours |
| | Laramon Tours |
| | Ocean Adventures |

**CANOEING AND RAFTING**

| | |
|---|---|
| Orange River | Felix Unite |
| | Wildthing Adventures |
| | Kalahari Adventure Centre |
| Kunene River | Gravity Adventure Group |
| Epupa Camp | Kunene River Lodge |

**SEA KAYAKING**

| | |
|---|---|
| Walvis Bay | Eco-Marine Kayak Tours |

## ON LAND

**ROCK CLIMBING / ABSEILING**

| | |
|---|---|
| Spitzkoppe, Brandberg | Walkers Rock and Rope Adventures |
| | Guided Ascents in Africa |
| | Blue Mountain Adventures |

**HORSE TRAILS**

| | |
|---|---|
| Windhoek, Lüderitz and Namib | Reit Safari Namibia |
| | Klein Aus Vista |
| | The Desert Homestead |
| Swakopmund | Okakambe Trails |
| Etosha | Epacha Horse Trails |

**CAMEL RIDING**

| | |
|---|---|
| Windhoek and Namib | Reit Safari Namibia |

**HIKING**

| | |
|---|---|
| Namib-Naukluft Trail and Fish River Canyon | Tok Tokkie Trails |
| | Canyon Adventure Trail |
| | Klein Aus Vista |

**GAME VIEWING**

| | |
|---|---|
| Windhoek | Harnas Wildlife Foundation |
| Etosha | Namibia Wildlife Resorts |

Kunene
Ruacana Falls
Uutapi (Ombalantu)
Ruacana
Osh
Otjijandjasemo Hot Spring
Opuwo
Spring
Dorsland Trekkers Monument
Etosha Nat Park
Seal Colony
Skeleton Coast Park
Old German Fort
Ongongo Falls
Karos Cons. Area
ATLANTIC OCEAN
Kamanjab
Terrace Bay
Bergsig
Petrified Forest
Khorixas
Twyfelfontein Rock Engraving
Burnt Mountain
Ving (Rock
Huab
Ugab
Ugab Guided Trail
White Lady Painting
Uis
Messum Crater
National West Coast Tourist
Diego Cão Cross
Cape Cross Seal Reserve
Recreational Area
Roc Pair
B2
Henties Bay
Tsaobis Le Nature
Goanikontes
Swakopmund
Old Railway Station
Walvis Bay
Dune 7
Na
Old Rhenish Mission Church
Namib-Naukluft Park
Zebra P
Kuis
Conception Bay
Sesriem C
Sossu
St Francis Bay
Namib Natu Rese
Spencer Bay
Koi
Dias Cross Site Lü
Kolmanskop Ghost Mining Town
Elizabeth Ghost Mining To
ATLANTIC OCEAN

| **4X4 TRAILS** | |
|---|---|
| Countrywide | JJ 4x4 Adventures |
| Kalahari | Namib Eco 4x4 Route |
| Lüderitz | Coastway Tours |
| Windhoek | Windhoek-Okahandja 4x4 Trail |
| | Uri Adventures |

| **QUADBIKING** | |
|---|---|
| Swakopmund and | |
| Walvis Bay | Outback Orange |
| | Dare Devil Adventures |
| | Namibia Quadbike Adventures |
| Sossusvlei | Sossusvlei Eco Quad |

| **MOUNTAINBIKING** | |
|---|---|
| Countrywide | Outside Adventures |
| | Boundless Adventures |

| **OVERLAND SAFARIS** | |
|---|---|
| Countrywide | Chameleon Safaris |

| **FLYING FOX (FOEFIE SLIDE)** | |
|---|---|
| Rossing Mountain | Dare Devil Adventures |

| **HOT-AIR BALLOONING** | |
|---|---|
| Countrywide & Sossusvlei | Namib Sky Adventures |
| | Francolino Flyins |

| **SKYDIVING / SOARING** | |
|---|---|
| Swakopmund | Skydive Swakopmund |
| Namib | Bitterwasser Lodge & Flying Centre |

| **SCENIC FLIGHTS AND HELICOPTER RIDES** | |
|---|---|
| Countrywide | Pleasure Flights and Safaris |

**10 GREAT ADVENTURES**
1. Sandboarding
2. Horseriding / camel riding
3. Fishing for sharks
4. Quadbiking
5. 4x4 trails
6. Hiking
7. Climbing
8. Sea kayaking
9. Skydiving
10. Canoeing / whitewater rafting

# Kaokoland

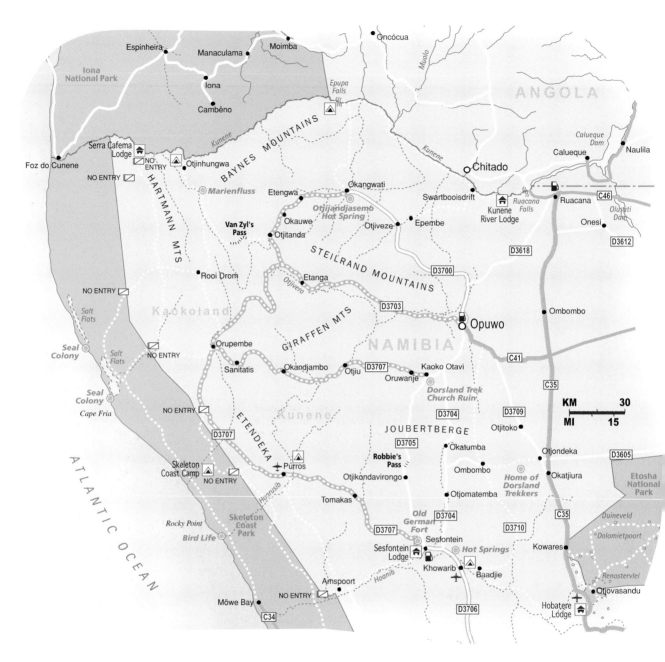

## KAOKOLAND

Kaokoland refers to the vast rocky, mountainous terrain bordered in the north by the Kunene River and by the Hoanib in the south, and immediately inland of the northern Skeleton Coast. It is a wild and unpredictable wilderness populated largely by the Himba and Herero-speaking people (who gave the area its name). Kaokoland's rivers are home to crocodiles, while small herds of Kaokoland elephant roam the desolate landscape, which fell victim to devastating drought in the 1970s. Much of its wildlife was decimated, but the land is slowly recovering and Kaokoland, especially its lumbering great elephants, remains a popular tourist drawcard.

## DRIVING THROUGH KAOKOLAND

The nearly 50,000km² (19,500 sq. miles) of rough roads and mountain terrain are not immediately inviting to the traveller. The tracks are unpredictable and difficult to navigate, and the landscape is wild and, to a large degree, empty of inhabitants other than the local Himba. Still isolated from Western influence, the Himba are simple subsistence farmers who remain true to custom, so problems with your vehicle here are not going to be solved by the locals. Indeed, the locals are friendly, approachable and hospitable, but it is best not to rely on them for anything more than a welcome drink and a cheery smile. At the same time, however, they know their home

## 26

## KAOKOLAND IN A NUTSHELL

Best times: Moderate to hot all year, best times are from May to August.
Climate: Winters are moderate but cool; heavy summer rains (Jan–Mar).
Risk factor: Isolated and inhospitable to the ill-prepared traveller. Party of at least two 4x4s essential on roads that are essentially dust tracks. Professional assistance in planning is advised.
Health: Malaria is endemic to the northern area. There is a risk of AIDS and bilharzia in this region.
Pack: Sunscreen and comfortable lightweight clothing, first-aid supplies, water rations and vehicle parts.
Facilities: Although locals are generally accommodating, guesthouses are few and far between – visitors need to be entirely self-sufficient. Some reliable tour operators service this area.

best and if you find yourself lost – and can decipher the elaborate hand gestures (few people here speak English) – you may decide to ask for directions. Remember, however, that locals have different names to those on maps.

### THE FAMOUS DESERT ELEPHANTS

Apart from the perils of the desert landscape, the natural splendour remains the attraction. Namibia's desert-dwelling elephants, although mistakenly considered an entirely separate species from the African elephant, have simply adapted to the harsh Kaokoland. The most notable deviations from other elephants is, of course, their diet. Here they browse on the indigenous Ana trees. The elephants may spend days in search of water trudging in excess of 60km (37 miles) for a drink. Other wild animals, too, will make their way from one water supply to another as the supplies dwindle in the dry season. Travellers should be aware that their instinct to find water sources has been honed over millennia: you are advised to take your own reliable water rations!

### RIVER-RAFTING ON THE KUNENE

The mighty Kunene in the north of Namibia forms part of its border with Angola for about 325km (200 miles). Winding and twisting through a rough primeval landscape, the great river is characterized by fearsome crocodiles, thundering waterfalls, tranquil streams and the raging whitewater rapids that have made this river one of the continent's premier rafting destinations. The river's untamed waters (almost entirely white in parts from the turbulence that roars beneath the surface) cascade over long-time popular adventure thrills like the renowned Epupa and Ruacana falls. Nail-biting rapids such as those at Enyandi and Ondorusu test you out before you arrive at the more treacherous rapids like The Crusher, Dead Man's Grave and Smash.

### GREAT AFRICAN RAFTING SPOTS

| | |
|---|---|
| Burundi | Luvironza River |
| Zambia | Zambezi River |
| Malawi | Lake Malawi |
| Namibia | Kunene River |
| South Africa | Orange River |
| South Africa | The Garden Route |

Left: Kaokoland desert elephant.
Top to bottom: Himba woman; Kaokoland landscape; the endangered white rhino.

# Skeleton Coast

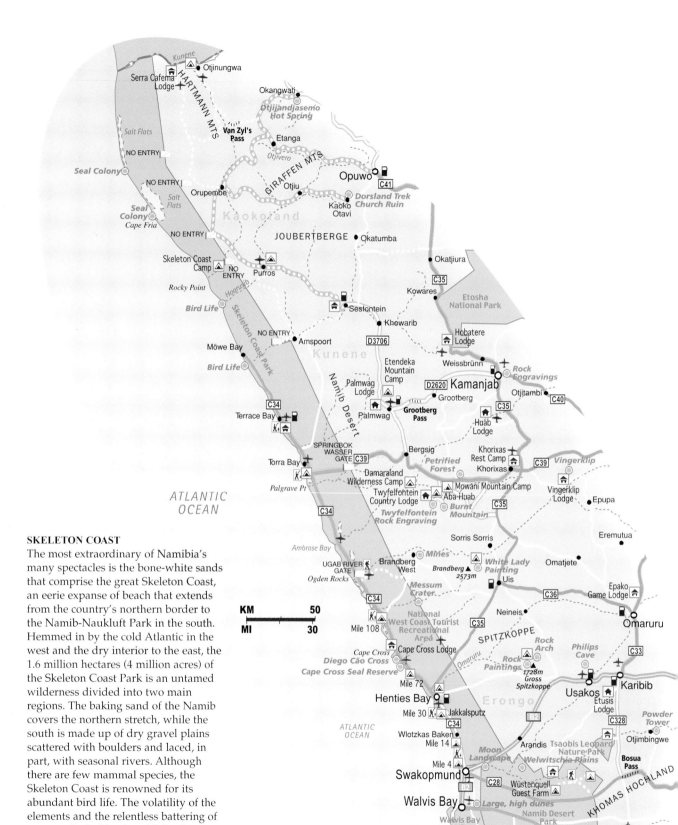

## SKELETON COAST

The most extraordinary of Namibia's many spectacles is the bone-white sands that comprise the great Skeleton Coast, an eerie expanse of beach that extends from the country's northern border to the Namib-Naukluft Park in the south. Hemmed in by the cold Atlantic in the west and the dry interior to the east, the 1.6 million hectares (4 million acres) of the Skeleton Coast Park is an untamed wilderness divided into two main regions. The baking sand of the Namib covers the northern stretch, while the south is made up of dry gravel plains scattered with boulders and laced, in part, with seasonal rivers. Although there are few mammal species, the Skeleton Coast is renowned for its abundant bird life. The volatility of the elements and the relentless battering of wave and wind lend to this landscape an almost surreal beauty. The coast can be shrouded in mist for days, which helped to earn it the reputation as the world's largest shipping graveyard – over 100 vessels have run aground here.

## 27

## DRIVING THE SKELETON COAST

The Skeleton Coast is an extensive wilderness and a traveller's paradise. Although sparsely vegetated, it boasts a unique array of life forms that have made unusual adaptations to life on this sandy, dry and wind-blown shore that stretches from the country's northern-most border with Angola down to the dry and dusty plains of the Namib Desert in the Namib-Naukluft Park.

## FUN ON FOUR WHEELS

The rocky coast is battered by the winds and pummelled by the ocean waters, and much of it is traversed over bumpy dirt roads or tarred roads in a sad state of disrepair. The southern reaches are covered by the sandy dunes of the Namib, and the gravel plains of the north are liberally sprinkled with boulders, rocks and rivers. The hardy surfaces here pose potential problems for foolhardy drivers: visitors travelling in a 4x4 through the region are advised to drive carefully, particularly in areas that have seen no rain for some time. Sometimes they have had too much rain! The scenic beauty of the colours and contrasts that dot the seascape along the sandy coastline might seem idyllic to romantic-at-heart adventurers, yet these quiet and lengthy stretches of beach sand are considerably less hospitable when you are stranded and helpless under the blazing sun. Despite the aridity of the broader region, the Namibian coast and inland areas are a haven for adventurers, but the golden rule is: do your homework first so that you are prepared for any eventuality.

## SKELETON COAST PARK INFO

Best times: May–August.
Climate: Generally moderate, often misty. Heavy summer rains. (Jan–March) with flash floods and high temperatures.
Risk factor: Private trips should be well planned, taking into account the volatility of desert and ocean.
Pack: Warm clothing for the fog-laden coast; sunscreen is essential; comfortable lightweight clothing for hot days.
Facilities: Some plush private operations, but generally simple to rustic camping and overnight facilities.

## WALVIS BAY

Positioned between the searing sands of the Namib in the south and the windswept shore of the Skeleton Coast in the north, Walvis Bay is the unofficial capital of Namibia's coastal stretch. Much of the social and economic activity of this little city centres on its vital natural harbour, the deepest in southwestern Africa. For centuries, small indigenous settlements remained undisturbed in this forgotten corner until Dutch, German and British colonial powers stumbled across the treasure that is its natural harbour. Walvis Bay acts as a vital instrument in the national economy (servicing the freight and fishing industries) and is a convenient base for some adventure activities that are on offer at certain times of the year, including four-wheel-drive and desert exploration, as well as birdwatching. Take the popular lagoon drive to enjoy an eyeful of flamingoes, pelicans, storks and cormorants. If you're there at the right time the lagoon will be pink with flamingoes!

Top to bottom: Skeleton Coast stretching into the horizon; a pelican at Walvis Bay; cormorants nesting on one of the many wrecks dotting the Skeleton Coast.

# North East - Etosha to Caprivi

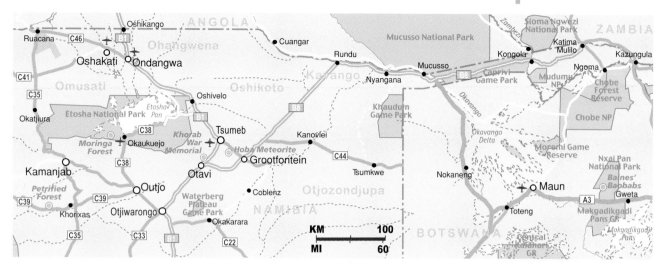

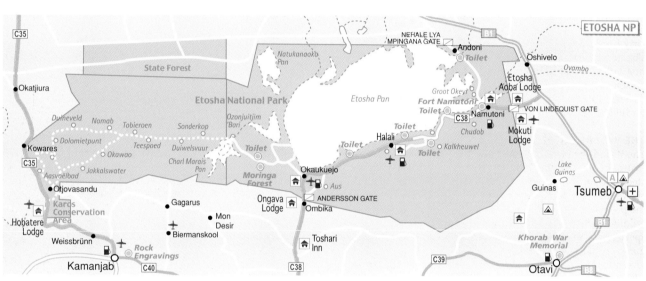

## ETOSHA NATIONAL PARK

Etosha ('great white place' in Herero, due to the bright sun) is one of the finest game reserves to be found in Southern Africa and is a vital game reserve for the entire region. The park is home to 114 species of mammal, 340 bird species, 110 different reptiles, 16 species of amphibian and yet just one fish species … and all of this is found in the 22,000km² (13,670 sq. miles) that make up the park named after the massive pan that covers a vast 5,000km² (3,107 sq. miles), stretching roughly 120km (74.5 miles) from east

### AN IDEAL BASE CAMP

Katima Mulilo boasts really good facilities for travellers and is an excellent base to explore and embark on adventure activities, as it's located on the banks of the mighty Zambezi River, and it is an easy base to hop into Zambia, Zimbabwe or Botswana.

to west and some 70km (43.5 miles) across at its widest point. The pan seldom boasts much water (if any) as it is fed by the rains rather than reliable rivers, and even when the rains fall hard, few areas fill up or flood due to the incredibly high rate of evaporation. Etosha is best explored in your own car without a guide. The roads are good and the open landscape allows for excellent wildlife spotting, although there are also sections that are thick, bushy and wooded. Oryx (or gemsbok) tend to congregate around Etosha's waterholes. The rainy season signals the arrival of summer migrants in the form of mammals and birds. In good years the pan will be alive with thousands of flamingoes. The western reaches of Etosha feature some unique areas, including the fascinating Moringa Forest or Haunted Forest, dubbed Sprokieswoud in Afrikaans. The Haunted Forest is littered with weirdly contorted moringa trees which were,

quite possibly, shaped by browsing herds of elephant and giraffe. Etosha has three main rest camps (Namutoni, Halali and Okaukuejo) with perimeter fencing and superb floodlit waterholes which can be visited 24 hours a day. The park walked tall as the world's largest game reserve until the 1960s, when its surface area was (over time) reduced by nearly 80%. Nonetheless, Etosha remains one of Africa's largest and greatest parks.

### KHAUDUM GAME PARK

Khaudum is wild, four-wheel-drive country and while its remoteness might add to its charm, it also demands travelling in a group with adequate supplies. The lack of fencing around Khaudum (with the exception of the boundary with Botswana) allows animals to leave the park in search of fresh grazing and water during the rainy season, thus ensuring a proliferation of wildlife to watch, particularly wild dogs and roan

## 28

## TOP TRIPS
• An hour outside Otjiwarongo are fossilised footprints that date back around 200 million years! You will stare in awe at the massive set of prints made by a very large two-legged dinosaur.
• A 2km (1.2 mile) drive out of Otavi will bring you to the Khorab War Memorial. Erected in 1920, it marks the spot where the German forces capitulated to General Louis Botha's SA forces in 1915.

antelope. Artificial waterholes provide some of the best wildlife spotting. Winter is best for game viewing, but you'll need patience: free-roaming animals don't take kindly to noise, particularly from humans and loud vehicles! The heavier summer rain thickens the dry woodland savanna (which is located on settled parts of the Kalahari's sand dunes), which encourages a vibrant birdlife for 'twitchers' to focus on.

### THE WATERBERG PLATEAU
The Waterberg Plateau Game Park dominates the surrounding landscape, its steep cliffs rise hundreds of metres above the surrounding plains, making the plateau something of a refuge for wildlife. Many of Namibia's endangered species have been rehomed here to safeguard them from poachers and predators, and this animal paradise towers 1,800m-plus (1,1118ft) above sea level. Due to its conservation success it supplies rare species of game and wildlife to many of Namibia's other parks. Its amazing biodiversity also allows this small park to support a wide array of animals. You can drive around the park on one of the organised game drives but NOT on your own: the animals prefer it

that way! Walking in the park provides incredible scenery and game viewing, with 200 bird species (black eagles and Cape vultures), age-old dinosaur tracks and San rock art.

### TSUMEB
Attractive and laid back, Tsumeb's name can be translated to mean "to dig a hole in loose ground", appropriate for one of Namibia's key mining towns which has attained a worldwide reputation in the mining community. The Tsumeb Museum offers visitors a window into the past while the Tsumeb Cultural Village is an open air museum that allows a first-hand look at what tribal life is all about in Namibia.

### GROOTFONTEIN
Meaning 'large fountain' for its natural springs, Grootfontein's fascinating Old Fort Museum has interesting historic photographs, gems, rocks and a display on the old art of wagon and cart manufacture. The 60-ton Hoba meteorite (the largest recorded on earth) can be found 50km (31miles) outside town. Almost 3m² (9.8ft²) and between 75–122cm (30–48in) thick, it may have celebrated in the region of 200 to 400 million birthdays. Hoba found its home here around 80,000 years ago.

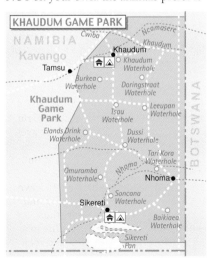

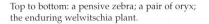
Top to bottom: a pensive zebra; a pair of oryx; the enduring welwitschia plant.

# Central Namibia

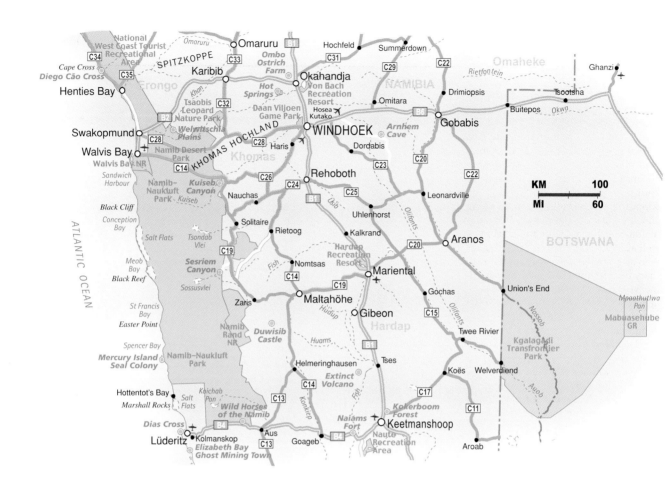

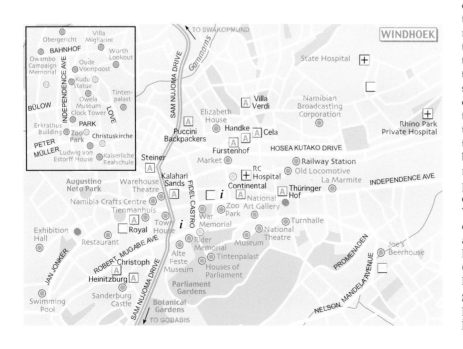

## WINDHOEK

Albeit relatively small and underdeveloped, the Namibian capital is the great tourist centre and economic hub of the nation, a vibrant, colourful and relatively modern city catering for international travellers. The nightlife is lively, the facilities adequate and the infrastructure impressive, while the colours, cultures and panoramic vistas are a photographer's dream, and in recent years there has been a healthy resurgence in the tourism market. Windhoek has become every inch the modern city and remains the gateway to the adventures promised by the coast, desert and wild expanse beyond waiting to be explored. The nearby Daan Viljoen Game Park is equipped for travellers and sedan cars are able to negotiate its roads. The park has three main trails: Wag-'n-Bietjie (Buffalo-thorn) Trail, Rooibos (bushwillow) Trail and Sweet-Thorn Trail, the game spotting is good and the birdlife prolific (including the Damara rockjumper and the rosy-faced lovebird).

## NAMIB-NAUKLUFT PARK

Larger than Switzerland, the 50,000km²-plus (31,070 sq. miles) of fantastically scenic desert landscape occupied by the Namib-Naukluft Park ranks it with the biggest in all of Africa. It represents a vital conservation effort to retain the pristine nature of the Namib desert, which vies with the Atacama Desert in South America for the title of oldest on earth. You'll need plenty of time to enjoy all that the park has to offer, so keep your itinerary flexible. The Namib has an amazing array of wildlife, despite the aridity, and the plantlife in the mountainous region is surprisingly prolific (albeit hardy). This is an area enjoyed by the rare Hartmann's mountain zebra as well as leopards and other shy animals who appreciate the vegetation and sanctuary offered by the caves, gorges and rocky terrain. Numerous small nocturnal delights (insects and reptiles) are to be found in the area. Birdwatchers will delight in the bustling air traffic around the deep kloof which has water year-round. Horseriding and hiking are popular ways to traverse much of this region. Hikes range from a few hours up to the more advanced eight-day, 120km (74 miles) Naukluft Hiking Trail.

## OKAHANDJA

Okahandja might be small, but it boasts some of Namibia's finest open-air markets specializing in souvenirs such as wood-carvings (notably enormous hippos, huge giraffe and up to 2m / 6.5ft tall human busts) as well as art from all around Southern and Central Africa. The Herero's administrative 'capital', Okahandja hosts a large and colourful annual festival in August to honour the Herero forefathers. There are numerous historic sights in and around town, including Moordkoppie (Murder Hill, the scene of the 1850 Herero massacre) and many graves of local leaders from the last 100 years (including that of the Oorlam leader Jan Jonker Afrikaner).

### NAMIBIA'S NATURAL WONDERS

• Namibia's massive parkland covers approximately 11.22 million hectares (27.7 million acres)
• Etosha Pan's amazing wildlife which hangs out at the huge salt depression
• The dramatic dunes of Sossusvlei
• Age-old rock engravings
• The Fish River Canyon
• The vast Namib Desert
• The unforgiving Kaokoland
• The ancient Petrified Forest
• The ominous Spitzkoppe hills

## MARIENTAL

Forget peace and tranquillity: Mariental suffers from an unhappy climate. Atrocious summer heat, biting winter cold, and the changes in season bring strong winds that blow dust everywhere. Local industry focusses on cultivating animal fodder, fruit and vegetables, as well as ostrich meat and karakul pelts, aided by its proximity to the Hardap Dam (Namibia's largest reservoir, enjoyed by anglers, hikers, birders and boating enthusiasts). Herman Brandt, the first colonial settler in the area, made his wife happy by naming it Marie's Valley (Mariental in German).

## GOBABIS

Gobabis has a special charm for passing tourists on this vital route through to Botswana. There are pretty old church buildings in town and a golf course. A statue of a bull at the town's western entrance bears testament to the importance of cattle to the Omaheke region.

## HENTIES BAY

Hentie van der Merwe first started fishing here in 1929, and little did he know that a town would grow here and adopt his name. A sleepy hollow, Henties wakes up for the summer season to welcome the 10,000-plus visitors who flock to this fisherman's paradise, many with an eye on casting a line into the ocean or swinging their clubs at the 9-hole golf course that runs through a valley down towards the beach. The town has plenty of petrol stations to cater for the lack of supply further north.

Top to bottom: Christuskirche; animal tracks on the face of a dune; climbing in the Namib-Naukluft National Park.

# South & Fish River Canyon

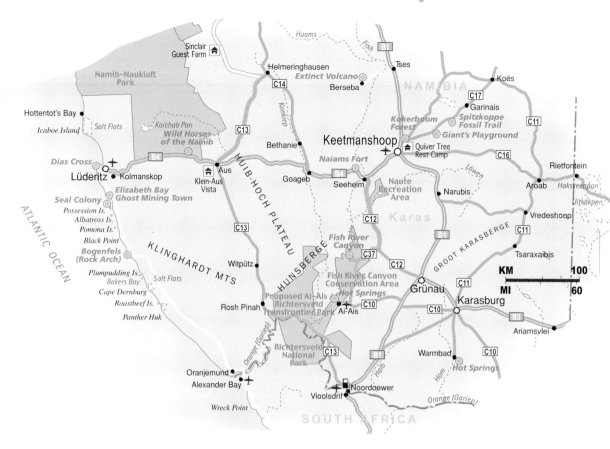

## FISH RIVER CANYON

The Fish River Canyon comprises wind-carved depressions, inclines and rock formations moulded from the inland plateau. The Canyon is dramatic in its simplicity, with valleys and gullies slicing through its ancient geological foundations. Its grandeur lies more in the spectacle than in the geological records and data that make up this natural phenomenon. The Fish River Canyon's steep inclines and roughly hewn rock faces, eroded over time by the forces of nature and its ravaging elements are second in size only to the Grand Canyon.

## HIKING THE FISH RIVER CANYON

The Fish River rises in the Khomas Hochland Mountains southwest of Windhoek and flows some 800km (500 miles) before it meets the Gariep – aka Orange – far to the south. The remarkable rock erosion has carved a network of paths and trails into the rock and sand. The last 160km (100 miles) of the river's fierce and often turbulent course winds through a deep canyon that forms the backdrop to Namibia's most challenging hiking trail. Although this trail is popular with ardent walkers and climbers, it is not standard tourist fare and remains entirely unspoiled – unlike

**FISH RIVER CANYON FACTS**

| | |
|---|---|
| Estimated age: | 2,000,000 years |
| Length: | 160km (100 miles) long |
| Widest point: | 27km (17 miles) |
| Deepest point: | 600m (2,000ft) |
| Smaller than: | Only the Grand Canyon in North America is bigger than the Fish River Canyon. |

the mass-oriented tourist drawcards of the big cities. For the first 65km (40 miles) of its course, the gorge of the Fish River Canyon is, in effect, a canyon within a canyon, making for some remarkable walking. Almost in retaliation against the forces that shifted the rocks and sediment millennia ago, the Fish River began to cut a deep channel in the bed of the original trough – only much deeper, narrower and far more spectacular. In places, the canyon floor is more than 500m (1,640ft) below the level of the plateau. Fortunately, it is a relatively gentle world of placid pools and mighty boulders strewn across beds of sand, with little evidence of life. Naturally, this sort of isolation (in a spot that is relatively inhospitable) presents dangers of its own. As long as wary travellers use their common sense and take no chances, there should be little to worry about – just the endless stretch of undulating path that lies ahead (albeit not always particularly well signposted, but the river is an able guide!).

## KEETMANSHOOP
Keetmanshoop (shortened to 'Keet' by the locals) is a small sunny town with a few examples of attractive German colonial architecture, pretty gardens and a rustic museum. 'Keet' lies almost 500km (310 miles) south of Windhoek and is roughly 1,000m (3,281ft) above sea level. The original church was built in 1866 but, sadly, 24 years later a freak flood washed the entire building away! Its replacement (the current town museum) was put up five years later … this time on somewhat higher ground!

## KOLMANSKOP GHOST TOWN
The desert ghost town of Kolmanskop lies just 10km (6 miles) from Lüderitz. The diamond rush saw this town spring up in 1908 and become the centre of the region's diamond industry. During its boom years the streets and businesses bustled with determined and starry-eyed prospectors, readily diving into the desert sands in search of their personal fortunes. It is today a tourist stop to explore the sand-ravaged houses and buildings that have been deserted for over 40 years. Naturally, you won't be able to enjoy the town's former facilities of an ice factory and casino, but the theatre and skittle alley have been restored to working order.

## LUDERITZ PENINSULA
A trip around the peninsula (in calm weather) will present some fabulous views and swimming possibilities at one of the many bays along the coast (Dias Point and Griffith Bay offer stunning views), while the rusted remnants of Sturmvogel Bucht's 'deceased' Norwegian Whaling Station is worth a look. A friendly, small town with slow-paced hospitality, rich in German tradition and history, Lüderitz is worth the effort to visit for a day. Sitting more than 360km (223 miles) from Keetmanshoop, Lüderitz is literally and figuratively isolated from the rest of the world, but it's not cut off completely: it has public telephones that seem to pop up on every corner. Part of Lüderitz's charm is that its isolation for so many years has left the town with much original architecture and characterful buildings from the 1900s. The town has an element of fun in the garishly bright colours of the houses and the midday siren that doubles as a fire alarm! Kolmanskop and Elizabeth Bay ghost towns are a comfortable drive from Lüderitz and are both worth the effort.

## FISH RIVER CANYON INFO
Best time: May–September
Climate: Summers are blistering; winter night temperatures can plummet.
Risk factor: Terrain is hard-going and tough, with plenty of dangers for the uninitiated. Professional assistance in planning is advised.
Pack: Sunscreen and comfortable lightweight clothing are essential, as are comprehensive first-aid supplies and plenty of water rations.

Top to bottom: Sossusvlei's dramatic dunescape; the vast expanse of the Fish River Canyon; majestic quiver trees (koker boom).

# Botswana

## ADVENTURING THROUGH BOTSWANA (See Contact Details 92-95)

### ON LAND

**GAME VIEWING**
Chobe National Park, Okavango Delta

Adventure Safaris
Uncharted Africa Safaris
Abercrombie & Kent
Moremi Safaris and Tours

Mashatu Game Reserve — Mala Mala (Mashatu)

**ELEPHANT SAFARIS**
Okavango Delta

Moremi Safaris and Tours
Elephant Back Safaris

**WALKS WITH BUSHMEN**
Chobe National Park

Moremi Safaris and Tours

**HORSERIDING**
Okavango Delta

Okavango Horse Safaris
African Horseback Safaris

Tuli Block — Limpopo Valley Horse Safaris

**BIRDING**
Moremi Game Reserve — Moremi Bird Safaris

**GAME TRACKING ON FOOT**
Moremi Game Reserve — Department of Wildlife and National Parks

**CAVING**
Drotsky's Cave (Gcwihaba) — Department of Tourism

### ON WATER

**GAME VIEWING IN *MOKOROS* (DUGOUT CANOES) AND MOTORBOAT SAFARIS**
Okavango Delta — Uncharted Africa Safaris
Abercrombie & Kent
Moremi Safaris and Tours

### ON WHEELS

**4X4 TRAILS**
From Maun through Okavango Delta — Botswana Parks and Reserves
Chobe National Park to Vic Falls — Botswana Parks and Reserves

**MOUNTAINBIKING**
Mashatu — Mashatu Game Reserve
180 Degree Adventures

**QUADBIKING**
Makgadikgadi Pans — Bush Bandits
Jacks Camp

## 31

**BOTSWANA**
Capital: Gaborone
Area: 600,372km² / 231,805mi²
Population: 1.6 million
Main ethnic groups:
• Tswana (75%)
• Shona (12%)
• San (3%)
• White (1%)
Main languages:
• English
• Tswana
• Shona
• San
• Ndebele
Main religions:
• Traditional beliefs (50%)
• Christian (mostly Anglican) (50%)
Currency: Pula (100 thebe)

IN THE AIR

**AERIAL GAME VIEWING / SCENIC FLIGHTS**
Okavango Delta and Chobe National Park      Moremi Air Services

**HOT-AIR BALLOONING**
Countrywide      Moremi Safaris and Tours

**TOP 10 ADVENTURES**
1. Game viewing
2. Canoeing (*mokoros*)
3. Caving
4. Horseback safaris
5. Hot-air ballooning
6. Scenic flights
7. Birdwatching
8. Quadbiking
9. Elephantback safaris
10. Walks with bushmen

# The Okavango River

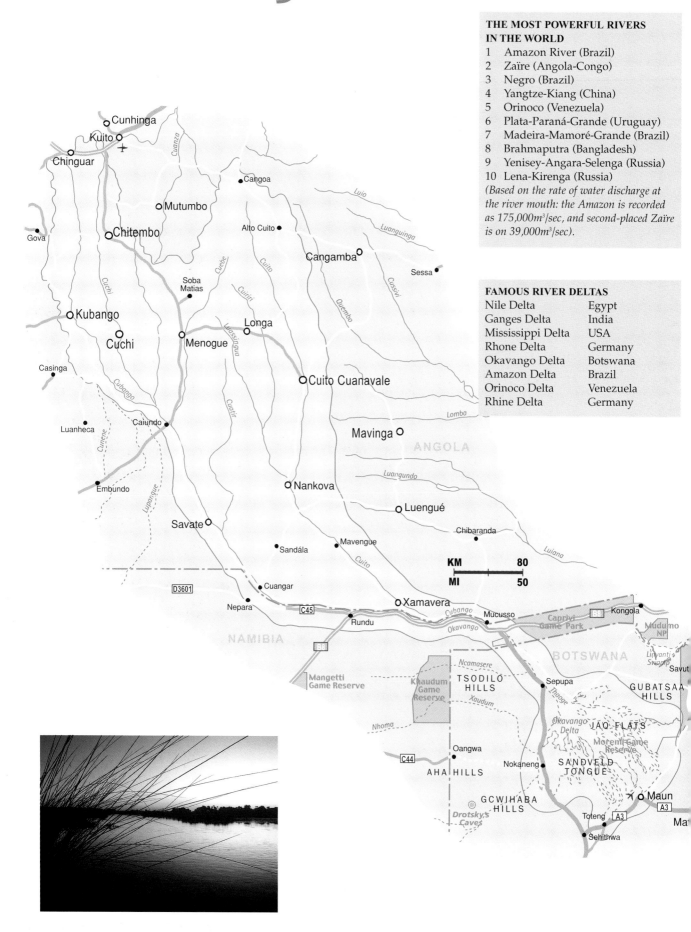

**THE MOST POWERFUL RIVERS IN THE WORLD**

1. Amazon River (Brazil)
2. Zaïre (Angola-Congo)
3. Negro (Brazil)
4. Yangtze-Kiang (China)
5. Orinoco (Venezuela)
6. Plata-Paraná-Grande (Uruguay)
7. Madeira-Mamoré-Grande (Brazil)
8. Brahmaputra (Bangladesh)
9. Yenisey-Angara-Selenga (Russia)
10. Lena-Kirenga (Russia)

*(Based on the rate of water discharge at the river mouth: the Amazon is recorded as 175,000m³/sec, and second-placed Zaïre is on 39,000m³/sec).*

**FAMOUS RIVER DELTAS**

| | |
|---|---|
| Nile Delta | Egypt |
| Ganges Delta | India |
| Mississippi Delta | USA |
| Rhone Delta | Germany |
| Okavango Delta | Botswana |
| Amazon Delta | Brazil |
| Orinoco Delta | Venezuela |
| Rhine Delta | Germany |

KM  80
MI  50

## 32

## OKAVANGO DELTA

The Okavango Delta is the world's largest inland delta, spreading over 15,000km² (5,790 sq. miles) during dry years, while higher rainfalls can fan out the delta over a monstrous 22,000km² (8,500 sq. miles). This wetland wilderness creates a vast green oasis in the middle of otherwise inhospitable terrain. It is here that the waters of the country's only perennial river, the Okavango, spread across its flood plain, soaking deep into the surrounding lands. The river should fulfil all Botswana's water requirements, but not only is it shared with Namibia, much of the water is also lost to evaporation. Drawing on the water supply for irrigation and domestic consumption also reduces the delta's waters. Conservationists are fighting to have the delta declared a World Heritage Site to secure its protection.

## HIGHS AND LOWS

Ironically, the river's highest levels are achieved during Botswana's dry season, reaching their peak in June and July. In Botswana's rainy season (spreading from October to March) the Okavango's pans and the many rivers and streams are dry; the formerly lush and wet water channels also become inaccessible by boat. All this is a result of the delta's dependence on the Angolan section of the river: the rain that falls during Angola's own rainy season provides the watery lifeblood to the Okavango's main tourist sections.

## SOUTHERN AFRICA'S GREAT RIVERS

| | |
|---|---|
| Breede | South Africa |
| Cuanza | Angola |
| Fish | Namibia |
| Groot | South Africa |
| Kuiseb | Namibia |
| Cunene | Angola, Namibia, Botswana |
| Kwando | Namibia (aka Linyanti and Chobe) |
| Limpopo | Mozambique, SA, Zimbabwe, Botswana |
| Okavango | Botswana, Namibia, Angola (as "Cubango") |
| Orange | South Africa, Lesotho, Namibia |
| Tugela | South Africa |
| Vaal | South Africa |
| Zambezi | Angola, Zambia, Namibia, Zimbabwe, Mozambique |

## THE AHA HILLS

The hills, one of Botswana's remotest and most difficult to reach places of interest, lie slap in the middle of a massive dunefield, creating a fascinating landscape. The hills straddle the border with Namibia and form a plateau stretching 245km² (151 sq. miles), the bulk of it made up of limestone, dolomite and marble. The rocks stretch back to a time some 700 million years ago, and their name is an onomatopoeic derivative from the Bushman word for the abundant barking geckos that live in the area.

## TSODILO HILLS

For centuries the inhabitants of these hills (aka the 'Mountains of the Gods') in the remote northwestern corner of Botswana have held them in symbolic and religious reverence. The rich tapestry of rock art created by the early inhabitants has earned the area the nickname 'The Louvre of the Desert', and the mystery and mystique surrounding the hills leaves an indelible impression on you long after you return home. In Bushman folklore the three hills represent the male, female and the child. Perhaps appropriately (although somewhat darkly) a fourth hill off to the side represents the male's first wife.

## DROTSKY'S CAVE & GCWIHABA HILLS

The Gcwihaba Hills are reached via an interesting circular route running from Nokaneng to Tsau, a route which also takes you through Aha Hills. It's a journey of at least 150km (93 miles) to the cave, whichever way you approach, and the circular trip is around 320km (198 miles), so be prepared for an overnight stay, make sure your tank is full of petrol and that the spare tyre is in good nick. Drotsky's Cave is officially known as Gcwihaba Cave (in the Bushman tongue Gcwihaba means 'hyena's lair'). This two-million-year-old site has dramatic stalactites, stalagmites and flowstones, particularly in the large chamber. There are hours of enjoyment to be had here, the highlight being a 45-minute walk in the dark after walking through a cave filled with bats and their soft and squishy droppings!

Opposite page: wetlands sunrise.
Top to bottom: aerial image of the Okavango; red lechwe herd on flood plains; *mokoro* (dugout canoe) as transport.

# Okavango Delta

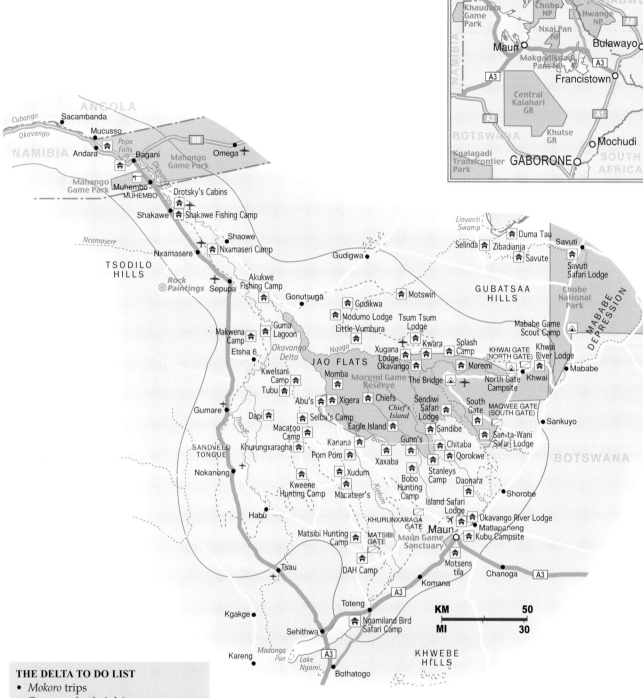

## THE DELTA TO DO LIST
- *Mokoro* trips
- Open-roof safari drives
- 4x4 drives
- Elephantback safaris trails (the Fish Eagle Trail starts at Maun and ends at Victoria Falls)
- Horseback safaris
- Running with the game (also on horse-back)
- Nature walks
- Game viewing
- Birdviewing (hides to view birds at close range, as well as game)

**GABORONE**

Botswana's capital is a relatively small, compact city, and although there may be few conventional tourist sites, Gaborone has enjoyed phenomenal growth since it was appointed the official hub of the new nation in the 1960s. Back then, the rather insignificant village had no more than a scattering of homes, but it boasted one important resource – water.

As a result, it was declared a city within 20 months of becoming the capital and, largely because of its considerable mineral wealth, is one of the fastest-growing urban settlements on the African continent. Gaborone's road infrastructure lends it a modern appearance, with impressive restaurants, hotels, casinos and other entertainment centres.

## 33

## AROUND GABORONE

The modern city has retained at least some of its distinct African flavour – its side streets are filled with craft markets and vending stalls, and few other urban centres of similar status can boast the same number of small reserves and conservation land on their doorstep. Mount Kgale (aka 'the sleeping giant') overlooks Gaborone, with a relatively easy walk along the Lobatse Road being all that separates you from great views of the capital. Just 12km (7.5 miles) south of Gaborone is Mokolodi Nature Reserve, set on 3,000 hectares (7,410 acres). Mokolodi offers wildlife education for children, guided two-hour wildlife walks as well as protecting a wide range of Botswana's wildlife (the highlight being their two resident white rhino).

## LOBATSE AND MOCHUDI

The town of Lobatse is found in a lovely setting 68km (42 miles) south of Gaborone, yet the town itself is dull, with its highlights being the national mental hospital, the country's largest abattoir (not related!) and the somewhat more impressive St Mark's Anglican Church with its unusual thatch roof. Mochudi, on the other hand, is one of southeastern Botswana's more interesting villages. The Kwena first settled themselves here back in the 1500s – the stone walls of their ruined former dwellings provide forensic evidence of their presence in this area. In the 1870s the people of the Kgatla tribe settled here after moving to avoid migrating Boers, and today the Phuthadikobo Museum (one of Botswana's finest) proudly displays the Kgatla's history, as well as that of Mochudi itself.

## MAUN AND ITS MINI GAME RESERVE

Maun is one of your typical frontier towns, although its 'romantic' image as a 'Wild West town' is being lost as development sees the town westernise itself to cash in on the tourist market. The town is getting a large-scale face-lift, although some of its original character still pops out from behind the glowing lights of western fast-food joints. Maun has a big population of Herero people and is a banking and administrative hub. The Herero are former Namibian refugees, and their women are stunning photographic subjects in their traditional dress … but be sure to 'negotiate' permission to take their photograph! The Nhabe Museum is worth a visit, as is the Craft Centre, while on the Shorobe Road craft-savvy visitors will enjoy the Okavango Ceramics and the Shorobe

OKAVANGO DELTA IN A NUTSHELL

**Climate:** The dry season from June to September offers the best conditions (albeit very, very hot), with the water levels at their highest, although the delta experience is fantastic year-round. Horse safaris run from March to November.

**Risk factor:** A clear head and some degree of swimming ability would be helpful in the unlikely event that your mokoro overturns. Horse safaris aren't for the beginner, as you will spend hours in the saddle. With masses of game in fairly close proximity, be vigilant and cautious … and should you have a face-off with a lion, many advise that you don't run (it's faster than you!).

**Health:** Malaria is a problem, but the disease is season-dependent (the dry season is considered fairly safe). The risk is highest when the rains fall, from October to February.

**Pack:** Binoculars will add to your game-viewing experience. Plenty of sunblock, long-sleeved shirts to shield off insect bites and provide relief from sunburn (as well as good headwear). The evenings can get quite cool (notably when on a night drive), making warm jackets or a fleece a necessity.

Basket Co-Operative. Maun's tiny game reserve takes up just 3km² (1,8 sq. miles) where it lies on the Thamalakane River. It is geared around wildlife education and houses a variety of antelope. The nearby Matlapaneng Bridge connects up with the village of Matlapaneng, a haven for tourists seeking budget accommodation and camp sites.

Top to bottom: elephant safari; Mabokushu tribe members fishing; African fish eagle.

# Chobe

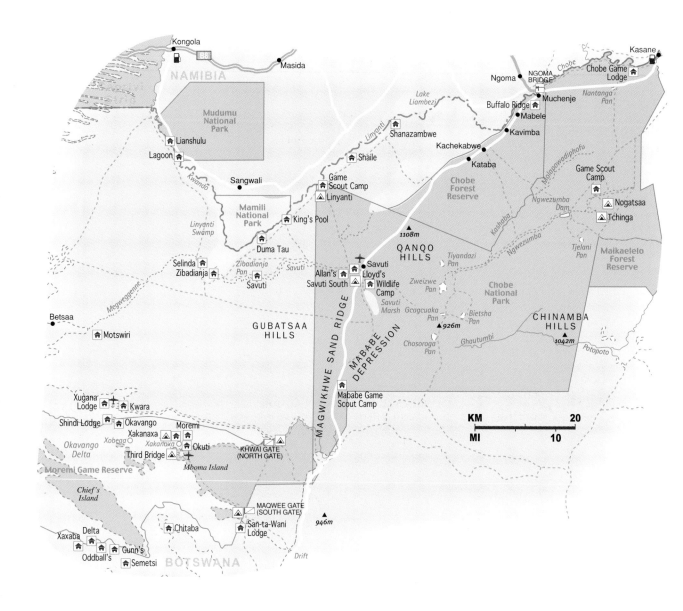

**CHOBE AND MOREMI RESERVES**
Whereas the Okavango region is predominantly wetland, the Moremi Game Reserve is a vast 2,000km² (770-sq.-mile) expanse of contrasts: flood plain and lagoon, dry bushveld and mopane woodland. The Moremi is roamed by big-game species such as lion, leopard and cheetah, elephant, buffalo and wild dog, kudu, tsessebe and Botswana's ubiquitous lechwe. Like Moremi, Chobe National Park's habitat is varied, alternating between swamp and grassland, flood plain and bushveld. The northern border of its 10,000km² (3,800 sq. miles)

wilderness is carved by the Linyanti-Chobe river system. The Chobe is Botswana's only perennial river and, although more than 30km (19 miles) of its banks have been commandeered by responsible tourism, it continues to act as the life force for much wildlife. Most notable are the more than 35,000 elephants, but there are also over 450 bird species. One of the most remarkable attempts to accommodate local communities has found fruition in the arid Kgalagadi Transfrontier Park between South Africa and Botswana. In an effort to preserve the natural habitat and its

characteristic game species, government and conservation officials established this cross-border park, which is home to an amazing range of plant, mammal and bird life. Covering an area of more than 2 million hectares (5 million acres), Kgalagadi effectively united South Africa's Kalahari Gemsbok National Park and Botswana's Gemsbok National Park – Africa's first formally gazetted transboundary reserve.

## 34

## MOREMI IN A NUTSHELL
Climate: Game viewing is good all year, with the dry season (May to November) offering the best pickings. Birders will delight at the influx of migrant species during the summer months. There's an added bonus in the scores of foaling antelope.
Risk factor: After any heavy rains many of the tracks can become totally impassable. Drive with care, have provisions and spares, as well as time, on hand – do not try to rush your way out of a bad position.
Health: Moremi is in a malaria area.
Pack: Fuel is only available at Maun and Kasane; remember that your fuel consumption is higher in sandy areas.

## CHOBE IN A NUTSHELL
Climate: Riverside conditions are good year round (best from May to October), while further inland conditions are best from November to May.
Health: Chobe is in a malaria area.
Risk factor: Drive with caution in any densely wooded areas: you may stumble across the path of an elephant!
Pack: Fuel is only available at Maun and Kasane.

## NAMIBIA'S MAMILI NATIONAL PARK
The 32,000ha (79,000 acres) Mamili National Park was opened at the same time as Mudumu (1990), and are the eastern Caprivi's only protected areas. The Linyanti Swamp is a major drawcard when the Kwando River is running full (often flooding around June), opening up lazy *mokoro* (dugout) forays to the forested islands, wetlands and reeded channels. Naturally, the birdlife is abundant (more than 430 species). Other wildlife ranges from elephant to lion, giraffe and hippo, along with numerous buck. *Mokoro* and 4x4 are the only way to get around Mamili and this is not the place to take personal risks, as help can be a long time coming. There are rangers on patrol throughout the park, but they might not cross your path in time if you find your way into a spot of bother. Game viewing is best before the rainy season, which can start as early as October. The best birding opportunities are between December and March when the migrants move in, but then the 'black cotton' clay (road) tracks could become totally inaccessible.

## NAMIBIA'S MUDUMU NATIONAL PARK
Spread across 100,000ha (247,000 acres), Mudumu is hugged to the west by the Kwando River, which is alive with crocodile, hippo and numerous water-loving buck such as sitatunga, red lechwe and reedbuck. Covered in mopane woodlands, the reserve is well-populated with elephant, giraffe and zebra, in addition to impala, kudu, red lechwe and the somewhat uncommon roan antelope species. These animals enjoy the shelter and foliage offered by the abundant mopane. Birdwatchers will fall in love with Mudumu, especially if they get to spot the African fish eagle, the Narina trogon, Pel's fishing owl, or any of the many species found nowhere else in Namibia. It's best to explore Mudumu by 4x4, but Lianshulu Lodge and Lianshulu Bush Lodge offer guided walks. For a cultural diversion, visit the Lizauli Traditional Village just outside Mudumu to learn about traditional Caprivi lifestyles (from food to farming methods, medicine to crafts and toolmaking). Lizauli is one of many local upliftment programmes and is worth supporting if you are environmentally or culturally sensitive.

Top to bottom: male lion; tented camp at Linyanti; game cruise on the Chobe river; sunset over the Zibadianja lagoon.

# Makgadikgadi

## MAKGADIKGADI IN A NUTSHELL

Climate: Generally sunny and hot. Heavy summer rains from December to February. The best time to visit is during the winter months, from May to August, although night-time temperatures are freezing in winter.

Risk factor: Private excursions are ill-advised; thin-crusted pans are very dangerous; inexperienced bikers can cause severe environmental damage.

Health: Malaria is endemic, so prophylactic treatment is essential. Tickbite fever is common after the first rains, and there have been reports of hepatitis A. AIDS and bilharzia are widespread.

Pack: Sunscreen and lightweight protective clothing are essential. A 4x4 vehicle is essential.

## MAKGADIKGADI PANS

The world's largest natural salt pans, Makgadikgadi once formed part of a massive inland lake, but all that exists today on the remaining plains is an endless sea of empty, cracked, salt-encrusted pans, most notable among them Makgadikgadi's Sowa, Ntwetwe and Nxai pans. Following climatic changes and immense seismic shifts, the waters that once covered this landscape receded to leave the 12,000km² (4,600 sq. miles) seasonal salt pans. Summer rains fill the depressions, becoming the lifeblood of the wildlife that is drawn here during the rainless winter. The plains of the Makgadikgadi and Nxai Pan National Park cover 7,500km² (2,850 sq. miles). Established operators know the region and are quick to warn of the dangers of the dry pans and the havoc they wreak.

## QUADBIKING IN MAKGADIKGADI

The general mode of transport here is the quadbike, a small, sturdy but reliable four-wheel vehicle with limited impact on the sands – almost all other vehicles tend to cause irreparable damage to the ecosystems. Because of the unforgiving terrain, travellers (usually in pairs) are given impromptu lessons on how to handle quadbikes – but be warned that it is not as simple as pushing the pedal and steering. Beyond Kibu Island, mirages appear and disappear under the harsh sun as the 'quadbike caravans' negotiate shallow but bone-rattling gullies and crests on the hard salty clay – a deceiving 'lid' over water lying below the surface. This is clearly no ride in the park, and there are pitifully few, if any, landmarks by which to navigate. Don't drive on, hoping to stumble onto

the correct course: every inch further into the pans could mean another inch further away from help. Travellers making their way across the pans need to be supremely self-sufficient. Plan for the unplannable! Even if you have the foresight to bring a winch, there's nothing in the pans to which you can attach the rope! It's essential to travel in a group. Tour operators have learned the hard way, and should know all the tricks; paying for their services and expert advice is in your long-term interests!

## ON HORSEBACK THROUGH TULI

The Tuli Block comprises reserves, concession areas and agricultural land covering 12,000ha (30,000 acres). This is indeed big game country, and the primitive landscape has contributed much to making Botswana one of Africa's top wildlife safari destinations. Riding horseback through Tuli is one of those experiences that can overshadow even the plushest private safaris. The open veld, wide blue skies and plethora of wildlife in an untamed wilderness call to you: lion, leopard, cheetah, Burchell's zebra, wildebeest, hippo and the Tuli elephant all have a home here. The horizon is punctuated with clusters of boulders and baobabs, while impala, klipspringer, honey badgers and bat-eared foxes dart in and out of sight. Much of the land here is private, so venturing off gravel roads is not encouraged, but there are also adventure operators offering diversions into the wilds.

## TULI IN A NUTSHELL

Risk factor: Private excursions are ill-advised, and visitors are required to be competent riders: outfitters will refuse to take novices through what is essentially treacherous territory.
Pack: Sunscreen and lightweight protective clothing is essential.

## NO NEED TO ROUGH IT

While some established concerns pride themselves in providing every luxury, the smaller ones offer the most tactile and memorable experiences, stretching from three to 10 days. Night drives are not permitted in Botswana, and the Tuli trail is reserved for days only. Most family cars are able to negotiate the well-signposted roads, but game viewing is rather limited from there: horseback safaris increase your chances of encountering wild animals! No inexperienced horseriders are permitted on the trails, and even those who are fairly well versed in horsemanship should heed the warning of guides. In most cases, even the horses are carefully screened for their controlled temperament and ability to withstand the perils of the veld. Groups are advised to stick to the tracks already etched into the dry riverbeds.

## BAINES' BAOBABS

The stands of baobabs that dot pockets of the otherwise empty interior symbolise the grandeur of this sparse country. From the outskirts of settlements to the featureless pans, the horizon is broken by the silhouette of these indigenous residents who have lived here for centuries. The most prominent are the Seven Sisters referred to as Baines' Baobabs. This cluster of 'upside down' trees is named after Thomas Baines, the artist and explorer who captured them on canvas in 1862. Baines' Baobabs stand on the rim of Kudiakama Pan.

Top to bottom: ilala palms in the Makgadi-kgadi pans; brown hyena; one of the famous Baines' Baobabs.

# Kalahari

**THE WORLD'S GREATEST DESERTS**
- Sahara Desert — *North Africa*
  9,065,000km² — 3,500,000mi²
- Gobi Desert — *Mongolia-China*
  1,295,000km² — 500,000mi²
- Kalahari Desert — *Southern Africa*
  582,000km² — 225,000mi²
- Great Victoria Desert — *Australia*
  338,500km² — 150,000mi²
- Great Sandy Desert — *Australia*
  338,500km² — 150,000mi²

## KALAHARI DESERT

The Kalahari is the largest continuous stretch of sand in the world. Flat, dry and empty, it covers more than 80 per cent of Botswana, stretching from the Orange River towards the more equatorial regions. This wide-open expanse – whipped by clouds of dust, lashed by the summer rains and baked by the sun – was formed 200 million years ago when the supercontinent Gondwana began to break up to form the landmasses of the southern Hemisphere.

## A KALAHARI SAFARI

The tourism industry is currently one of Botswana's most lucrative, and a vital element of this burgeoning business is ecotourism, an increasingly popular

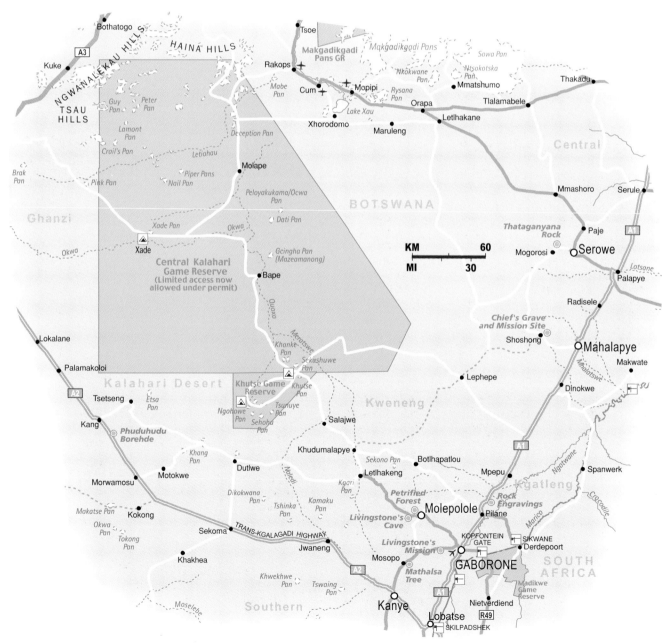

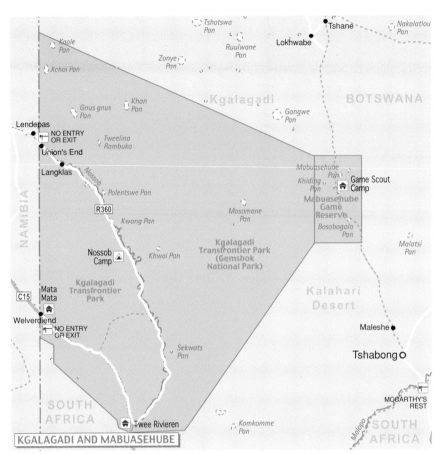

## 36

KGALAGADI AND MABUASEHUBE

trend throughout Africa. Eco-tourism has rapidly usurped the position of Botswana's hunting industry as one of the country's top foreign-exchange earners. It is now one of Africa's leading destinations. The sandy tracks first cut through this countryside by early explorers have given way, in parts, to a more developed infrastructure, but gravel and dust roads are still the paths most travelled in Botswana's wild areas. This adds to the rustic mood of untrammelled wilderness so sought after by travellers to Africa.

### A SENSITIVE ECOLOGY

As so much of Botswana's land cover comprises arid and sparsely vegetated terrain, the ecological balance is a sensitive one, easily destabilized, yet it is this parched land, unusually rich in game and bird species, that proves the great attraction. Game viewing is at its finest in the dry winter from May to August, when wildlife congregates at the remaining water sources. Wet summers provide the animals with an abundance of water, at which time they are far more reclusive. Summers also introduce a greater risk of malaria.

### KHUTSE & MABUASEHUBE

Hugging the southernmost border of the Central Kalahari Game Reserve, Khutse Game Reserve is a small santuary located fairly close to Gaborone. Made up largely of undulating savannah within typical pan countryside, Khutse is four-wheel-drive territory (like it or not!) and its numerous pans yield good wildlife sightings. The birdlife, too, is rich. Mabuasehube Game Reserve (now part of the Kgalagadi Transfrontier Park) is located in a remote region that is time-consuming and costly to reach ... yet it yields rich rewards for those who invest the time and money to enjoy what it has to offer: the simple beauty of the stark pans, the natural burnt ochres and browns of the desert, as well as reliably abundant game. The rare brown hyena is frequently spotted in the area, while wildebeest, hartebeest, eland, springbok and gemsbok are seen around the countless pans, particularly during the rainy season (which holds out from October to April). During the drier months game (and, as a result, most of the tourists!) is concentrated largely around three of the major watering points, Lesholoago Pan, Mpaathutlwa Pan and Mabuasehube Pan.

Opposite page: Springbok grazing.
Top to bottom: gemsbok; Nossob dry riverbed; suricates on the lookout.

# Zimbabwe

## ADVENTURING THROUGH ZIMBABWE (See Contact Details 92-95)

### ON LAND

**HIKING AND CLIMBING**
Countrywide
Chimanimani National Park

Zimbabwe Tourist Office
Zimbabwe National Parks and Wildlife

**GAME VIEWING AND WALKING SAFARIS**
Gonarezhou Park, Chiredzi
Zambezi Escarpment, above Mana Pools
Mana Pools National Park
Hwange, Matusadona

Zimbabwe National Parks and Wildlife
Chipembere Safaris
Natureways
Wilderness Safaris

**HORSE TRAILS**
Mavuradonha Wilderness
Victoria Falls
Matobo National Park

Natureways
Zambezi Horse Trails
Zimbabwe National Parks and Wildlife

**ELEPHANTBACK SAFARIS**
Nakavango Estate, Victoria Falls
Matopos Hills, Bulawayo

Shearwater Adventures
Camp Amalinda

### ON WHEELS

**4X4 TRAILS**
Countrywide

Taggallong

**DIY TRAILS**
Kariba
Mana Pools
Hwange National Park

all arranged through
Zimbabwe National
Parks and Wildlife

### ON (OR IN) WATER

**WHITEWATER RAFTING**
Batoka Gorge, Zambezi River

Adrift
Frontiers Rafting
Safari Par Excellence

**RIVER SPEEDBOAT TRIPS**
Zambezi River / Victoria Falls

Jet Extreme
Shearwater Adventures

**RIVER BOARDING, WHITEWATER (AND TANDEM) KAYAKING**
Batoka Gorge, Zambezi River   Safari Par Excellence

**CANOE SAFARIS**
Lower Zambezi/Mana Pools

Cansaf Adventures and Canoeing Safaris
Karibu Safaris
Natureways

**TIGER FISHING AND HOUSEBOATING**
Lake Kariba

Sengwa Safaris
River Horse Safaris
Taga Safaris
Zimbabwe National Parks and Wildlife

**INLAND SCUBA DIVING**
Chinhoyi Caves

Pro Divers

## 38

**BUNGEE JUMPING**
Victoria Falls Bridge      Shearwater Adventures

**GORGE SWING / FLYING FOX**
Rapid 4, Batoka Gorge      Adrift

**HELICOPTER FLIPS 'FLIGHT OF ANGELS'**
Victoria Falls      Shearwater Adventures
            Safari Par Excellence
            Batoka Sky

**MICROLIGHT FLIGHTS**
Victoria Falls      Batoka Sky

**ZIMBABWE**
**Capital:** Harare
**Area:** 390,580km$^2$ / 150,800mi$^2$
**Population:** 12.3 million
**Main ethnic groups:**
• Shona (71%)
• Ndebele (16%)
• White (1.5%)
• Asian (0.5%)
**Main languages:**
• English
• Shona
• Ndebele
**Main religions:**
• Syncretic (combination
   Christian/traditional
   beliefs) (50%)
• Christian (26%)
• Traditional beliefs (24%)
**Currency:** Zimbabwean
          dollar (100 cents)

**10 GREAT ADVENTURES**
1. Whitewater rafting
2. Bungee jumping
3. Fishing
4. Game viewing
5. Houseboating
6. Hiking
7. Horseriding
8. Elephant safaris
9. Scenic flights
10. Canoeing

# Victoria Falls

## VICTORIA FALLS ADVENTURES

Everything is bigger and better, deeper and steeper at the much-publicised junction of Zimbabwe and Zambia. Whitewater rafting can be breathtaking, bungee jumping terrifying, elephant-back safaris out of this world and the scenic flights by plane or helicopter are the stuff of lifetime memories. There are also walking routes, hiking trails, 4x4 excursions, sundowner cruises and game-viewing safaris. The Zimbabwean side is particularly well serviced by the hospitality industry and is, therefore, not cheap. The Zambian side is less 'developed' and not as spectacular, but it does offer a different, less glitzy view, with a better opportunity to get close to the waters of the falls.

## RAPID FIRE

Victoria Falls provides a daunting yet breathtaking backdrop for the site's highly challenging but massively rewarding rapids. It's natural that great whitewater rafting is centred around impressive waterfalls. Africa has a good number to speak of.

- Blue Nile Falls        Ethiopia
- Murchison Falls        Uganda
- Augrabies Falls        South Africa
- The Great Usutu        Swaziland
- Oribi Gorge Falls      South Africa
- Braganca Falls         Angola
- Epupa Falls            Namibia
- Ruacana Falls          Namibia
- Kagera Falls           Burundi

## THE SMOKE THAT THUNDERS

The mighty Victoria Falls (aka Mosi-oa-Tunya, 'the smoke that thunders') is one of Africa's greatest natural wonders, a vast and remarkably rugged vista of rainforest and riverine landscape. As the focal point of adventure in both Zambia and Zimbabwe, tour operators abound in and around Victoria Falls and the Zambezi Gorge, which is rated one of the world's wildest whitewater rafting destinations. The section between Lake Kariba and Victoria Falls is considered among the least tamed of the river's course (as well as one of the most spectacular) and is also the home territory of crocodiles and hippos, with even the occasional elephant spotted along the rugged banks.

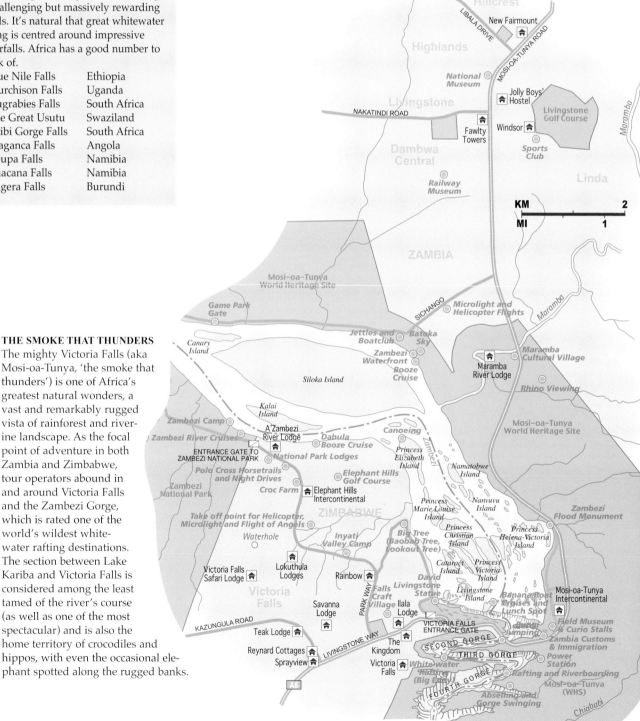

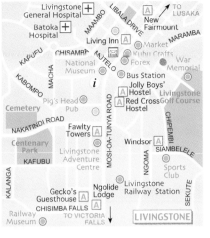

## 39

## VIC FALLS IN A NUTSHELL

**Climate:** Hot and humid all year. The falls are at their best from Feb-Aug.
**Risk factor:** Risks are plentiful, like dodging hippos and battling some of Africa's most fearsome rapids. Some excursions require little more than determination; others can be deadly and require considerable water skills.
**Health:** Malaria is rife; AIDS remains a concern; waterborne diseases (bilharzia) are a risk; bumps, grazes and bruises are par for the course!
**Pack:** Antimalarial medication and water purification tablets and protective, waterproof clothing. Reliable tour operators provide the necessities.

but, depending on the rains, are restricted to July and early August, while low-water runs are tackled between mid-August and the end of December. While the waters above the falls are shallow, more than 20 rapids punctuate the waters below. When the waters are low, the dangers are greater, and August to December are graded 5 – extremely demanding (Grade 6 is given to rapids that are unrideable!). The three-day, 65km (40 mile) whitewater trail from Kazungula ends at Big Tree at the falls.

## HIGHLIGHTS OF THE FALLS

Highlights are undoubtedly the awesome 110m (360ft) bungee jump, hailed as the highest commercial bridge leap in Africa. Queues may be long, the wait frustrating and the cost expensive, but the experience is unbeatable. Another unforgettable experience is the much vaunted Flight of Angels over the falls in a seaplane, helicopter, microlight or a twin-engined aircraft. Prices depend on the agent, aircraft and how long you stay airborne, but the experience is exhilarating, although frowned upon by conservationists. The main attraction is, however, the whitewater rafting, and the Zambezi Gorge is known to be one of the wildest whitewater spots in the world. High-water trips are available from the Zimbabwean or Zambian sides,

## VICTORIA FALLS NATIONAL PARK

The dramatic Falls and surrounding rainforest lie at the heart of the Victoria Falls National Park, a small but green and thriving 2,300 hectares (5,680 acres) of walking trails, woodland and riverine habitat. The forest that borders the falls is a thick jungle with dense undergrowth and a high canopy filled with ferns and orchids. Stands of wild fig and sausage trees are alive with bird calls. Small primates also inhabit these wooded slopes.

## VICTORIA FALLS VILLAGE

Within relatively easy walking distance of the thundering waters is Victoria Falls Village, which is still rather rustic in appearance. Expeditions into the forest, elephantback safaris, bungee jumps and cycling excursions can be arranged here; visitors' amenities crowd the 'village'. Considerably more tame is the quaint little Zambezi Nature Sanctuary, a small but rewarding haven for some of the region's indigenous wildlife, notably some 5,000 of the Nile crocodiles.

*Opposite page: canoeing on the Zambezi.*
*Top to bottom: microlighting over Victoria Falls; Victoria Falls aerial view; a section of the main falls; bungee plunge off the Zambezi River bridge.*

## THE WORLD'S HIGHEST FALLS

| | | |
|---|---|---|
| Angel Falls, Venezuela | 979m | 3,212ft |
| Tugela, South Africa | 850m | 2,800ft |
| Utigord, Norway | 800m | 2,625ft |
| Monge, Norway | 774m | 2,540ft |
| Mutarazi, Zimbabwe | 762m | 2,499ft |
| Yosemite, United States | 739m | 2,425ft |
| Espelands, Norway | 703m | 2,307ft |
| Lower Mar Valley, Norway | 655m | 2,151ft |
| Tyssestrengene, Norway | 647m | 2,123ft |
| Cuquenan, Venezuela | 610m | 2,000ft |

# Kariba

## LAKE KARIBA

Constructed between 1955 and 1958, and opened by Queen Elizabeth II in 1960, Lake Kariba remains one of the continent's most ambitious water projects, and is the third-largest artificial body of water in Africa. The massive walls span a perimeter of 579m (1,900ft) and stretch 282km (175 miles) across the landscape to cover a total of 5,000km² (1,930 sq. miles). The walls are 24m (79ft) thick at the base and 128m (420ft) high. A fascinating diversion is to take a walk along the top of the dam wall to feel the pounding of the massive turbines.

The shores of the great lake are a wildlife haven and are surrounded by some of Zimbabwe's finest parks, reserves and wilderness areas, all of which are popular drawcards for their game.

## LAKE KARIBA IN A NUTSHELL

Climate: Temperatures are the highest in the country and can be especially high on the water. Nights can, however, be cold, especially mid-year.

Risk factor: Aside from the presence of a good many crocodile, risks are few as the waters and shores of Kariba are well serviced by the local travel industry. Be vigilant to avoid becoming a victim of the usual pickpockets and adhere to standard water safety rules.

Health: Malaria, bilharzia and AIDS are prevalent throughout much of the country. Drinking water is fairly safe.

Pack: Malarial prophylactics, sunscreen and personal supplies.

Facilities: Amenities are generally very good to excellent.

## 40

## SAILING LAKE KARIBA

Lake Kariba straddles the Zambezi River and remains Zimbabwe's principal source of hydroelectricity. The heart of the lake's leisure industry is Matusadona National Park with its attractive resorts offering fine game viewing, walking trails, boat cruises and sailing safaris. The harvesting of fish such as kapenta is the mainstay of locals while sport fishing attracts tourists! There are plenty of marinas, boat yards and anchorages, and the game lodges on the water's edge boast excellent facilities, including yachting and fishing. Game viewing and bird watching from the water is rewarding, with crocodile, fish eagles, cormorants, kingfishers, darters and herons, and even elephant and buffalo. The water (filled with drowned trees) and the shores are a wildlife sanctuary, and the neighbouring parks of Matusadona and Chizarira have enjoyed good quantities of game in recent times. Given the lake's location and popularity, certain parts of the shore are very expensive. Prices vary from the outrageous to budget picnic cruises, many of which depart regularly from the lake's marinas.

## A FERRY GOOD TIME

The Chaminuka ferry leaves Kariba town once a week and takes two to three days to reach Binga. Costs are low and the game viewing very good, but amenities are usually basic and you should bring your own supplies. Trips on the 9m (30ft) *Searunner* trimaran skirt Chete Island and it is not unusual to spot wildlife from the deck. Other operators offer special day packages for small groups, usually including a day on the water. Accommodation, including tents, is not hard to come by, but you may want to book these in advance.

## MANA POOLS NATIONAL PARK

This magnificent park is deservedly a World Heritage Site. Wild, remote and still wrapped in its original beauty, Mana Pools ('mana' means 'four') is a great spot for fishing but even better for wildlife viewing, with hippo, croc, zebra, antelope and elephant all sure to be seen. Day visitors are welcome, but you'd definitely want to spend a few nights in one of the rustic camp sites or in a more upmarket lodge!

Opposite page: aerial view of Lake Kariba.
Top to bottom: drowned trees near Bumi Hills; crocodiles at the Kariba crocodile farm; dam wall and Nyaminyami statue.

# Great Zimbabwe Ruins

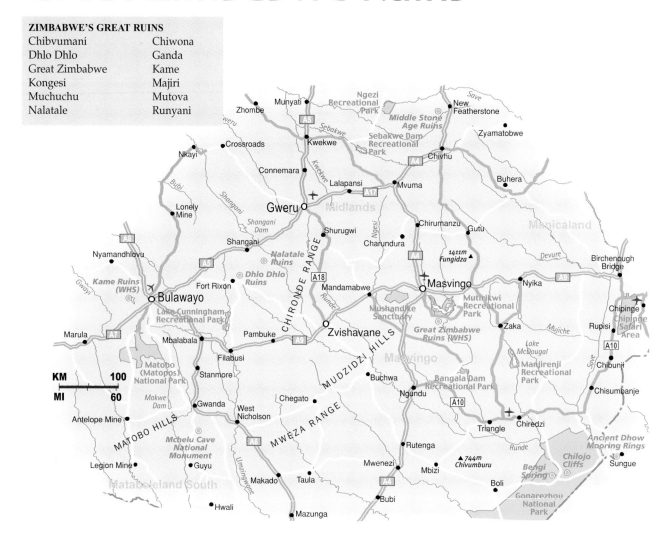

### GREAT ZIMBABWE

Perhaps the country's most significant legacy, the majestic stone-walled ruins of Great Zimbabwe comprise the most impressive medieval site in Africa south of the Sahara. This architectural and archaeological gem, about 30km (19 miles) from Masvingo, was established more than 1,000 years ago by the Karonga, ancestors of the local Shona, and comprises a fascinating series of stone walls. The walled city harboured no fewer than 10,000 citizens – a fatal mistake that led to overpopulation and the abandonment of the citadel in the 1450s. Excavation of the site has provided evidence that medieval Africa was indeed highly sophisticated. Guided tours take visitors through the Hill Complex (once known as the Acropolis) which is thought to have been the monarch's residence. The walls of the Great Enclosure are 5m (16ft) thick and 11m (36ft) high and were built with nearly a million stone 'bricks' over 100 years in the 14th and 15th centuries.

### EXPLORING CHIMANIMANI

Relatively small, Zimbabwe's Chimanimani National Park (and the mountains and village that share its name) is the focal point for excellent walking and is especially popular with backpackers. Today, it is probably the most popular hiking destination in Zimbabwe. The region is blessed with an extraordinary splendour, and a rich floral and faunal life, including baboons and antelope species such as klipspringer and blue duiker. Within easy reach are two of the area's top attractions: the wildlife of Chimanimani Eland Sanctuary, and the natural beauty of the forest-enclosed Bridal Veil Falls. It is, however, the mountain range that lures hikers: a huge granite massif that towers some 2,200m (7,200ft) crowned by the impressive 2,436m (7,995ft) peak of Mount Binga (also known as Kweza), which lies on the other side of the Mozambique border. Virtually all the paths and trails are faultless, taking hikers through an unspoiled mountain

wilderness dotted with caves, gorges, streams, and slopes blanketed with grassy plains and dotted with msasa trees. To reach the lofty heights of Mount Binga can take up to four hours of arduous climbing, but access to the plateau via Bailey's Folly may require only two to three hours.

### MANY WAYS TO SCALE A PEAK

There are various hiking options, including a one-day walk to the Southern Lakes by way of the Banana Grove Trail and the relatively gentle walk up Skeleton Pass, which should take less than an hour. While many trails take one up (and/or down) some demanding inclines and may be considered challenging by most, some walks require only moderate fitness. Few should ever be tackled alone, though. Chimanimani has more than adequate visitor facilities, reinforced by the fact that walkers are scarce. About 20km (12 miles) from Chimanimani village is Mutekeswane Base Camp, the starting point of no

The Hill Complex

Cleft Rock Enclosure — Eastern Enclosure (Original Soapstone Birds Site) — Gold Furnace Enclosure — Recess Enclosure — Western Enclosure — Southern Enclosure

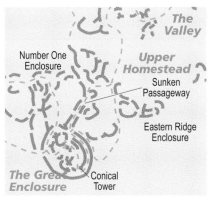

The Valley — Number One Enclosure — Upper Homestead — Sunken Passageway — Eastern Ridge Enclosure — The Great Enclosure — Conical Tower

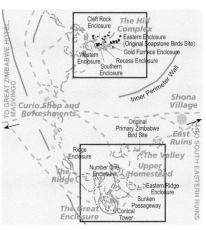

fewer than three separate mountain routes winding some 500m (1,640ft) up the slopes. Camp sites here have warm showers and basic overnighting requirements, but the most popular accommodation options are perhaps offered at caves such as Digby's Falls, North Cave and Peterhouse Cave. All provide easy access to some of the most spectacular hikes in the area. The good news is that Chimanimani National Park is well serviced by a sound tourist infrastructure such as shuttle services and well-informed operators, and even offers the services of search parties in case of emergencies.

Top to bottom: detail of stone wall; conical tower from the 11th century; Matobo Hills; aloes and western ridge stone wall.

## CHIMANIMANI IN A NUTSHELL

Climate: Best hiking is when it is sunny but not too hot (May–Sept). Nights can be windy and cold.

Risk factor: It is generally safe to walk Chimanimani, but never hike alone or in pairs and plan well. Watch for sudden changes in weather, keep to known routes (you may wander into Mozambique!) and leave your itinerary with park authorities.

Health: Malaria, bilharzia and AIDS are prevalent. Drinking water is relatively safe (even on the mountain), but take water purification tablets.

Pack: Take your own supplies such as food and equipment (collecting of firewood is prohibited, so you will need a gas cooker), warm clothes, sun protection and a sleeping bag.

Facilities: Amenities are generally good and overnight stays comfortable.

## MATOBO HILLS

Despite the stark beauty of their seemingly horizonless vistas, the granite hills of Matobo are best known in the Western world as the final resting place of Cecil John Rhodes, the mining pioneer and statesman who played a significant role in the troubled history of southern Africa. His grave tablet stands in the middle of a wide circle created from the boulders that lie strewn across the hillsides. The spot at Malindidzimu is known as the View of the World and provides one of the most impressive panoramas in southwestern Zimbabwe. Backed by austere, cold-faced mountains weathered by rain and wind and sand, the wilderness of Matobo National Park – 50km (31 miles) south of Bulawayo – is home to a relatively small assortment of wild and rare animals. Giant granite outcrops and precariously balanced rock formations characterise the landscape, and the area boasts one of the world's most astounding collections of indigenous rock art.

CHIMANIMANI — Mount Binga - highest point in Mozambique — Mt Binga 2436m — Chimanimani — ZIMBABWE — Chimanimani National Park — Rusito — MOZAMBIQUE

# Hwange

## A SUPER PARK

Zimbabwe's animal populations have been badly affected by irresponsible management and the lack of funds and infrastructure. During the 1980s, the continent's most expansive black rhino populations (around 3,000), were reduced to no more than 300 individuals as a result of poaching, but there have been efforts to curb poaching activities by dehorning the rhinos and hunting down poachers. Although the prohibition on the trade in rhino horn seems to have met with little success, there has been some attempt (with limited success) to translocate rhino and other species to safer grounds. Zimbabwe's elephant populations are now growing, some having been reintroduced with the establishment of the Gaza-Kruger-Gonarezhou Transfrontier Park, the 'Superpark' that spans the boundaries of three countries – South Africa, Zimbabwe and Mozambique. At an impressive 100,000km² (40,000 sq. miles), this is the world's largest conservation area and 'Operation Ark' saw some 1,000 elephants translocated from the Kruger National Park in South Africa to both Mozambique and Zimbabwe.

## HWANGE NATIONAL PARK

A former hunting reserve for Ndebele kings, Hwange was one of Africa's best-stocked parks until the 1970s, thanks partly to the creation of dozens of artificial watering holes. Located alongside the Kalahari Desert, it was created as a means of enticing people into viewing animals en route to the more famed Vic Falls nearby. The easy little two-hour 10 Mile Drive that loops through the best wildlife areas of the park is the staple attraction for most visitors, with the highlight being the Nyamandhlovu Viewing Platform above the popular (among the animals!) Nyamandhlovu Pan. More adventurous visitors will take their choice of the Ngwethla Loop, an overnight stay at Sinamatella Camp (with its amazing views and chilling night-time animal 'talk') or ranger-escorted walks.

## ZAMBEZI NATIONAL PARK

The Victoria Falls and Zambezi national parks preserve an incredible natural heritage that includes spectacular water-falls, thousands of hectares of protected land and some of Africa's most impressive wildlife populations. Much of Zimbabwe is still untamed, yet authorities have made considerable attempts to incorporate the requirements of the mass tourism market with the demands of land preservation. The Zambezi NP extends to over 56,000ha (138,350 acres) and is considerably larger than Victoria Falls NP. Zambezi is home to elephant, buffalo, rhino, zebra, lion, leopard and cheetah, in addition to countless other species that have made

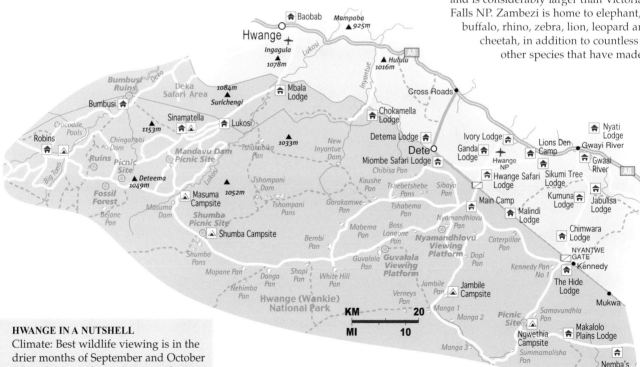

## HWANGE IN A NUTSHELL

Climate: Best wildlife viewing is in the drier months of September and October when the animals are driven to the artificial waterholes rather than spreading out around the vast park.

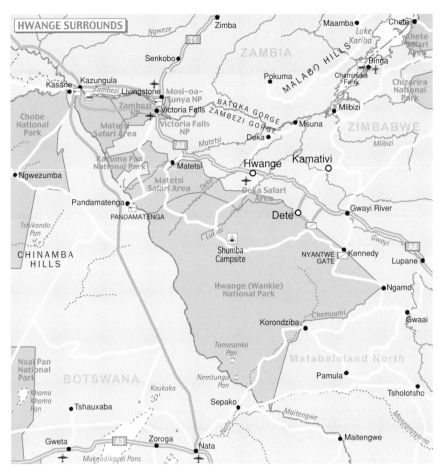

their home in the Zambezi Basin. Less developed than the rather tourist-oriented Falls, Zambezi National Park offers a taste of Zimbabwe at its finest.

## TACKLING THE ZAMBEZI

Depending largely on the season and the rains, the high-water expeditions are limited to late winter (July and August), while low-water runs are best between mid-August and December. The waters are not always easy to navigate – especially beyond the favoured tourist stopovers – and when the waters are low the existing risks are even greater. This is particularly true from August to December when Grade 5 rapids (Grade 6 means they are unsurpassable) are fraught with danger, to be tackled only by the exceptionally fit and equally skilled. Trip durations vary on the Zambezi, but the most popular are the 24-hour, 22km (14 miles) excursion with seven other 'sailors' on an inflatable rubber craft, and the less demanding three-day, 65km (40 miles) whitewater trail from Kazungula to Victoria Falls' Big Tree – a very different experience to the rather menacing whirlpools at Mupata Gorge, which require a lot more skill to negotiate and are potentially hazardous for the uninitiated.

## HARARE

Founded just over 100 years ago, Zimbabwe's capital was once hailed as the most African of the continent's principal cities. Harare (formerly known as Salisbury) was pronounced the official capital of Southern Rhodesia in 1923 and was declared a city in 1935. It has seen better days and is plagued intermittently with fuel shortages and barren supermarket shelves. Despite problems such as growing urban crime, the capital remains a beautiful city that has retained at least some of its charm. It also serves as an important centre for the country's arts and crafts industry, notably the soapstone sculptures, the best of which are found about 8km (5 miles) from town at Chapungu Kraal, a model Shona village that offers a glimpse of tribal life. Harare is set against an inspiring backdrop of bushveld savanna dotted with a series of rock formations (the most famous being the Epworth Balancing Rocks) and an impressive number of rock-art sites.

Opposite page: a pride of female lions resting.
Top to bottom: water lilies; 4x4 vehicle in flooded plain; ilala palms at sunset.

# Mozambique

## ADVENTURING THROUGH MOZAMBIQUE
### (See Contact Details 92-95)

### IN THE AIR

**MICROLIGHTING**
Zongoene Lodge          Mozambique Connection

**PARASAILING**
Parasailing          Praia do Sol

### ON WHEELS

**4X4 TRAILS**
Countrywide          Mozambique 4x4 trails
Pafuri Trail          Mozambique Connection
Inhambane Province          Mozambique Connection
Maputo Elephant Res.          Mozambique Connection

**QUADBIKING**
Barra Lodge
Guinjata Bay

**OFFROAD BIKING**
Extreme Biking Safaris

**MOZAMBIQUE**
**Capital:** Maputo
**Area:** 799,380km$^2$ / 308,642mi$^2$
**Population:** 19.6 million
**Main ethnic groups:**
• Makua-Lomwe (47%)
• Tsonga (23%)
• Malawi (12%)
**Main language:**
• Portuguese
**Main religions:**
• Traditional beliefs (60%)
• Christian (30%)
• Muslim (10%)
**Currency:** Metical (100 centavos)

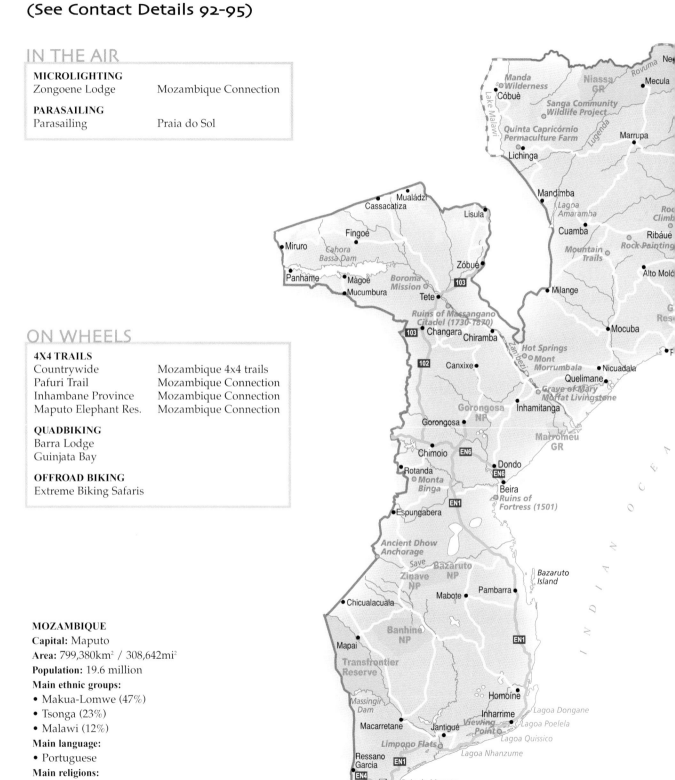

## 43

**SCUBA DIVING**

| | |
|---|---|
| Ponta do Ouro / Ponta Malongane | Devocean Diving |
| | Simply Scuba |
| | Hartley's Oceans and Islands |
| | Adventure Diving Safaris |
| Central Mozambique | Barra Lodge |
| | Guinjata Bay |
| Bazaruto Archipelago | Classic Sailing Adventures |
| | Island Quest Sailing and Diving |
| | Marlin Lodge |
| | Indigo Bay |
| | Hartley's Safaris |
| Northern Mozambique Archipelago | Pemba Beach Hotel |
| | Wildlife Adventures |

**SAILING**

| | |
|---|---|
| Central Mozambique | Barra Lodge |
| | Praia do Sol |
| Bazaruto Archipelago | Classic Sailing Adventures |
| | Island Quest Sailing and Diving |
| | Indigo Bay |
| Pemba/Northern Mozambique Archipelago | |
| | Wildlife Adventures |
| | Pemba Beach Resort |
| Inhaca Island | Mozambique Connection |

**SEA KAYAKING**

| | |
|---|---|
| Inhaca Island | Hardy Ventures |

**GAME FISHING**

| | |
|---|---|
| Along the coast | Charles Norman Safaris |
| | Marlin Lodge |
| Indigo Bay | Classic Sailing Adventures |
| | Safaris Unlimited |

**WATERSKIING**

| | |
|---|---|
| Countrywide | Praia do Sol |
| | Indigo Bay |
| | Classic Sailing Adventures |

**DOLPHIN SAFARIS**

| | |
|---|---|
| Ponta do Ouro | Dolphin Encountours |

**DHOW TRIPS**

| | |
|---|---|
| Inhaca Island | Mozambique Connection |

## ON LAND

**HORSERIDING**

| | |
|---|---|
| Bazaruto Island | Indigo Bay |
| | Barra Lodge |

**GAME VIEWING / SAFARIS**

| | |
|---|---|
| Countrywide | Hartley's Safaris |
| | Barefoot Safaris |
| Maputo Elephant Reserve | Mozambique Connection |

**DUNEBOARDING**

| | |
|---|---|
| Bazaruto Island | Indigo Bay |

**10 GREAT ADVENTURES**

1. Scuba diving
2. Dolphin safaris
3. Sailing
4. Game fishing
5. 4x4 driving
6. Horseriding
7. Quadbiking
8. Microlighting
9. Waterskiing
10. Sea kayaking

# Maputo Region & Surrounds

**MAPUTO CITY**

## THE LAND
Mozambique covers 799,380km² (308,561 sq. miles), which makes up more land mass than France and Great Britain combined. A relatively flat land, its average altitude is just over 350m (1,148ft), and it enjoys a spectacular coastline that runs for more than 2,500km (1,554 miles), which provides much of the country's tourist activity. The multitude of rivers and mountains create a wide and varied range of vegetation that opens itself up to hiking, walking, canoeing and rafting opportunities. The mighty Zambezi River flows through the Cahora Bassa Dam and runs across the central parts of the country, emptying into the Mozambique Channel and the Indian Ocean at the 100km-wide (62 miles) Zambezi Delta. The country's highest point is the 2,437m (7,993ft) Binga Peak, found in the Chimanimani mountain range, on the border with Zimbabwe (Mozambique shares a border with six other countries).

## MAPUTO
No more than a small, haphazard collection of temporary shelters in the 16th century, Maputo (known in fairly recent times as Lourenço Marques) is a lively port city criss-crossed by palm-fringed avenues lined with jacaranda and flame trees. Following a period of civil strife and political uncertainty that ended only in 1992, many of Maputo's grand palaces and synagogues, markets and museums, and even humble Creole-style homes (particularly in the larger urban centres) still bear the physical scars of civil war. However, Maputo is emerging from the ashes to slowly regain some of the glory of its heyday. It is home to a thriving population of bohemian artists and receives a steady trickle of travellers. It has a vigorous nightlife which centres on the late-night bars of Rua do Bagamoio, the revelry spilling over into the evening markets and brightly lit seafront. Rather dilapidated in parts, the city is dotted with historic Portuguese forts. A highlight is its must-see Museum of the Revolution.

## MAPUTO GAME RESERVE
Also known as Maputo Elephant Reserve, the protected area lies across Maputo Bay – an area of shimmering lakes, stretches of grassland and mile upon mile of unspoiled white sand beaches. There are not large herds of game, but elephants are relatively plentiful in the reserve (thanks to excellent conservation efforts). The birdwatching is excellent and the scenery spectacular. The coastline is rich in colourful tropical fish, coral and a host of marine life. It is also an important breeding ground for the amazing leatherback turtles that weigh in at around 646kg (1421 pounds). These maritime giants lay up to 1,000 eggs per season.

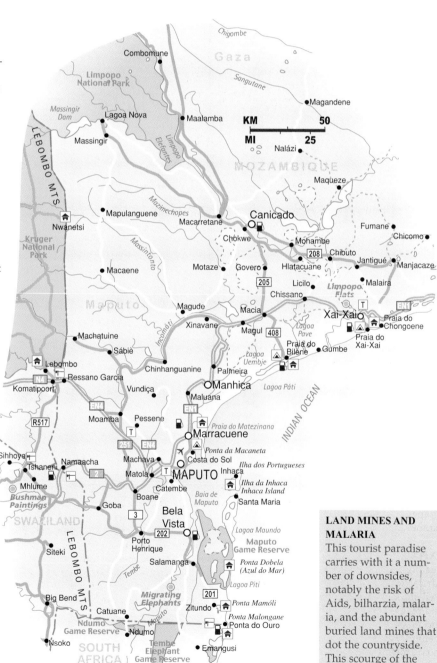

## LAND MINES AND MALARIA
This tourist paradise carries with it a number of downsides, notably the risk of Aids, bilharzia, malaria, and the abundant buried land mines that dot the countryside. This scourge of the civil war has taken a massive toll on thousands of civilians.

## 44

### INHACA ISLAND
An idyll of beautiful beaches whose shores are dotted with stands of mango trees and lined with brightly coloured offshore reefs, Inhaca Island is about 24km (15 miles) from the mainland and easily accessible via the ferries departing from the capital. It is the largest in the Gulf of Maputo and its pretty village presents a fascinating look at island life. Dominated by the upgraded Inhaca Hotel, the narrow streets have a good selection of restaurants and cafés interspersed with the odd (laid-back!) attraction. Situated in extraordinarily rich waters, the island's popular coastal attractions have proven to be its most magnetic drawcard. Apart from the marine research centre, which offers a different perspective to the conventional island idyll, Inhaca's shores are peppered with striking beaches and a fascinating reef life that offers some of the finest diving, snorkelling and underwater explorations on Africa's east coast.

### EXPLORING MAPUTO PROVINCE
Readily accessible by road from South Africa, Maputo province has everything: well-stocked reserves, historic old towns and magical beaches, outstanding diving and miles of endless road that create a memorable adventure playground. For most 4x4 enthusiasts – and this is the only real way to explore the south! – the departure point is Komatipoort in South Africa's Mpumalanga province, and entry is via Ressano Garcia in the far

### MAPUTO PROVINCE IN A NUTSHELL
Climate: Hot and humid; cool weather and coastal breezes June-Aug.
Risk factor: Experienced mechanics specializing in 4x4 maintenance are hard to come by; language is an obstacle. Roads are navigable but are generally in poor condition and best suited for 4x4 vehicles.
Health: Malaria is rife and AIDS is a real threat. Waterborne diseases include hepatitis, typhoid, cholera and dysentery. Water is not drinkable.
Pack: Lightweight summer clothing and sunscreen. Bottled water is vital. Be familiar with your vehicle's needs and bring your own spares! Beach driving requires a permit.

south. Life here centres on the capital that, although dilapidated, is well thought out yet charming in character and mood. The war-ravaged streets remain much as they were during the civil war, but are now peopled by laughing children, earnest street vendors and sarong-clad women.

### GETTING AROUND MAPUTO
Despite the tourist traffic, communication remains an obstacle even in the capital, and Portuguese (the official language) is spoken only by a few. Lined by groves of cashew trees and a series of villages of bamboo-and-palm huts, the scarred roads in the south are generally in poor condition, making four-wheel-drive vehicles preferable to sedans. Be on the lookout for potholes – a reliable warning sign is sandy patches gouged into the grass on the sides of the tarred roads, an indication that vehicles have been compelled to scramble off the road. Offroad, the sand is as fine as castor sugar and travellers reluctant to break a sweat are advised to pack up and go home. Even in the best-maintained areas, driving can be demanding and the slightest falter can end in spinning wheels and flying sand. This is especially true on the shoreline, where beach sand is very fine. The coast is extremely fragile, and a permit is required to drive along the beach. Edge forward very slowly, with diff-locks engaged and tyres deflated, and drive on the compact sand below the high-water mark.

Top to bottom: Natural History Museum in Maputo; mural depicting Samora Machel; early morning in the Maputo Elephant Reserve; the ferry crossing with its human tourist cargo from Catembe to Maputo.

# Bazaruto

## HISTORY AND MYSTERY

Mozambique has done duty as a Portuguese outpost, and numerous Portuguese and Arab traders and colonists have settled along the coast over the centuries since Vasco da Gama 'discovered' this land in 1497. The country's history is shrouded in the mystery of the legend of King Solomon's Mines; countless explorers have yet to stumble upon this vast stash of gold. Another myth was that of a fabulously wealthy empire, Monomotapa – the myth was aimed at motivating Portugal to bring peace to the land. The country also saw massive slave trading in the 1800s as well as pirate attacks on the mainland and islands. More recently, the brutal civil war decimated much of the land, infrastructure and wildlife until peace was declared in the early 1990s.

## TRIBAL LIFE

Mozambique features eight major tribal groups, the largest of which is the Makua-Lomwe (accounting for close to half the population). The next largest is the Tsonga (a quarter of the population), and other groups include the Shona and the Zambezi Valley tribes (the Chuabo, Sena and Nyungwe), as well as the Yao.

## INHAMBANE

Almost two million coconut palms grace the Inhambane area, also rich with a fabulous marine life and interesting local diversions such as dhow taxis and roadside stalls. The town itself provides a fascinating and welcoming glimpse back in time and is known for the hundreds of dhows that float on Inhambane Bay's tranquil waters. Reed baskets at the Mercado Municipal market make a fine purchase, along with hats and mats. The bell tower at the 200-year-old Cathedral of our Lady of the Conception offers magnificent views of the town and surrounding bay.

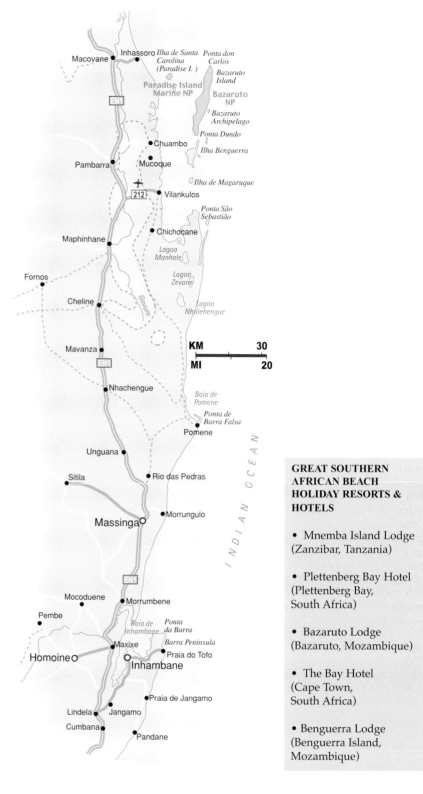

**GREAT SOUTHERN AFRICAN BEACH HOLIDAY RESORTS & HOTELS**

- Mnemba Island Lodge (Zanzibar, Tanzania)

- Plettenberg Bay Hotel (Plettenberg Bay, South Africa)

- Bazaruto Lodge (Bazaruto, Mozambique)

- The Bay Hotel (Cape Town, South Africa)

- Benguerra Lodge (Benguerra Island, Mozambique)

## BAZARUTO ARCHIPELAGO

The Bazaruto Archipelago is a chain of tiny islands roughly 20km (12 miles) off the Mozambique coast, which have been incorporated into the Bazaruto National Park. Its unique and isolated ecosystem ensures near-pristine diving conditions in warm waters heated by the Benguela current, with an amazing tropical sea life of brightly coloured corals, anemones, fish and turtles, while saltwater flyfishing is growing in popularity in the archipelago. Rehabilitated after the Mozambican conflict, the archipelago comprises four principal islands – Bazaruto Island, Magaruque, Benguerra and Santa

## 45

Carolina, perhaps better known as Paradise Island – and several smaller reef-lined islands, which make up the national park. Bazaruto, Magaruque and Benguerra are the largest of the group.

### THE ARCHIPELAGO IN A NUTSHELL
Climate: Humid and tropical, with high summer temperature and relatively moderate rains.
Risk factor: No real danger beyond the usual risks posed by ocean sports. Be prepared, take precautions, and be sensible, as rescue services are limited.
Pack: Winter evenings can be chilly, but carrying plenty of clothing should not be a priority! Take malarial prophylactics and sunscreen, as well as diving gear if you're on a budget (renting is costly).
Facilities: An upmarket destination (and pricey), facilities are adequate and most lodges and resorts range from good to excellent.

### DIVING BAZARUTO
Buffeted by fluctuating sea levels, powerful currents and strong winds, the unique ecosystem is relatively isolated and, as such, remains unscathed by development. The waters are crystal clear and splashed with colour in the form of tropical sea life that makes for a magnificent underwater experience and with wonderful spots to explore. The diving, outstanding beaches, upmarket accommodation, and fishing and birding opportunities have earned the archipelago a reputation as a favourite tourist spot. Idyllic Bazaruto is most popular among fly-in travellers, but only visitors with reservations at one of the lodges are permitted to overnight on the islands themselves. Access to these protected waters is via boat from Vilankulos, some 500km (300 miles) south of Beira. Camping is permitted but is not recommended, as there are so many choices for more comfortable lodgings on the magical islands.

### CAST AWAY
Mozambique is an angler's paradise with world-class catches up for grabs. Black marlin, sailfish and a host of game fish draw marine anglers, while freshwater angling offers great bass as well as tiger fish (notably at Cahora Bassa). Tourists and locals find spearfishing, snorkelling, scuba diving, sailing and sea kayaking (as well as many other water activities) highly rewarding here. Mozambique's numerous habitats and over 600 bird species should make 'twitchers' happy. After the internal strife and deterioration, national parks and reserves are being upgraded while four-wheel-drive routes are abundant, as are hiking and climbing trails.

### BARRA PENINSULA
Barra is the site of the province's capital, Inhambane. It is understandably among Mozambique's most popular holiday meccas: the azure waters, coves, bays and sands perfectly characterise the leisurely pace of beach holidays. The landscape of Barra and the adjoining Cape Inhambane are dotted with coconut plantations and mangrove swamps, and the wave-washed shores are a powerful lure to the marine wonderland. Beware though: the waters are warm but unpredictable, and powerful rip currents and volatile waves make it an exhilarating but particularly safe adventure experience.

Opposite page: local fishermen hauling their catch in from the tropical shoreline.
Top to bottom: Bazaruto Island lagoon and sand dunes; a young boy contemplates the next catch; lighthouse on Bazaruto Island.

# Beira Corridor

## BEIRA

Mozambique's second-largest city, Beira operates as a busy port yet is somewhat shabby and chaotic. It has, however, achieved fame for its lip-smacking prawns and inviting white-sand beaches, many of which offer excellent swimming. Beira's architecture is varied, ranging from the beautiful Catedral de Nossa Senhora de Rosário (1915, a functioning church), the neoclassical Clube des Chinês (1917, now the city archives) and Casa Infante Sagres. Colonial structures include the Casa Portugal, Banco Standard Totta, and the avant-garde exhibition hall, Casa dos Bicos. The 1,200-seater Cinema São Jorge is one of Africa's largest and most ornate cinemas. Beira also offers a clutch of interesting art galleries and a municipal market offering excellent seafood, and fruit and vegetables bigger than you've ever seen before. The best place to buy prawns is from the fishermen on Macúti Beach: the beach was named after the wrecked ship that was towed in front of the lighthouse to act as a breakwater.

## BEIRA CORRIDOR AND RAILWAY

The Beira Corridor is a 32km-wide (20 mile) corridor of land that follows the railway line from Mutare in Zimbabwe to Beira in Mozambique. The corridor and the railway line provide landlocked Zimbabwe with a vital trade and tourist link to the Indian Ocean. Closing

## FLORA AND FAUNA

Mozambique has a tropical to subtropical climate, and its landscape is dressed in temperate rainforest, mopane woodland, old baobab trees, woodland mahogany and the unique mangroves with their root systems running above and below the earth. Animal life includes masses of birds (over 900 species) and an abundant marine life (including the walrus-like dugong). The country's mammal populations are now increasing among species such as elephant, buffalo, lion and leopard as well as roan and sable antelopes.

the line was once used as a means of stifling the former Rhodesian government, and it has been repeatedly opened and closed over the years as a result of decades of civil war and armed conflict.

## GORONGOSA NATIONAL PARK

Following decades of liberation fighting and bloody civil war, Mozambique's wildlife was all but obliterated, with elephant, buffalo, blue wildebeest, hippo, Burchell's zebra, and waterbuck, all previously numbering in the thousands. The legacy of the armed conflict was that species numbers dipped into the low hundreds – or disappeared. Once considered one of the continent's greatest legacies, Gorongosa was originally set aside as a hunting area with the goal

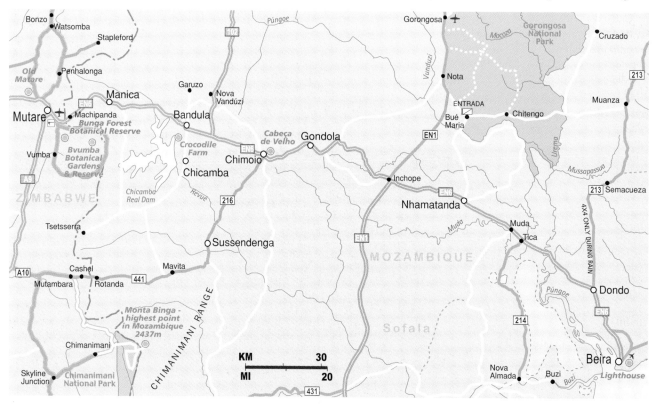

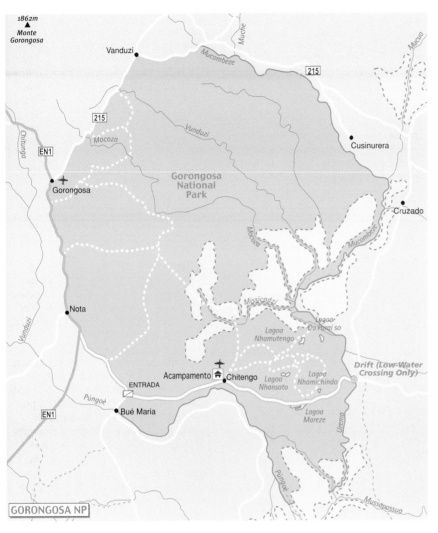

## 46

GORONGOSA NP

of providing game meat to thousands of workers on the burgeoning sugar and coconut plantations. Gorongosa's tourist appeal is its magnificent vegetation, which includes grasslands along Lake Urema, as well as vibrant forests of fever trees lining seasonal pans, and woodland and dense palmveld, all filled with a vibrant diversity of wildlife species. Gorongosa is a vital sanctuary for the Sofala zebra (a sub-species of the Burchell's zebra), whose numbers have plummeted from 30,000 down to around 50 over the last three decades. The park is also an attraction for birders, with the spotting of the palm-nut vulture a major feather in any twitcher's cap. Hundreds of other species include the collared palm-thrush, racket-tailed rollers, rufous-bellied herons, martial eagles and silvery-cheeked hornbills. Some of the park's favoured activities are guided canoe trips and walks (both organised and run by park management) as well as the 350km (217 miles) trip to Inchope which can be done by two-wheel-drive bakkies out of the rainy season.

## GORONGOSA IN A NUTSHELL
Climate: The cool months (May-Sept) are the best for visitors, rather than the hot and humid months (Oct-Dec) when early rains can make mudbaths out of dirt roads and tracks.
Risk factor: Summer rains can make large areas treacherous or totally inaccessible.
Pack: You'll need to ensure you're self-sufficient, so bring your own food (stock up at supermarkets in Beira or Chimoio). Manage your fuel reserves carefully as fuel is not available at Inchope or Gorongosa Village. Be sure to fill up at Save Bridge, Chimoio or Beira.
Facilities: Some basic facilities exist in the park, mainly camp sites with all the basic needs for weary travellers.

Opposite page: a local woman busy at work in her outdoor kitchen.
Top to bottom: Catholic cathedral in Beira; Mount Gorongosa under cloud; sunset over Mount Gorongosa.

# Cahora Bassa to Zambezi River Mouth

## CAHORA BASSA

The grand Cahora Bassa dam is situated around 500km (310 miles) north-west of the Mozambique coast. Built during the heady days of the 1970s, the grand dam represented one of Africa's largest-ever civil engineering projects, and is one of the larger dams on earth. Although the dam is a major producer of hydroelectric power for southern Africa, it has admittedly become something of a white elephant – it operates way below its capacity as a result of damage incurred during the civil war. The dam has in effect created Lago de Cahora Bassa (Lake Cahora Bassa), a monstrous 270km (170 miles) body of water that reaches all the way back to the conflu-ence of the Zambezi and Luangwa rivers on Zambia's border. The dam lies in a magnificent gorge and amidst glorious scenery. It's not a surprise, then, that the dam itself has developed into something of a tourist attraction with its superb scenery and views, as well as tours of the dam and the impressive turbine room, although the facilities and amenities for visitors are rather basic. Visitors can get to the dam by car or by the bus from nearby Songo, which acts as the dam's service town. *Chapas* (converted minivans) also run a few times a day from Songo to the dam, but the more energetic can take the high road and walk the 6km (3.7 miles).

## TETE

The nearest town of any decent size to Cahora Bassa is Tete, located southeast down the Zambezi, roughly 150km (95 miles) from the dam. A former vital trading outpost from the days before Portuguese 'rule', Tete remains a major cog in Mozambique's transport wheel – its position on the Zambezi aside, Tete is also on the A2 from Zimbabwe through to Malawi. The town also has an impressive suspension bridge that straddles the Zambezi River.

### POWER ON TAP

The 2,700km-long (1,678 mile) Zambezi River starts as a mere trickle in the northwest of Zambia, yet gathers enormous momentum as it winds through six southern African nations. Dams at Cahora Bassa and Kariba provide vast amounts of valuable hydroelectric power to the region.

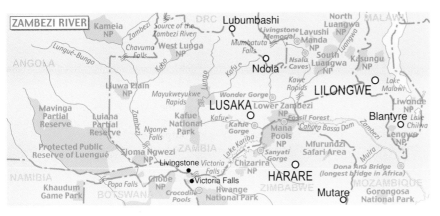

## 47

## THE ZAMBEZI DELTA

The 3,000km (1,860-mile) Zambezi River winds for 820km (510 miles) of its route across Mozambique before reaching the ocean. Its broad valley slices the country in two, beginning at Feira and ending, after having accumulated run-off waters from five other countries, in the wetlands of the delta. By the time the waters reach Mozambique they have been tamed by Zimbabwe's Lake Kariba and are again dammed by the 160m (525ft) walls of the 270km-long (170 mile) Cahora Bassa, Mozambique's most ambitious dam. Having coursed through the hinterland, and waters guarded by crocodiles and hippos, the Zambezi begins to disperse about 600km (373 miles) downstream on the buffalo plains of Marromeu, where it spreads into a network of streams, channels and tributaries covering 4,000km² (1,544 sq. miles). Today, the delta spans only 100km (62 miles), but is nevertheless a visual delight – especially from the air – and is home to big game such as elephant, buffalo, rhino and roan antelope.

## CHIMOIO & MANICA

The capital of Manica province, Chimoio has plenty to offer travellers. The Cabeca do Velho (a large rock that bears an uncanny resemblance to an old man's face) sits 5km (3 miles) out of town and provides marvellous views for anyone who takes the relatively short trip to the top. Roughly 35km (21 miles) west of Chimoio is Chicamba Real Dam, a popular weekend getaway and angling spot, while to the southwest on the border with Zimbabwe is Monta Binga, at 2,437m (7,990ft) the highest peak in Mozambique and a popular target for climbers (although it's best approached from Zimbabwe's Chimanimani National Park). Manica is a small settlement 70km (43 miles) to the west of Chimoio and has a rich history as a gold-trading area. Nearby attractions include the Chinamapere rock paintings, Vumba's mineral water springs and the Penha Longa Mountains (on the border with Zimbabwe).

## CLIMBING MOUNT NAMULI

Climbers intent on tackling Mozambique's second-highest peak – the 2,419m (7,934ft) Mount Namuli – kick off their journey at Gurúè, in lush surrounds and amidst tea plantations. The local Makua people regard the mountain as sacred, and hikers should respect local customs and traditions, which can include presenting the local chief with a gift of sorghum flour from which beer will be made along with offerings to the tribal ancestors.

### WE WISH YOU GOOD HEALTH!

Mozambique is the third-worst country in the world in terms of providing doctors for patients. For every 36,000 people in the country there is just one doctor! Malawi is by far the worst with almost 50,000 people queuing for each doctor. In terms of deaths per 1,000 members of the population, Mozambique ranks second in the world with 23 deaths per 1,000 people, behind Angola on 25.

| DOCTOR RATE | | DEATH RATE | |
|---|---|---|---|
| 1 | Malawi | 1 | Angola |
| 2 | Eritrea | 2 | Mozambique |
| 3 | Mozambique | 3 | Niger |
| 4 | Niger | 4 | Malawi |
| 5 | Ethiopia | 5 | Zimbabwe |
| 6 | Chad | 6 | Botswana |
| 7 | Burkina Faso | 7 | Zambia |
| 8 | Rwanda | 8 | Rwanda |
| 9 | Liberia | 9 | Swaziland |
| 10 | Ghana | 10 | Sierra Leone |

Top to bottom: Cahora Bassa dam wall; kapenta rigs on Cahora Bassa; woman drying and sorting kapenta.

# Mozambique Island

**ILHA DE MOZAMBIQUE IN A NUTSHELL**

Climate: Generally hot and humid, with cooler weather June to August.

Risk factor: Petty crime may be a problem in the south of the island. Vandalising historic sites in any way is punishable by law.

Health: Malaria is rife on the mainland and AIDS is a real threat. Waterborne diseases include hepatitis, typhoid, cholera and dysentery. Be sure to drink only bottled water.

Pack: Lightweight clothing should be sufficient, but be sure to pack good walking shoes. The Muslim community will frown on female travellers who expose any flesh. Sunscreen is recommended.

Facilities: Very, very basic to adequate.

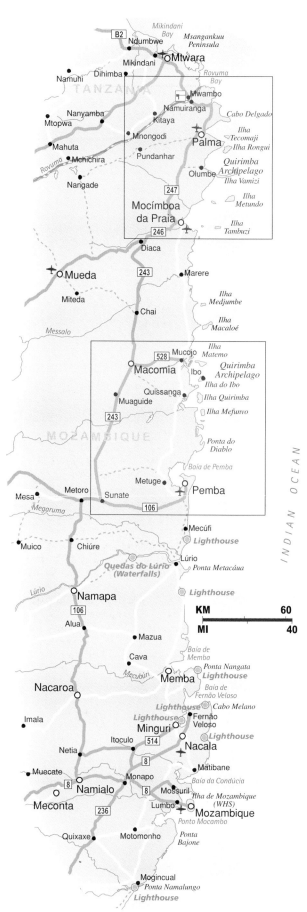

## 48

## MOZAMBIQUE ISLAND

Also known as Ilha de Mozambique (or simply Ilha!), Mozambique Island is a fascinating historical site that served the Portuguese and Arabs as a major fortified port city. It was declared a World Heritage Site in 1991 due to its rich seafaring history and architectural heritage. The island is just 2,500m (8,202ft) long and its widest point measures 600m (1,969ft), yet its size belies the rich and varied range of cultures, languages, religions and historical influences that occupies the island, all of which have earned it the label of Africa's 'meeting point of civilisations'.

## WALKING ILHA DE MOZAMBIQUE

Picture-postcard Ilha de Mozambique is linked via a bridge to the mainland 3km (2 miles) away, its coastline offering unsurpassed views across the Indian Ocean. Unfortunately, the waters here are severely polluted – a contrast to the diving spots further along the shore. Like much of Mozambique, the island that shares its name is impoverished, and conditions on parts of Ilha de Mozambique are no better than some of the worst on the mainland. Although most islanders in the southern reaches of the island live in small, tightly packed shelters in shack towns, the rest of the island – particularly the northern parts – comprises splendid colonial buildings, mosques, forts, palaces and churches. A reflection of its historic past, the streets and alleyways of the Old Town are edged by quaintly dilapidated structures that appear to have been standing here for millennia.

## WELL FORTIFIED

Although the urban heart is slowly losing its colonial atmosphere to the ambience of the traditional Muslim community that is reclaiming its stronghold on the island, there are still many remnants of yesteryear to be seen. The best preserved is the 16th-century Fort of São Sebastião, erected around a spring that remains the island's only reliable source of drinking water. Within its confines is the impressive Church of Nossa Señhora Baluarte, erected in 1522 and thus the southern Hemisphere's oldest European building still standing. Also notable in their exquisite detail and historical significance are the Palace and Chapel of São Paulo (which served as the governor's residence in the 18th century) and the Jesuit College of São Paulo, with its almost Gothic pulpit dating back to the days when Portuguese Catholics held the island.

## QUIRIMBA ARCHIPELAGO

Many of the islands on this vast archipelago have been settled for centuries, yet they remain somewhat removed from the mainstream tourist route, as access to the islands is not particularly easy and neither are facilities terribly impressive. Getting to and from the islands requires a bit of planning and help – boating in and out is heavily tide-dependent, and navigating the mangrove swamps that link many of the islands does require the help of someone with previous experience. Ibo is the most popular of the islands, but others worth visiting include Quirimba (a mission station and later a large coconut plantation), Matemo and Quisiva islands (both housing large Portuguese plantation houses), while Ilha das Rolas (aka Rolas Island) is a tiny speck in the ocean which serves as a useful seasonal settlement for local fishermen.

## ILHA DO IBO

Heavily fortified during its Portuguese occupation, Ibo has a history as the region's most important supplier of slaves to the sugar plantations of Île de France. The island has seen better days, but its wide streets are lined with quaint Mediterranean-style buildings. Many of these stately structures were erected in the 1800s and, although the whitewashed walls of the once grand but long abandoned Portuguese villas and palaces are fading, it is the very isolation that is the island's charm. The centuries-old churches and ancient bulwarks that fringe the streets and line the waterfront are but half the attraction — the other is the surrounding ocean, alive with turtles and dolphins that can easily be spotted from the dhows that ferry visitors around Ibo's romantic coastline.

Top to bottom: ghost crab; snorkelling at Santa Carolina Island; women fishing on the Quirimba Archipelago; coconut plantation.

# Zambia

## ADVENTURING THROUGH ZAMBIA (See Contact Details 92-95)

### ON LAND

**HIKING**
Batoka Gorge
Lower Luangwa River

Taita Falcon Lodge
Changa Changa
  Adventures

**ABSEILING**
Batoka Gorge

Abseil Zambia

**HORSERIDING**
Livingstone

Lusaka

Chundukwa
  Adventure Trails
Chaminuka Private
  Game Reserve

**PHOTOGRAPHIC / BIRDING SAFARIS**
South Luangwa

Robin Pope Safaris
Gwembe Safaris

**ELEPHANTBACK SAFARIS**
Countrywide

Safari Par Excellence

**GAME VIEWING / WALKING SAFARIS**
South Luangwa/Kafue

North Luangwa
Lower Zambezi
Lusaka

Livingstone

The Bushcamp
  Company Ltd
Chundukwa
  Adventure Trails
Shiwa Safaris
Chiawa Camp
Chaminuka Private
  Game Reserve
Wilderness Safaris

**10 GREAT ADVENTURES**
1. Walking safaris
2. Whitewater rafting
3. Jetboating
4. Fishing
5. Game viewing
6. Houseboating
7. Hiking
8. Gorge swing
9. Canoeing
10. Microlighting

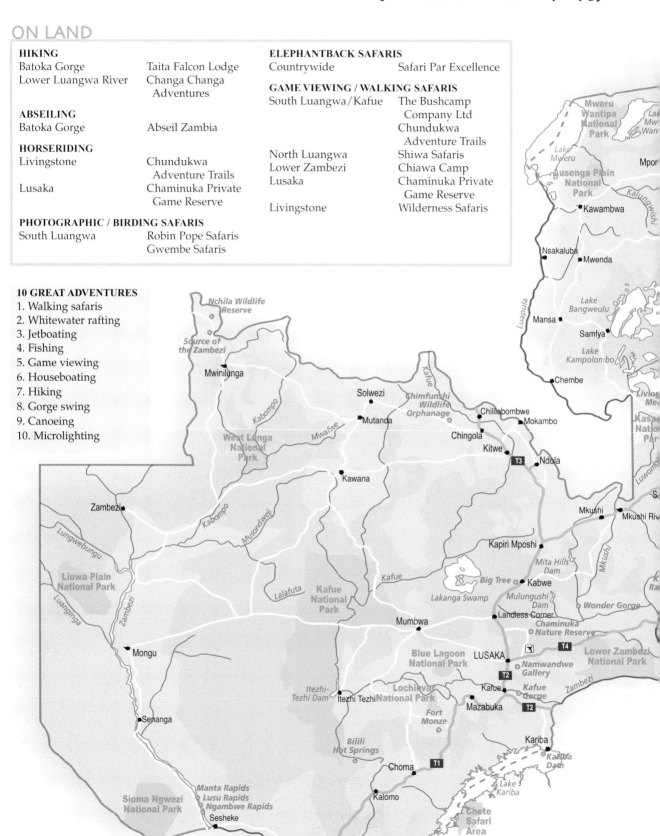

## 50

## ON WHEELS

**QUADBIKING**
Batoka Gorge          The Livingstone Quad Company

**MOUNTAINBIKE SAFARIS**
Countrywide          Boundless Adventures

## IN THE AIR

**MICROLIGHTING, HELICOPTER FLIPS & FLIGHT OF ANGELS**
Livingstone/Vic Falls          Batoka Sky
                               Safari Par Excellence
                               Shearwater Adventures

**BUNGEE JUMPING**
Victoria Falls Bridge          Shearwater Adventures

**FLYING FOX / GORGE SWING**
Batoka Gorge          The Zambezi Swing

**FLY-IN SAFARIS**
Countrywide          Ulendo Safaris

## ON (OR IN) WATER

**WHITEWATER RAFTING**
Batoka Gorge, Zambezi River          Bundu
                                     Safari Par Excellence

**JETBOATING**
Zambezi River, Livingstone          Jet Extreme
                                    Shearwater Adventures
                                    Safari Par Excellence

**RIVER BOARDING, WHITEWATER KAYAKING (AND TANDEM KAYAKING)**
Batoka Gorge, Zambezi River          Bundu Adventures
                                     Safari Par Excellence

**HOUSEBOATING**
Kariba          The Houseboat Company

**CANOE SAFARIS**
Livingstone/Vic Falls          Safari Par Excellence
                               Bundu Adventures
                               Chundukwa Adventure Trails
Lower Zambezi/Mana Pools          Mvuu Lodge
                                  Karibu Safaris
                                  Cansaf Adventures and Canoeing Safaris
                                  Chiawa Camp
Lower Luangwa River          Changa Changa Adventures

**RIVER CRUISES**
Zambezi River, Livingstone          Wild Horizons
                                    The African Queen
                                    Victoria Falls River Safaris
Kariba River          Gwembe Safaris

**FISHING**
Lower Zambezi          Mvuu Lodge
                       Chiawa Camp
                       Zambezi Royal Chundu Fishing and
                         Safari Lodge
Upper Zambezi          Tiger Camp
Lake Tanganyika          Nkamba Bay Lodge
Kariba          Gwembe Safaris

**SCUBA DIVING**
Lake Tanganyika          Tanganyika Lodge

**ZAMBIA**
**Capital:** Lusaka
**Area:** 752,610km² / 290,584mi²
**Population:** 10 million
**Main ethnic groups:**
• Bemba (36%)
• Maravi (18%)
• Tonga (15%)
**Main languages:**
• Bemba • Tonga • Nyanja • Lozi
• Lunda • English
**Main religions:**
• Christian (63%)
• Traditional beliefs (37%)
**Currency:** Zambian Kwacha (100 ngwee)

# The Zambezi Source to Cahora Bassa

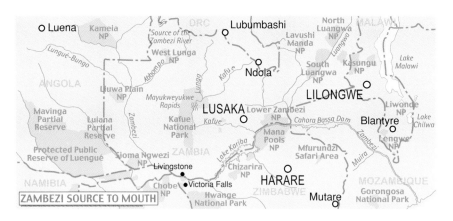

ZAMBEZI SOURCE TO MOUTH

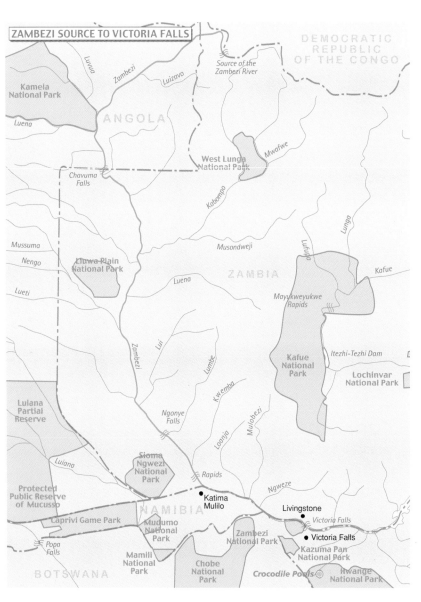

ZAMBEZI SOURCE TO VICTORIA FALLS

## LUSAKA

Having originated as little more than a single general store serving workers building a railway siding in the early 1900s, the modern city – succeeding Livingstone as the nation's capital in 1930 – has mushroomed into a hub of activity conveniently situated at one of the most important crossroads in southern Africa. Lusaka is every inch a modern urban settlement with all the charm and scourges that entails: open-air markets, tree-lined boulevards and dusty side streets lurking with muggers and less innocuous criminals. In reality, apart from a network of travel-oriented facilities such as the airport, bus terminals and tourist offices, there is little to attract the casual sightseer. Lusaka's citizens are nevertheless widely acknowledged as the friendliest and most hospitable on the continent.

## ON THE WATERS OF THE ZAMBEZI

The majesty of the Zambezi River is surpassed only by the thrill of its waters, and it's the favourite playground of watersport adventurers in southern Africa. While the river can be gentle and tranquil in parts, it can also be venomously fearsome in others and, as a result, offers something for everyone. As it is the focal point of river adventure in both Zambia and Zimbabwe, tour operators abound. The gentler option is canoeing or kayaking the way local inhabitants have done for centuries. The level of skill required is basic and, as long as you don't have a fear of water, this can be enjoyed by all. Canoeing and kayaking the gentler waters above the famed Victoria Falls is the most popular choice, and several adventure companies are based here. Excursions last from a few hours on the water to four days or even more than a week, covering about 20km (12 miles) a day. A number of Zimbabwe-based trips launch from the Kariba vicinity, and may take you as far as Chirundu, with a further three days to Mana Pools and another three days to Kenyamba. A more daring option would be to tackle the whirlpools at Mupata Gorge, but these demand considerably more skill to negotiate and can be very hazardous for the inexperienced.

| AFRICA'S LONGEST RIVERS | | |
| --- | --- | --- |
| Nile River | 6,695km | 4,160 miles |
| Congo River | 4,667km | 2,900 miles |
| Niger River | 4,030km | 2,505 miles |
| Zambezi River | 2,350km | 1,650 miles |
| Shabeelle River | 2,490km | 1,550 miles |
| Orange River | 1,860km | 1,155 miles |

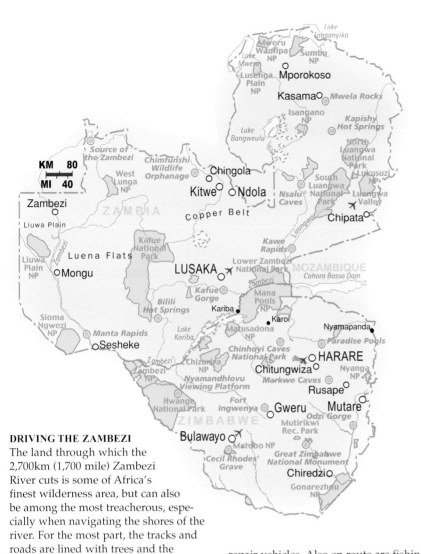

## 51

## DRIVING THE ZAMBEZI

The land through which the 2,700km (1,700 mile) Zambezi River cuts is some of Africa's finest wilderness area, but can also be among the most treacherous, especially when navigating the shores of the river. For the most part, the tracks and roads are lined with trees and the escarpment on both the Zimbabwean and Zambian sides can be steep and dangerous. Some roads and paths have been forged along the river, but certain sections have fallen prey to erosion and, occasionally, flooding. All 4x4 drivers should take precautions and ensure they have vehicle spares. During the arid season, flood plains are dry, grass cover minimal, and a fine dust covers much of the land. Although lush after the rains, the rushing waters can be hazardous, and the wildlife present their own risks, while armed poachers may follow in their tracks. The route of the Zambezi is not an easy drive, but areas such as the Mana plains may be less challenging. Mana is renowned for its hiking and foot safaris under the protection of armed guards. The region is well developed, so facilities are good with regular opportunities to refuel, restock and repair vehicles. Also en route are fishing camps and other tourist activities. While the section below Kariba is one of the least tamed, much of the hospitality industry centres on Mana Pools NP. The terrain varies from the rocky Zambezi escarpment to plains, and although it may be explored on foot, it is closed to the public from May to October. An alternative route is the Zambian wilderness between Mongu and Mwinilunga. Known as the Source of the Zambezi, the *veld* varies from a relatively comfortable drive over level ground to some extremely demanding stretches that require considerable driving skill.

Top to bottom: the Victoria Falls Bridge over the Zambezi River connects Zambia and Zimbabwe; Kuomboka ceremony; Zambezi riverboarding; sunset over Cahora Bassa.

| AFRICA'S GREAT RIVER SOURCES | | | | |
|---|---|---|---|---|
| RIVER | FROM | TO | DISTANCE | |
| Nile | Lake Victoria | Mediterranean Sea | 6,690km | 4,180 miles |
| Congo | Lualab & Luapula rivers | Atlantic Ocean | 4,371km | 2,716 miles |
| Niger | Guinea | Gulf of Guinea | 4,184km | 2,600 miles |
| Zambezi | Zambia | Mozambique Channel | 2,736km | 1,700 miles |
| Orange | Lesotho | Atlantic Ocean | 2,092km | 1,300 miles |

# Luangwa National Park

**THE LUANGWA VALLEY**

The Luangwa Valley follows the course of the Luangwa River: one side is wild, unpredictable and remote, the other a picturesque expanse of nature reserve where wild animals abound. The northern reaches of the valley, occupied mostly by the Bemba people, are dominated by the untamed wilderness of North Luangwa National Park: difficult to access, nature reigns supreme in the park. Predators and scavengers lurk in murky waters and scour the plains. It is

from the fauna-rich miombo woodlands of the Zambian plateau that the escarpment dips 1,000m (330ft) to the floor of the Luangwa Valley. Hippo and crocodile still inhabit the Luangwa River, but along the 200km (124 miles) that separate North Luangwa from its southern counterpart there is a noticeable change. South Luangwa National Park is one of Africa's best reserves and is far more developed than the north. Although no 'walk in the park', it is much more accessible, dry river beds and hard-baked

soils opening into woodland and grassy plains populated with lion, leopard, elephant, buffalo, zebra and Thornicroft's giraffe. The Save the Rhino Trust continues to combat the poaching of elephant and rhino in the area.

**WALKING SOUTH LUANGWA**

More easily reached than its northern neighbour, South Luangwa National Park is most popular among fly-in visitors, but may also be accessed by road, from Malawi via Chipata or from

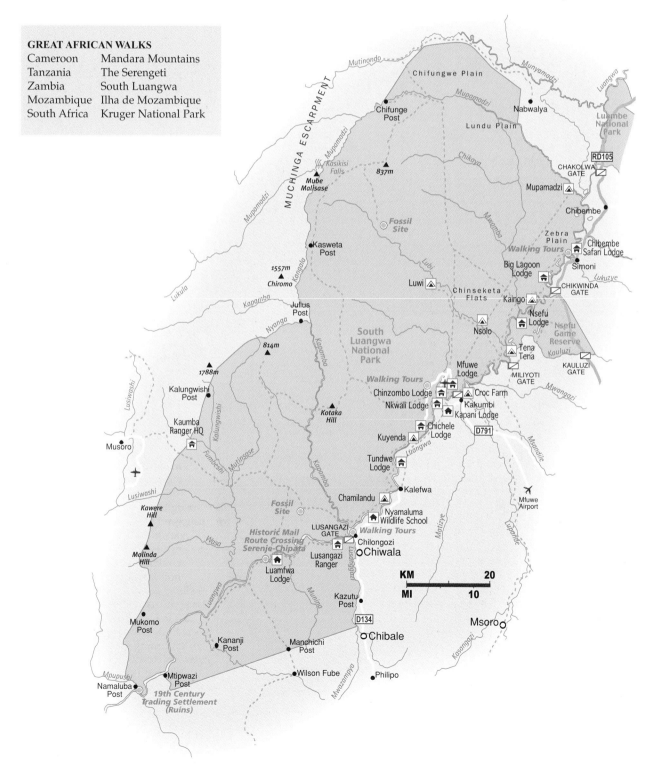

## 52

Lusaka along the Great East Road. The latter is worthy of its name, but certain areas remain tricky to navigate and, despite the repair work, are riddled with potholes. For hikers on walking safaris, this poses few problems, but the undulating roads offer some suggestion as to what the wilderness may offer. The ground varies from soft sand to hard-baked stretches that can take their toll on the legs on five-day guided walks or even shorter excursions. Hikers and self-drivers will have to cross stretches of scrubby veld and dry river beds and, because there are no accessible bridges, this takes some stamina (and, for drivers, considerable skill behind the wheel). Generally, guides stick to open areas, where it is easier to spot predators and where escape routes are open. Both the vegetation and the wildlife vary enormously, and South Luangwa is rightfully renowned for its lion, leopard, elephant, buffalo, zebra, puku, crocodile and hippo. The park has seen some development and is no longer as pristine as before. Increasing visitors are focused on experiencing the birdlife, including herons, storks, goliath heron, egrets, marabou, jacana and ibis. There are a number of simple lodges and camp sites, but most safari-goers head for the lodges on the Luangwa River's eastern banks on the park's outskirts. Most have isolated fly camps within the park, which have been set up to cater for guests on walking safaris.

## SHIWA NGANDU

Virtually hidden in the miombo woodland, this 9,350 hectare (23,000 acre) grand private estate near Mpika is astonishing. In 1914 Stuart Gore-Brown, ex-soldier, mentor and explorer, laid claim to 4,900ha (12,000 acres), later adding 4,450ha to the property. He went on to play a pivotal role in the story of Zambia and remains the only European

### SOUTH LUANGWA IN A NUTSHELL
Climate: September to November can be unbearably hot in the valley, but June to November are dry and thus provide the best game viewing.
Risk factor: Distances are vast and may be challenging in parts, with the usual risks posed by wilderness safaris, so it is best to take a pre-arranged tour with guides.
Health: Malaria is rife all year round, as are waterborne diseases.
Pack: Anti-malarial medication, water purification tablets, protective clothing and good hiking shoes.
Facilities: Facilities are good (even impressive) in the lodges, but some hiking stopovers can be quite basic.

settler to have been honoured with a state funeral and to be buried according to the ritual reserved for a tribal chief. The grand old Shiwa House is in a sad state of disrepair, but the surrounding wilderness is quite beautiful.

## BAROTSELAND

Fiercely independent and devout followers of tradition, the people of Barotseland remain one of the most authentic indigenous groups in Zambia. Barotseland once extended far and wide, but now centres on the Zambezi's flood plains. The most engrossing feature of the region is the rituals of its people, epitomised in the Kuomboka, a lavish parade that sees the Lozi king take to the waters in an ornate barge in his ceremonial evacuation of the flood plain in favour of higher ground. The ritual is repeated every year as a highlight of the ceremonial calendar.

Top to bottom: Burchell's zebra; a herd of buffalo in the southern region; sunset over the Luangwa River.

# Kafue National Park

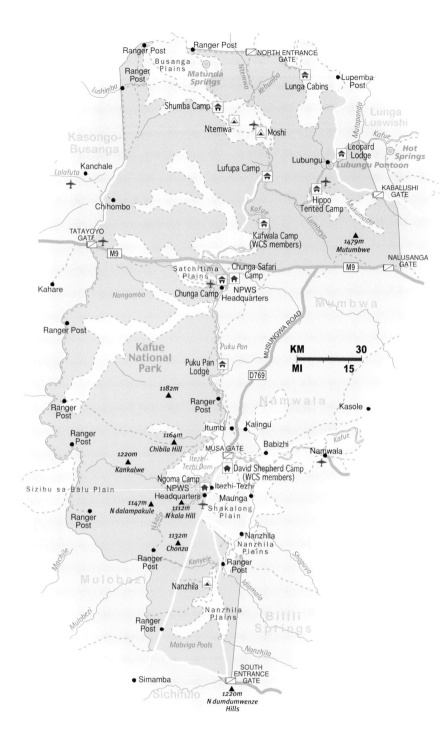

Map labels:
Ranger Post · Ranger Post · NORTH ENTRANCE GATE · Busanga Plains · Matunda Springs · Ntemwa · Kebumbo · Lunga Cabins · Lupemba Post · Lunga Luswishi · Shumba Camp · Kasongo-Busanga · Ntemwa · Moshi · Mattaponda · Kafue · Hot Springs · Lalafuta · Kanchale · Lufupa Camp · Lubungu · Leopard Lodge · Lubungu Pontoon · Chihombo · Kafue · Hippo Tented Camp · Mukumashi · KABALUSHI GATE · TATAYOYO GATE · Kafwala Camp (WCS members) · M9 · 1479m Mutumbwe · NALUSANGA GATE · Satchitima Plains · Chunga Safari Camp · M9 · Kahare · Nangamba · Chunga Camp · NPWS Headquarters · Mumbwa · Ranger Post · Kafue National Park · Puku Pan · Puku Pan Lodge · D769 · Namwala · 1182m · Ranger Post · Kasole · Ranger Post · Itumbi · Kalingu · Kafue · Ranger Post · 1164m Chibila Hill · MUSA GATE · Babizhi · Namwala · 1220m Kankalwe · Itezhi-Tezhi Dam · David Shepherd Camp (WCS members) · Sizibu sa Balu Plain · Ngoma Camp · NPWS Headquarters · Itezhi-Tezhi · Maunga · 1147m Ndalampakule · 1112m Nkala Hill · Shakalong Plain · Ranger Post · 1132m Chonza · Nanzhila · Nanzhila Plains · Machile · Ranger Post · Kanyele · Ranger Post · Shapuya · Mulobezi · Nanzhila · Idiomolo · Bilili Springs · Mulobezi · Ranger Post · Nanzhila Plains · Mabvigo Pools · Nanzhila · Simamba · SOUTH ENTRANCE GATE · Sichifulo · 1220m Ndumdumwenze Hills

KM 30
MI 15

## AMAZING NATIONAL PARKS

With kilometre after endless kilometre of wide-open plain, vast stands of indigenous woodland and lush riverine vegetation – most of which remains mercifully unblemished and packed with enormous herds of game and an abundance of predators – it is no surprise that Zambia enjoys much acclaim as one of Africa's finest wildlife destinations. Not only are its national parks and game management areas set in what may well be some of Africa's most authentic wilderness areas, but the backdrop of Zambia's landscape is arguably the most breathtaking in the subcontinent. Zambia covers an impressive 750,000km$^2$ (290,000 sq. miles) and has about 20 national parks, more than 30 game management areas and countless numbers of small private and state-run reserves. Perhaps because most are separated from each other by vast distances and, in some cases, are virtually inaccessible or difficult to get to, they represent some of southern Africa's most pristine wilderness areas.

## KAFUE NATIONAL PARK

Zambia's top parks include some of Africa's finest, such as South Luangwa and Kafue (the most accessible of the parks) and Lower Zambezi and Victoria Falls. These most popular parks have seen considerable development in the way of roads and other infrastructure, with the establishment of a number of camp sites and exclusive private lodges, most of which are affiliated to safari operators. The superb wilderness areas harbour massive herds of game, including Africa's most recognized wildlife species such as lion, leopard, buffalo and elephant. Throughout the history of Zambia, wildlife resources were traditionally controlled by tribal laws and custom; however, with the settlement of Europeans and the increase in poaching, game reserves were set aside to control hunting, poaching and the growth of population numbers. Kafue itself lies around 200km

## LARGEST PARKS OF THE WORLD

| | |
|---|---|
| Fiordland | New Zealand |
| Kafue | Zambia |
| Kruger | South Africa |
| Bidwell | USA |
| Namib-Naukluft | Namibia |
| Canaima | Venezuela |
| Tsavo | Kenya |
| Etosha | Namibia |

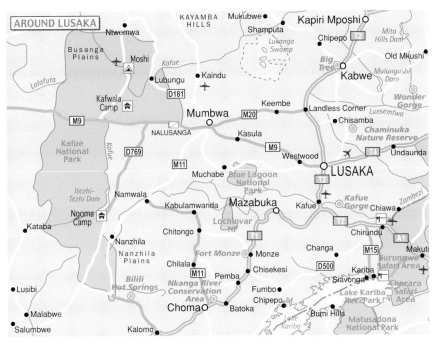

## 53

AROUND LUSAKA

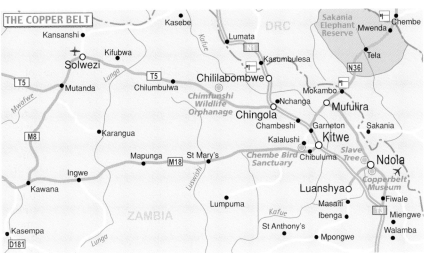

THE COPPER BELT

(124 miles) west of Lusaka and is one of the world's largest parks, clocking in at an astounding 22,000km² (12,400 sq. miles). Wildlife is prolific and Kafue offers fantastic walks and drives to see the wide-ranging flora and fauna. Kafue is richly laced with rivers and lakes, but be careful as they are the home of large groups of hippo and crocodile. The wetlands are a happy hopping ground to numerous small buck as well as being a habitat enjoyed by more than 400 species of bird.

**THE COPPER BELT**
Steeped in a long and erratic history of colonial occupation, Zambia and Zimbabwe were once known as Northern and Southern Rhodesia respectively. Ethnically diverse and culturally extremely rich, both Zambia

and Zimbabwe rely to a large degree on the land that has since been reclaimed from colonial powers. Zambia's greatest asset is its copper reserves and even though these are gradually declining, copper exports still account for in the region of 80 per cent of the nation's foreign income. Zimbabwe, on the other hand, has historically relied almost entirely on the harvest of its cash crops, most notably tobacco, which once created one of the most broadly based economies of the region.

Opposite page: tourist boat on the Lunga river. Top to bottom: Lunga River Lodge; greater kudu in Kafue National Park; the sleek African darter.

## ADVENTURING THROUGH MALAWI (See Contact Details 92-95)

### ON LAND

**HIKING**

| | |
|---|---|
| Countrywide | Land & Lake Safaris |
| Mulanje Mountains | Mulanje Mountain Conservation Trust |
| Nyika Plateau | Nyika Safaris |
| Liwonde National Park | Central African Wilderness Safaris |
| Lengwe National Park | Jambo Africa Tours |
| Nyala Park | Jambo Africa Tours |
| Zomba Plateau | Jambo Africa Tours |

**CLIMBING**

| | |
|---|---|
| Mulanje Mountains | Mulanje Mountain Conservation Trust |

**GAME VIEWING**

| | |
|---|---|
| Lengwe National Park | Jambo Africa Tours |
| Nyala Park | Jambo Africa Tours |
| Zomba Plateau | Jambo Africa Tours |
| Shire River | Central African Wilderness Safaris |
| Liwonde National Park | Central African Wilderness Safaris |
| River Safaris | Land & Lake Safaris |
| Nyika Plateau | Nyika Safaris |
| Vwaza Marsh | Nyika Safaris |

**HORSERIDING**

| | |
|---|---|
| Nyika Safaris | Barefoot Safaris |

### IN THE AIR

**FLY-IN SAFARIS**

| | |
|---|---|
| Countrywide | Ulendo Safaris |

### ON WHEELS

**MOUNTAINBIKING**

| | |
|---|---|
| Countrywide | Boundless Adventures |
| | Land & Lake Safari |

### ON (OR IN) WATER

**SCUBA DIVING / SNORKELLING**

| | |
|---|---|
| Lake Malawi | Scuba Shack |
| Club Makokola | Kayak Africa |
| Kaya Mawa | Kayak Africa |

**KAYAKING**

| | |
|---|---|
| Lake Malawi | Kayak Africa |

**SAILING**

| | |
|---|---|
| Lake Malawi | Danforth Yachting |
| | Barefoot Safaris |
| | Lake Malawi |
| | Marathon |

**FISHING**

| | |
|---|---|
| Lake Malawi | Danforth Yachting |
| | Land & Lake Safaris |

**RIVERBOAT SAFARIS**

Shire River
Liwonde National Park
Central African Wilderness Safari

**MALAWI**
**Capital:** Lilongwe
**Area:** 118,480km$^2$ / 45,745mi$^2$
**Population:** 10.9 million
**Main ethnic groups:**
• Maravi (55%)
• Lomwe (17%)
• Yao (13%)
• Ngoni (7%)
**Main languages:**
• English
• Chewa
**Main religions:**
• Protestant (34%)
• Catholic (32%)
• Traditional beliefs (18%)
**Currency:** Malawian Kwacha (100 tambala)

## 54

Chitipa
Kaporo
Karonga
Chisenga
Uledi
M1
*Nyika NP*
○*Nyika Plateau*
Mkondowe
Katumbi
*Vwaza Marsh Wildlife Reserve*
Rumphi
*Kasitu*
Mzuzu
Euthini
Nkhata Bay
Chintheche
*Chizumulu Island*
Mzimba
○*Historic Mission*
*Likoma Island*
*Rupashe*
Jenda
Dwangwa
M1
*Dwangwa*
*Nkhota-Kota Wildlife Reserve*
*Kasungu NP*
Kasangu
Nkhotakota
*Bua*
*Rusa*
Ntchisi
*Lake Malawi*
Mponela
Senga
Makanjila
Mchinji
*Lake Malawi NP (WHS)*
M12
✈ LILONGWE
Monkey Bay
*Lilongwe*
M1
Dedza
Chiponde
Mangochi
○*Fort Mangochi*
*Lake Malombe*
*Lake Chiuta*
*Livulezi*
Ntcheu
*Liwonde NP*
Nayuchi
Liwonde
*Lake Chilwa*
M1
Zomba
M3
Nambazo
M6
*Tedzani Falls*
Mwanza
*Shire*
*Majete Wildlife Reserve*
✈ Blantyre
*Kapichira Falls*
Mulanje
M2
*Lengwe NP*
*Mwabvi Wildlife Reserve*
Bangula
Nsanje

**9 GREAT ADVENTURES**
1. Scuba diving or snorkelling
2. Sailing
3. Kayaking
4. Climbing
5. Horseriding
6. Game viewing
7. Mountainbiking
8. Fishing
9. Hiking

# Lake Malawi – North

## LAKE MALAWI

Lake Malawi – which borders Malawi, Mozambique and Tanzania – is one of the subcontinent's most valuable assets, yet it remains one of its most threatened, and its precious resources are at constant risk from human intervention. The 23,000km² (8,900 sq. mile) Lake Malawi is the third-largest inland body of water on the continent and covers nearly half the country's territory. The 585km (364 miles) of its length along the southern Rift Valley comprise a diversity of habitats for an array of wildlife. As a result, the waters of the lake – encircled by mountain slopes – have formed the mainstay of the nation's economy and the nucleus of Malawi's tourism industry.

## THE COUNTRY

Malawi is a desperately poor nation, with the bulk of its rural people engaged in farming, and the majority of citizens living on the shores of Lake Malawi (aka Lago Niassa in Mozambique and Lake Nyasa in Tanzania), depending on its waters for subsistence and livelihood. Malawi is covered by large stretches of endless savannah and has proven remarkable in its resilience. Malawi, the landlocked 'Warm Heart of Africa' is a traveller's dream: wild animals crossing an unspoiled wilderness easily accessible to visitors, and all very, very cheap. The country's diverse cultural heritage is an eclectic mix of fascinating customs and traditions still practised with enthusiasm by the vast majority of the country's population.

## THE LIFE OF THE LAKE

Blessed with tranquil beaches, the most important human settlement along the shore is the fishing community at Chember, who depend on Lake Malawi for their livelihood. Numerous dugout vessels ply the lake surface, netting fish which form the staple diet of Malawi. The lake has one of the world's richest populations of freshwater fish and many of the species found here are endemic. Casual angling is forbidden in areas, including Cape Maclear National Park and the surrounding islands, although water-based leisure activities are encouraged. Conservation remains a precarious occupation, even when tackled with the best of intentions and, sadly, Lake Malawi seems to be one such failure. The great lake, with about 350 endemic cichlid species and some 650 others, is home to a precious freshwater fish population faced with almost certain extinction if the situation on its shores is allowed to persist. The destruction of the ecosystem has been environmentally catastrophic, and the dire need for both education and environmental control is raising alarming concerns for the lake's future.

## 55

# NYIKA NATIONAL PARK

Almost hidden in the northwestern reaches of the country, Nyika is Malawi's greatest national park, certainly in terms of size. The wild, high-lying terrain comprises hill and valley virtually enclosed by the inclines of the surrounding escarpment. Nyika's varied vegetation has given rise to an equally varied array of animal and plant species, from endemic orchids and chameleons to the highest number of leopards in southeast Africa. The park is home to zebra, reedbuck, roan antelope, eland, klipspringer, duiker, jackal and hyena, as well as 250 bird species.

# THE NYIKA PLATEAU

At an altitude of about 2,000m (6,560ft) above sea level, the face of Nyika Plateau (part of Nyika National Park) is unlike anything you may see elsewhere in Malawi. Its flat, horizonless plains, waving with high savanna grasses interrupted only in the distance by the occasional forest grove and a lone hill, dip down into rugged gorges. A series of jagged mountain peaks neatly encircles the grassy plateau and lends the wilderness a quiet, even melancholy feel. Road access to Nyika is somewhat lacking, providing a rather uncomfortable journey to the national park along the more established route which, although short in distance, can take longer than five hours. Many roads – particularly those in, around and to the park – are impassable during the wet season, yet road travel is your only choice, and no visitors (no matter how brave the attempt) are allowed to enter the park on foot.

# NYIKA'S WILDLIFE

Although wildlife populations are well represented at Nyika, hikers following the numerous walks and trails that cross the plateau tend to lose out on sightings of zebra, roan antelope, reedbuck, waterbuck, eland, and kudu. The high, golden grasses provide ample camouflage for

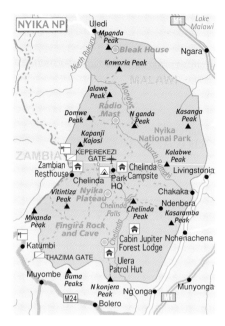

these animals and, in addition, provide shelter to about 450 bird species, among them wattled cranes and francolins. As a result, horseback safaris have proven to be the best way to spot the various game species scattered across Nyika National Park. Quite at home here are herds of elephant, buffalo, kudu and plenty of roan antelope, plus the occasional lion and leopard.

# RIDING NYIKA

Exploring Nyika on horseback is the most rewarding vantage point from which to experience the wide, open veld of Nyika and view the carpets of wild flowers that blanket its spring landscape. Atop a steed, high above the tall grasses, the wilderness and its creatures are far more accessible to the eye and camera lens. Private operators (such as those at Chelinda) keep their own stables and offer various routes and trails that include excursions to a number of different sites, among them Lake Kaulime, the plateau's only natural lake. Nyika's horseback trails can take a few hours, a few days, or even a few weeks to enjoy, provided your pocket and levels of endurance are up to the physical and financial limits. Most operators insist that you take a mounted guide: these scouts are friendly, knowledgeable, willing to assist with all requests and are invariably an enormous help.

## NYIKA IN A NUTSHELL

Climate: Moderately warm to hot, temperatures range from 20°C (68°F) to 27°C (80°F) throughout the year.
Risk factor: Risks are few, but most horseback safari operators will insist clients have some skill on horseback.
Health: Malaria is a real threat and water sources may contain bilharzia.
Pack: Drink only bottled water, and keep a supply of purification tablets.
Facilities: Horseback safaris means that you will be roughing it!

Top to bottom: Kaya Mawa beach (Likoma Island); camping on Kande beach; a local fishing boat.

# Lake Malawi – Central

## KAYAKING ON LAKE MALAWI

The shores of Lake Malawi have one of the worst records of malaria infection in the African interior, and bilharzia is a constant threat, yet the lake's waters remain the region's favoured leisure destination. The hospitality industry has found a well-established home here: an ever growing number of hotels, lodges and camp sites offer anything from windsurfing and kayaking to sailing, snorkelling and diving. The best way to experience the lake's varied habitat is by kayak, exploring the fish-filled waters and shoreline caves and stopping to snorkel among the luminous creatures. Most of the lake's islands offer guided kayaking expeditions, and the sport is fast gaining popularity among adventurers. Private operators have, in recent years, been permitted to lead kayaking trips between the islands in the concession areas, and basic camps have been established on some of the stopovers. There is little to beat the gentle sway of a hammock and the warm showers provided by water buckets well placed among the lower branches of trees. The camp sites at Domwe and Mumbo offer a welcome base for energetic kayakers returning from their demanding lake activities, hopping from island to island, rock to rock, and flitting from one pool or cove to the next, especially when the sun is high and the water bottle is low. Stopovers on the islands may be occupied by rock climbing, beachcombing, bird-watching, and even swimming. Be warned: there is the possibility of a chance encounter with a crocodile!

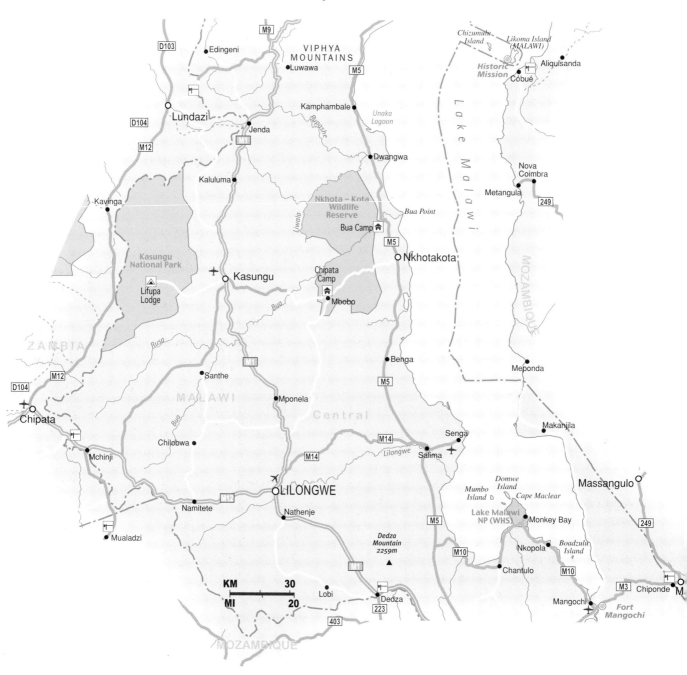

## 56

## LIKOMA ISLAND

Although Likoma lies just off Mozambique, the island remains the property of Malawi, its coastline (dotted with lone baobabs alongside crystal waters) taking on the flavour of the motherland. The sandy 17km² (6.5 sq. mile) island, with its mango trees and rugged mountain peaks, is otherwise flat and unprepossessing, but its languid beaches are lapped by clear waters. Lying in splendid isolation off the mountain-backed beach of Mozambique's mainland, Likoma can be difficult to reach and the only proper (albeit rather unreliable) way to reach it is via the *MV Ilala II*, the dilapidated but enchanting old lake steamer that ferries passengers between Likoma and Mozambique once a week. The island is tranquil and laidback and, apart from the weekly performance of the *malipenga* dancers pandering almost exclusively to a tourist audience, there are few notable landmarks.

The most significant is the cavernous St Peter's Cathedral, built along the lines of Winchester Cathedral by Anglican missionaries in the early 1900s.

St Peter's remains the focal point of the island today, with many of the locals working virtually all year every year on maintaining the colossal remnant of Likoma's colonial past.

## LILONGWE

Although Malawi's vast natural heritage is the country's enduring drawcard, the appeal of its large centres (in particular its capital at Lilongwe) should not be underestimated. Blantyre stretches for about 20km (12 miles) into Limbe, and is the social and commercial heart of Malawi. Lilongwe, on the other hand, is gentle, laid-back and utterly predictable in character. Although only of limited interest to the casual visitor, the sprawling city is home to about half-a-million Malawians and offers a refreshing mix of old and new, with little clutter, noise or commotion. The older sectors of Lilongwe have retained much of their original charm, while the modern parts are a surprisingly sedate collection of malls, tourist traps and official buildings merging well with the islands of green that form the residential districts. A notable example is Capital City, initiated by President Banda with the financial assistance of the South African government during the height of the latter's apartheid regime. Not only is the climate of the city moderately warm, but Lilongwe is very accessible, very cheap and, in the heart of southern Africa, a convenient base from which to explore the subcontinent.

### LAKE MALAWI IN A NUTSHELL
Health: Malaria is a very real threat, as is pollution and diseases such as bilharzia. Swimming and snorkelling can pose a health risk! Drink bottled water, and carry purification tablets.

Top to bottom: local children at Senga Bay; lodge overlooking the Shire River; canoeing near Mumbo.

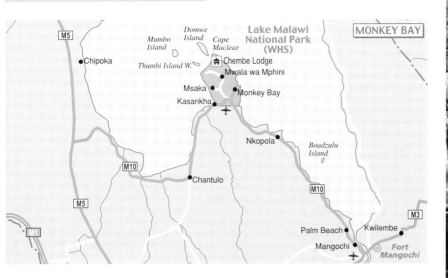

# Lake Malawi – South

## SHIRE RIVER

The 596km (370-mile) Shire, flowing from Lake Malawi through Malawi and Mozambique to the Zambezi, is the country's longest river. It winds through Malawi's Liwonde National Park, crossing some of the country's most abundant wildlife territories and its wild open spaces. The waters are the hunting and grazing habitat of crocodile and hippo, while the surrounding wilderness has a small but healthy population of elephant and even two black rhinos, introduced into the area in recent years. The shallows, wooded shores and expansive sky are home to waders, waterfowl and migrant birds during the summer months. Although much of the Shire offers boat rides for visitors, the southern valley remains largely undiscovered, top attractions being the wild expanses of Majete Wildlife Reserve and Lengwe National Park.

## CONSERVATION IN MALAWI

Traditionally, Malawi placed much importance in protecting its wildlife heritage, and an impressive expanse of its land cover is designated as protected land. The reserves and parks cover about 20 per cent of the country, and yet Malawi's national parks have never really featured among its top attractions. Many of the country's wildlife areas are not particularly well developed, and a near disastrous combination of limited resources and a lack of commitment from officials had meant that these parks failed to realise their potential. Until recently poaching was a major concern as many wild species were hunted, poached or raided from traditional lands. Funds from donor countries have helped reintroduce species to traditional roaming grounds, as well as establishing a better overall conservation climate and infrastructure.

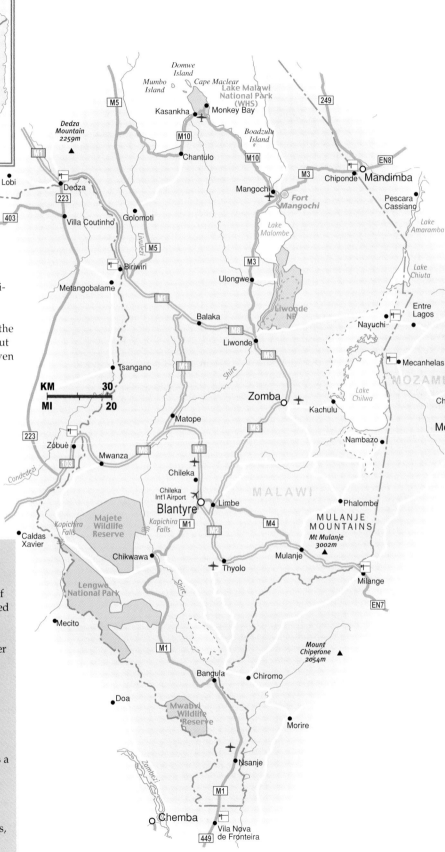

## 57

## LIWONDE NATIONAL PARK

The smallest, most accessible and most rewarding of Malawi's parks, Liwonde National Park is also the best managed. Drastic improvements in the training of rangers and other staff have meant the park is better patrolled than ever. Once plagued by poaching and suffering rapidly declining wildlife populations, the ranging staff today encounters fewer and fewer traps, and the threat of poaching has been curtailed, although perhaps inevitably some subsistence poaching continues. There has been a discernible increase in mammal numbers, and elephant herds have more than quadrupled in under 30 years. Today the 548km² (212 sq. mile) stretch of land is home to more than 600 elephant, 500 sable antelope and nearly 3,000 hippo.

## LIWONDE'S OTHER FAUNA

Liwonde boasts healthy herds of bushbuck, impala and waterbuck, along with troops of vervet monkeys and yellow baboons. There are leopards and there have been good sightings of the elusive spotted hyena, yet the numbers of predators seem to be declining; the lions that were once common prowlers on these plains have been eradicated. However, following the success of reintroduction programmes focusing on zebra, eland, reedbuck, buffalo and even black rhino, attempts will be made to reintroduce lion once officials are satisfied that they can be contained within park borders.

Top to bottom: colourful fabrics at Blantyre market; St Michael and All Angels' church, built between 1888 and 1891; local girl from the Ngoni tribe carrying a basket on her head.

## MOUNT MULANJE IN A NUTSHELL

Climate: Climbing is best in the dry months April–November. Summer rains render many roads impassable without 4x4 vehicles.
Risk factor: The only real dangers will be faced by foolhardy hikers.
Health: Malaria is a real threat; many water sources may be contaminated.
Pack: Water purification tablets, malarial prophylactics and a mosquito net. Drink only bottled water.
Facilities: Overnight accommodation in the mountain huts is basic and hikers and trekkers are advised to be self-sufficient even when with a guide.

## MOUNT MULANJE

The Mulanje region in the south of the country lies at the heart of Malawi's tea industry. The slopes of the Mulanje massif are covered with a patchwork of verdant plantations, yet the majestic highlands that stretch up from the Zomba Plateau are ideal hiking territory. Mulanje and Zomba towns offer spectacular views of the country's highest peak, Mount Mulanje, towering 3,002m (9,850ft) over the region.

## CLIMBING MOUNT MULANJE

The network of walks and trails (with many undiscovered routes) provides endless opportunities to wonder at Malawi's natural heritage. All are accessed via well-marked and reliable paths, dotted intermittently with a good number of well-maintained and serviced small huts for overnight stops. The remarkable panorama and good facilities that characterise Mount Mulanje have made it the country's top hiking destination, as well as a reserve (hikers must obtain permission at Likabula Forest Station).

## FAIRLY EASY GOING

The going is seldom too tough for even the moderately fit (certain sections require determination, rock-climbing skill and perseverance), and a number of short, relaxed meanders in the lower reaches of the montane forest will satisfy casual walkers. To reach the top will take a full day, but it is not too arduous and offers great rewards. Local weather is volatile and it is easy to get lost on the mountain. The peak is often wrapped in billows of cloud and can be virtually impenetrable on foot; thick mist, heavy cloud cover and relentless precipitation can cause drastic drops in night temperatures. Consult the officers at Likabula or knowledgeable climbers affiliated to local mountain clubs.

# Tanzania

## ADVENTURING THROUGH TANZANIA (See Contact Details 92-95)

### ON LAND

**SAFARIS**
Serengeti, Ngorongoro and Lake Manyara — Serena Active
Wild Frontiers
Adventure Dynamics International
Hartley's Safaris

Selous and Ruaha national parks, Mufinidi and the northern parks — Ruaha Ruaha River Lodge
Hartleys Safaris

**BIRDING**
Selous, Lake Manyara and all major parks — Birding & Beyond Safaris

**HIKING**
Countrywide — Serena Active
Ngorongoro area — Wild Frontiers

**MOUNTAINEERING**
Mount Kilimanjaro and Mount Meru — Savage Wilderness Safaris
Wild Frontiers
Guided Ascents in Africa
Blue Mountain Adventures

**MARATHON RUNNING**
Kilimanjaro — Kilimanjaro Marathon

### ON WHEELS

**MOUNTAINBIKING**
Ngorongoro, Serengeti, Lake Manyara — Serena Active
Dar es Salaam and Zanzibar — Boundless Adventures

### ON (OR IN) WATER

**SCUBA DIVING**
Zanzibar — East Africa Diving and Watersport
One Ocean The Zanzibar Dive Centre
Zanzibar Beach Resort and Dive Centre
Hartley's Oceans and Islands

**CANOEING**
Lake Manyara — Serena Active

**SAILING**
Zanzibar — Zanzibar Beach Resort and Dive Centre

**BOATING**
Lake Tanganyika — Barefoot Safaris

**SEA KAYAKING**
Zanzibar — 180 Degree Adventures
Zanzibar Beach Resort

**TANZANIA**
**Capitals:** Dar es Salaam (administrative), Dodoma (legislative)
**Area:** 945,087km$^2$ / 364,900mi$^2$
**Population:** 37.2 million
**Main ethnic groups:**
• ± 120 Bantu groups (99%)
**Main languages:**
• Swahili
• English
**Main religions:**
• Traditional beliefs (42%)
• Muslim (31%)
• Christian (27%)
**Currency:** Tanzanian shilling (100 cents)

## 59

## IN THE AIR

**BALLOONING**
Serengeti National Park          Serengeti Balloon Safaris

**PARAGLIDING TOURS**
Rift Valley          Wild Frontiers

**10 GREAT ADVENTURES**
1. Safaris
2. Hot-air ballooning
3. Mountainbiking
4. Canoeing
5. Hiking
6. Mountaineering
7. Sea kayaking
8. Scuba diving
9. Marathon running
10. Birding

# Arusha

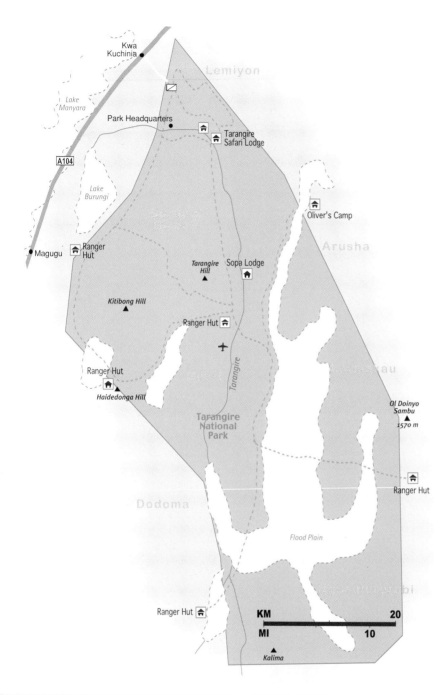

## ARUSHA NATIONAL PARK

To the northeast of Arusha town is Arusha National Park, a relatively tiny conservation area spread over just 137km² (50 sq. miles). It preserves a unique and individual natural world. Named after the Warusha people who have inhabited the area for generations, the park offers impressive gameviewing and natural environments, ironically 'surrounded' by fairly densely populated areas. Much of the park's interesting natural formations are a result of former volcanic activity in the region. There are three distinct landscapes within the park: Ngurdoto Crater, the Momela lakes and Mount Meru. Ngurdoto is an extinct volcano and the Momela Lakes came about following volcanic activity on the now dormant Mount Meru, a popular three-day climb (although it is possible to do it in a day!). Arusha offers

**KINGS OF CONSERVATION**

Tanzania can justifiably claim to have one of the most remarkable conservation records in Africa. Approximately 30 per cent of its land is dedicated to conservation efforts concentrated in wildlife sanctuaries made up of more than 35 parks, reserves and conservation areas. These range from the tropical coast to the semi-arid central plateau, and the semi-temperate highlands to forested woodlands. Tourists and safari-goers bring sought-after foreign currency into the country and, by visiting the reserves, help to preserve vital habitats such as the savannah grasslands and endless plains that are home to some of Africa's most recognised wildlife. Tanzania's tourist infrastructure is relatively sophisticated, and travel in and around the game reserves, national parks and World Heritage Sites (such as Arusha, Gombe, Kilimanjaro, Tarangire, Selous and the world-famous Serengeti and Ngorongoro) is generally a pain-free and quite luxurious experience.

## ARUSHA TOWN'S SIGHTS & SOUNDS

- Uhuru Monument
- Arusha International Conference Centre (AICC)
- The clocktower roundabout
- The bustling city market bursting with fruit and veg
- The National History Museum with its exhibition on the evolution of man
- The Cultural Heritage Complex (on the Dodoma road out of Arusha)
- Meserani Snake Park, 25km (15 miles) outside of Arusha
- Ol Donyo Orok Gallery and Crafts

## ARUSHA TOWN

The centre of trade and commerce in northern Tanzania, Arusha is one of Africa's fastest-growing cities. Not blessed with marvellous sightseeing opportunities, Arusha is, however, a great base for kick-starting your Tanzanian safari adventure. Located around 1,540m (5,053ft) above sea level, Arusha is surrounded by fertile lands that yield marvellous crops of coffee, maize, flowers and bananas. The city is watched over by nearby Mount Meru (popular with climbers): on clear days you can see snow-capped 'Kili' in the distance.

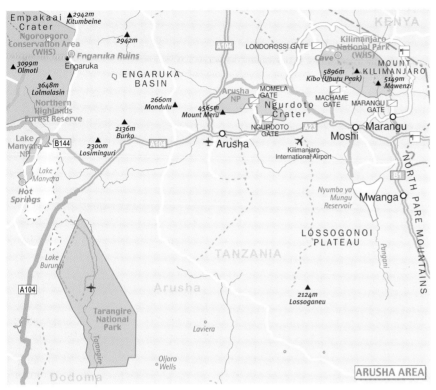

great day-tripping safaris and expeditions, with plenty of observation hides and picnic sites, although there are good overnight facilities in the form of lodges and camp sites. There are truly magnificent views from the rim of Ngurdoto Crater. Early risers will get the best views in the morning light, the eye feasting on the crater, the surrounding areas as well as Mount Kilimanjaro.

*Top to bottom: camel safari; Momela Lake; traditional dhow.*

## TARANGIRE NATIONAL PARK

Tarangire offers 2,600km² (1,000 sq. miles) of rolling hills, riverine forests, acacia woodlands and ancient baobabs. The Tarangire River provides the only permanent water in southern Maasailand, and this makes the park a wildlife-spotter's paradise during the dry season (from June to September). The park's ecosystem is based on patterns of annual migration and it plays a big part in preserving the country's wildlife, which includes an abundance of birdlife.

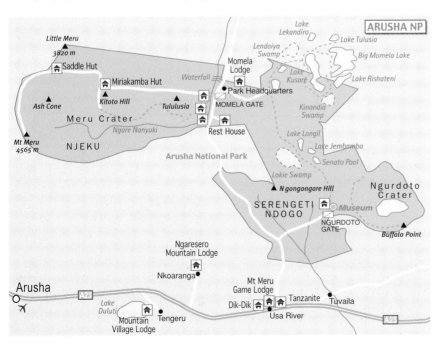

# Kilimanjaro

**THE HIGHEST MOUNTAIN ON EARTH**
The world's highest mountain is, in fact, Mount Kea (10,203m/ 33,476ft), but as it stands on the ocean seabed, it is mostly unreachable by travellers. The oceans cover nearly three-quarters of the Earth's surface and, despite countless research and conservation efforts, constitute some of the least explored areas of the planet's natural life.

**MOUNT KILIMANJARO**
Mighty Kilimanjaro, with an altitude of 5,895m (19,340ft), emerged 750,000 years ago as a result of volcanic activity. 'Kili' is the world's highest freestanding mountain. The precise origin of Kili's name remains lost in time – the local word *kilima* (from which the name apparently stems) means 'hill' rather than 'mountain'. Rising from the plains of the Masai, the mountain peak – a dormant volcano – is snowcapped (although just 3º south of the equator) and the make-up of the slopes varies enormously. From the foot to about 1,800m (5,900ft), the inclines comprise volcanic soils; the vegetation up to

2,800m (9,200ft) is rainforest, which receives over 2,000mm (79in) of rain; followed – to an altitude of 4,000m (13,100ft) – by a moorland of heather and giant lobelias.

**AFRICA'S GREAT MOUNTAIN ICONS**
- Mount Cameroon   Cameroon
- Mount Elgon   Kenya
- Mount Kenya   Kenya
- Mount Kilimanjaro   Tanzania
- Mount Sinai   Egypt
- Mount Stanley   Uganda
- Table Mountain   South Africa

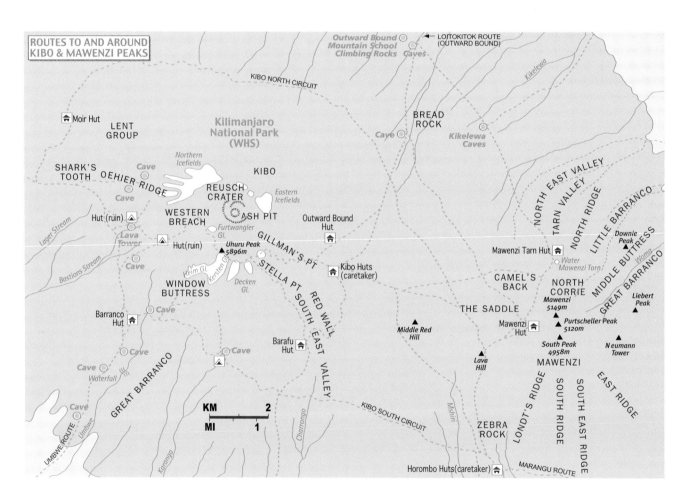

**HIGHEST MOUNTAIN BY CONTINENT**
(aka The Seven Summits)

| | | | |
|---|---|---|---|
| • Asia | Mount Everest | 8,850m | 29,028ft |
| • South America | Aconcagua | 6,959m | 22,826ft |
| • North America | Mount McKinley | 6,194m | 20,316ft |
| • Africa | Kilimanjaro | 5,895m | 19,335ft |
| • Europe | Mount Elbrus | 5,642m | 18,505ft |
| • Antarctica | Visson Massi | 4,897m | 16,062ft |
| • Australia | Mount Kosciuszko | 2,228m | 7,307ft |

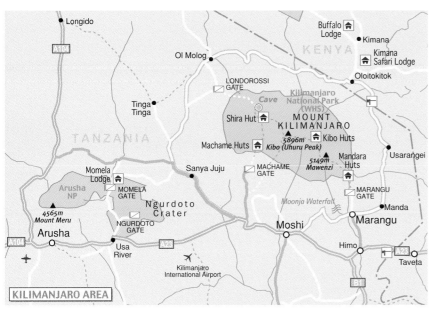

## 61

## CLIMBING KILIMANJARO

Although there are difficult areas on
Kili's slopes, it is unlikely you will need
ropes, ice axes and picks, and the more
followed routes are relatively trouble-
free. In fact, the greatest challenge is
overcoming the heat of the sun and the
icy chill of the summit – the most reported danger is the altitude sickness that
sets in at about 3,500m (10,500ft). The
only way to combat it is to climb slowly
and stop often to allow your body to
acclimatise. Climbing Kilimanjaro is an
expensive exercise: although tour operators should see to transfers, accommodation, and equipment, you need to hire
registered guides and porters as well as
pay the US$20 rescue fee. There are also
park and camping fees, yet the standard
five-day climb is so popular that it can
be overbooked (the park sees 20,000 visitors pass through a year). The first day
of the ascent departs from the park and
comprises an undemanding three- or
four-hour hike through rainforest to the
A-frame huts at the first rest stop. You
then plough on to the night stop at
Mandara Hut, from where you will
progress to Horombo on day two where,
at 3,720m (12,200ft), the first signs of
altitude sickness strike. The day's five-
hour trek will take you to the rim of
Maundi Crater and up an incline to the
highlands. The trek becomes tougher by
the third day as you pass the Last Water
and Zebra Rocks and move onto The
Saddle, the bridge connecting the peaks
of Kibo and Mawenzi. The last stretch of
the six-hour walk up to Kibo Hut at
4,700m (15,4400ft) can be arduous. Kibo
is dreary and cold, and the last two days
are mentally and physically demanding.
In the icy morning, you head for

**KILIMANJARO IN A NUTSHELL**
Climate: Avoid the rains in April, May
and November.
Risk factor: Cheap package deals may
be less reliable and less safe than
established operators. Irresponsible
tourists are degrading the trail in
Kilimanjaro National Park through
constant use.
Health: Exhaustion, fatigue and altitude sickness are the most serious
complaints. Be vaccinated against
cholera, tetanus, hepatitis and polio.
AIDS is prevalent.
Pack: Warm, waterproof and wind-
proof clothes, sturdy hiking boots, a
sleeping bag, sunscreen and water.
Sweets help maintain energy. A head
torch for the early-morning stretch. A
kikoi (sarong) that can act as a scarf
and pillow.
Facilities: Reliable operators offer the
best service and provide equipment.

Gillman's Point on the crater. Oxygen is
very thin, making the walk tougher, but
a mere 210m (700ft) further is the great
reward: Kilimanjaro's true summit,
Uhuru Peak.

Top to bottom: Mount Kilimanjaro;
Kibo crater; ice cliffs on Kibo.

# Dar es Salaam & Zanzibar Region

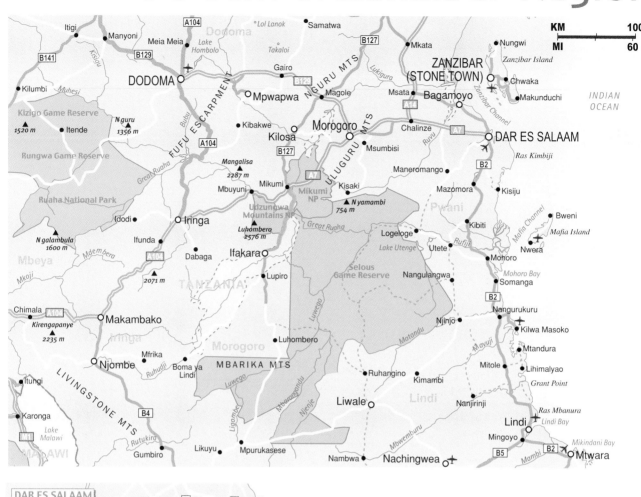

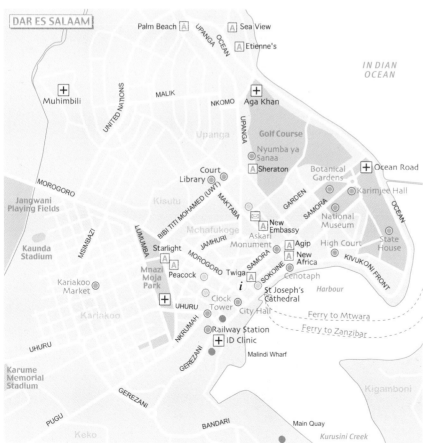

## 62

## DAR ES SALAAM

When it comes to African cities, Dar es Salaam (aka Dar), as a rather young city, is Tanzania's most strategic harbour and the largest urban settlement in the country. While Dodoma and Dar es Salaam are both capital cities of the country, it is Dar es Salaam that is its very exciting heart. Established in 1870 as a 'Haven of Peace' by the Sultan Majid, today's thriving, modern city has remained true to its nature as a bustling African hub but also has the cosmopolitan flavour that seems to infiltrate so many of Tanzania's urban centres. Dar is the axis on which the national economy pivots. With its striking backdrop and string of breathtakingly beautiful (and famous) beaches, even the inner city is also punctuated here and there with patches of emerald green. While the urban chaos that pervades so much of metropolitan Africa has not escaped Dar, there is an overriding sense of the quaint and the charming in the city centre. The city has a long legacy of colonial intervention but this, combined with the remarkable spirit and conviviality of its people, makes for an even more fascinating adventure. English and German colonists left behind a wonderful amalgamation of architecture that combines well with the indigenous flavour of the city. Dar plays host to a number of plush hotels, fine restaurants and upmarket shopping haunts, but is also the home of an unusual collection of cathedrals and churches, museums and markets, galleries and boutiques – all haphazardly interspersed with many important cultural sites that are only decades old.

### EXPLORING ZANZIBAR'S WATERS

Some 85km (53 miles) long and 25km (16 miles) wide, Zanzibar's coast of rocky coves, mangroves, lagoons, pristine beaches and astonishing coral reefs is home to many leisure activities, from kayaking to deep-sea game fishing and, more recently, diving and snorkelling. Visibility from a kayak is virtually unobstructed and you will see right down to the corals and reefs. Not for nothing is this area known as The Sunrise Coast, and this is most true of Bwejuu and Makunduchi. There are numerous boat trips to offshore islets and even Pemba, and exploring these by boat provides a unique glimpse of coastal Tanzania. It also offers some of the best scuba diving and snorkelling in East Africa. The corals are virtually unscathed and the reefs teem with sea creatures. Although diving is extraordinary, few operators are based on the eastern shore so conditions here are better. Because it is so sheltered, too, visibility makes for excellent diving. The beach at Chuumbe Island Coral Park is punctuated with 'eco-bungalows', and a network of walking and diving trails laces the coast. There are also wrecks, and the Stone Town harbour is dotted with 200 of them, but conditions in the harbour are poor and it is best to explore wrecks elsewhere on the coast. The east coast of Zanzibar Island remains undeveloped, and most lodgings are rustic, but tour operators also offer other rewards, including increasingly popular big game fishing and deep-sea diving, as well as the magical opportunity to dive with dolphins and turtles – and even the occasional shark.

### ZANZIBAR'S COAST IN A NUTSHELL

Requirements: Some diving excursions may require qualifications.
Climate: Tropical and hot, so best times are December–January (peak holiday season) and June–October. Ocean conditions vary according to location, and the best time to dive is from October to November.
Risk factor: Theft and mugging are becoming more frequent. Exposure to the sun is exacerbated by wind and sea. Malaria remains a threat. Currents on the east coast may be dangerous.
Facilities: Many hotels have local guides and a number of operators in Stone Town offer water-based excursions, many running PADI courses.

Opposite page: market day in Zanzibar.
Top to bottom: Lutheran church, Dar es Salaam; Dar es Salaam sunrise; a palm weaver.

# Zanzibar, Pemba & Mafia

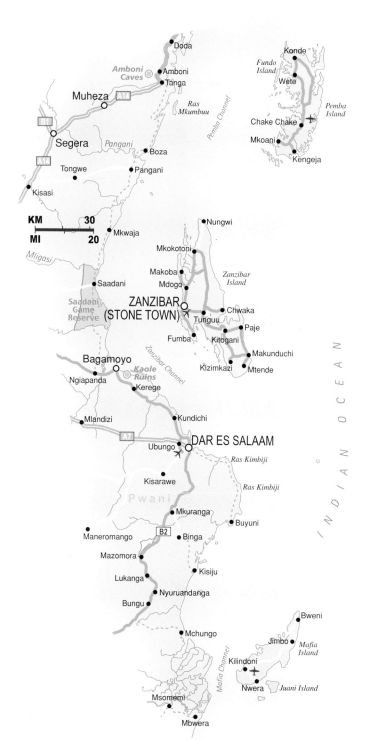

**Doda**
**Amboni** *Amboni Caves*
**Tanga**
**Muheza** A1
*Pangani*
B1
**Segera**
A14
**Boza**
**Tongwe** **Pangani**
**Kisasi**
*Mligasi*

KM ——— 30
MI ——— 20

**Mkwaja**
**Saadani**
*Saadani Game Reserve*
**Ngiapanda**
**Bagamoyo** *Kaole Ruins*
**Kerege**
**Mlandizi**
**Kundichi**
A7
**Ubungo**
**DAR ES SALAAM**
*Ras Kimbiji*
**Kisarawe**
*Pwani* *Ras Kimbiji*
**Mkuranga**
**Maneromango**
**Binga**
**Buyuni**
B2
**Mazomora**
**Kisiju**
**Lukanga**
**Nyuruandanga**
**Bungu**
**Mchungo**
**Msomemi**
**Mbwera**

*Ras Mkumbuu*
*Pembu Channel*

**Konde**
*Fundo Island*
**Wete**
*Pemba Island*
**Chake Chake**
**Mkoani**
**Kengeja**

**Nungwi**
**Mkokotoni**
**Makoba**
**Mdogo**
*Zanzibar Island*
**ZANZIBAR (STONE TOWN)**
**Tunguu**
**Chwaka**
**Fumba**
**Kitogani**
**Paje**
*Zanzibar Channel*
**Makunduchi**
**Kizimkazi**
**Mtende**

*INDIAN OCEAN*

**Bweni**
**Jimbo**
*Mafia Island*
**Kilindoni**
**Nwera** *Juani Island*

## PEMBA ISLAND

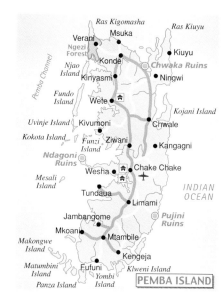

*Ras Kigomasha*
**Verani** **Msuka**
*Ras Kiuyu*
*Ngezi Forest*
**Konde** **Kiuyu**
**Kinyasmi** *Chwaka Ruins*
*Njao Island*
*Pemba Channel*
*Fundo Island*
**Wete** **Ningwi**
*Uvinje Island*
**Kivumoni**
*Kojani Island*
*Kokota Island*
**Ziwani** **Chwale**
*Funzi Island*
**Wesha** **Chake Chake** **Kangagni**
*Ndagoni Ruins*
*Mesali Island*
**Tundaua** **Limami**
**Jambangome** *Pujini Ruins*
*Makongwe Island*
**Mkoani** **Mtambile**
*Matumbini Island*
**Kengeja**
**Fufuni**
*Panza Island* *Yombi Island* *Klweni Island*

*INDIAN OCEAN*

## ZANZIBAR ISLAND

*Lighthouse*
**Nungwi** *Ras Nungwi*
*Tumbatu Island*
*Mvuleni Ruins*
**Jongowe** **Potowa** *Mnemba Island*
*Shirazi Ruins*
**Mwanahaza**
**Mkokotoni** **Matemwe**
**Makoba**
*INDIAN OCEAN*
**Mahonda** **Pwani Mchangani**
*Slave Caves* **Kinyasini** **Kiwengwa**
*Kichwele Forest*
**Mdogo** **Ndagaa**
**Mawimbini** **Tamarind**
*Changuu Island* *Persian Baths Ruins* **Uroa**
**Dunga** **Uroa**
*Ras Michamwi*
**Pingwe**
*Dunga Ruins*
**ZANZIBAR (STONE TOWN)**
**Tunguu** **Chwaka** **Dongwe**
**Chukwani**
*Chumbe Island* **Kikungwi** *Jozani Forest*
**Kitogani** **Paje**
**Fumba** *Uzi Island*
*Kwale Island* **Jambiani**
*Menai Bay*
*Zanzibar Channel*
*Shirazi Mosque* **Makunduchi**
*Pungume Island* **Kizimkazi** **Mtende**
*Ras Kazim Kazi*

## MAFIA ISLAND

*INDIAN OCEAN*
**Bweni**
**Jimbo**
*Mafia Channel*
*Mafia Island*
**Baleni**
**Kilindoni**
*Ghole*
**Nwera** *Kua Ruins*
*Juani Island*

**ZANZIBAR IN A NUTSHELL**
Climate: Tropical and hot, the best time to dive is during October and November.
Risk factor: Theft and mugging are becoming more frequent – keep an eye on equipment and accessories. Currents on the east coast may be dangerous. Zanzibar is Muslim, so exposed flesh is frowned upon beyond tourist spots.

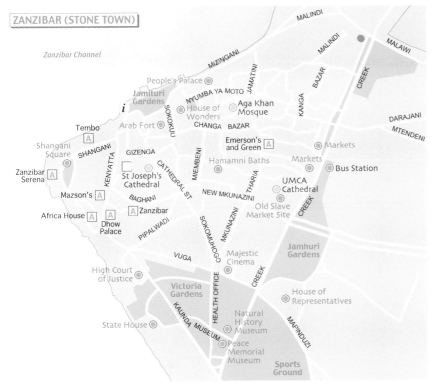

## 63

**ZANZIBAR (STONE TOWN)**

## ZANZIBAR

Although the name may conjure up romantic images of exotic destination inaccessible to all but locals and only a handful of intrepid adventurers intent on discovering Africa's legendary city, Zanzibar is in fact one of East Africa's most significant tourist destinations. Spread across two separate islands some 40km (24.8 miles) from Tanzania's mainland, the most famous is the island of Zanzibar (aka Unguja). The other is Pemba just kilometres to the northeast. The word 'zanzibar' is said to originate from an early, all-encompassing name given to much of East Africa's extended coast by Arab traders. This stretch of shore, it is said, was once commonly known as Zinj el Barr, meaning the Land of the Black People. Now called the Spice Island, Zanzibar is a coastal paradise, known for its spectacular beaches and the lingering ghosts of ancient Africa. At the island's centre stands Stone Town, the old quarter of Zanzibar Town. Most visitors agree that it is the heady aroma of spices and the intangible sense of history that is Stone Town's most alluring drawcard. The winding, mostly cobbled streets, alleys and footpaths criss-cross in a labyrinth not easily negotiated by the uninitiated, and the overriding buzz is a baffling combination of Arabic, Asian and

European languages, led by a barrage of Swahili. The architecture is an endearing hotchpotch of the romantic and the practical: minarets and Gothic-like arches of palaces and forts stand alongside markets and street stalls.

## PEMBA

The island of Pemba may not be as famous as its exotic neighbour, but it's more or less the same size, covering some 984km² (610 sq. miles) and is an equally picturesque beach idyll with plenty to offer, from natural splendour to the multitude of outdoor activities on offer. Pemba is best known for the abundance of cloves harvested here annually, and the unsurpassed quality of its diving and snorkelling. Sweltering in the heat and alive with its spice aromas, Pemba has also retained its centuries-old charm, remaining seemingly unchanged for hundreds of years – except for the tides and winds that continue to buffet the shores from seasonal monsoons! With a population of less than half a million, this tiny satellite of Tanzania also has a long and sometimes turbulent history of conquerors and colonists, and this has left an indelible mark on the island.

## MAFIA

Mafia (not linked to the Italian Mob) is an ideal spot for adventurers, with magnificent diving (notably at Chole Bay, a protected deep-water anchorage) and snorkelling, angling, dhow sailing, water sports and daydreaming on the beach.

Top to bottom: a diving dhow; view of Stone Town; Swahili door in Stone Town.

# The Serengeti & Ngorongoro Region

**SERENGETI IN A NUTSHELL**
Requirements: Travellers from South America and most of Africa must have yellow fever immunisation certificates.
Climate: Coolest from June to October, but this is also the busiest and most expensive time. January to February may be better: although hot, it's the best time to see migration in the southern park.
Risk factor: Day-to-day life is filled with the dangers of wildest Africa.
Health: Be vaccinated against cholera, tetanus, hepatitis and polio. Malaria is rife in the lowlands. AIDS is a threat.
Pack: Most operators supply basics; take light hiking gear, warm clothes, walking boots, and sun protection.

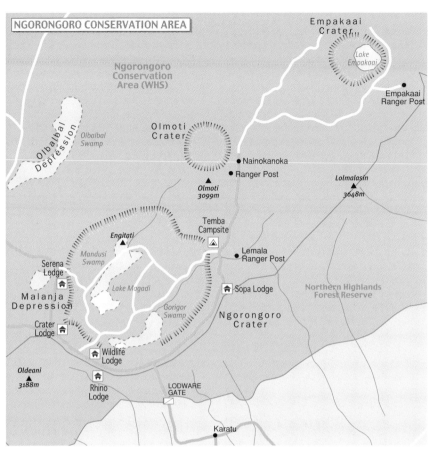

## 64

NGORONGORO CONSERVATION AREA

## SERENGETI

The dramatic natural arena in which Africa's greatest display plays itself out, the horizonless plains of the Serengeti are a spectacular wildlife sanctuary without parallel. Known by the local Maasai as 'The Great Open Place', the plateau of the 15,000km$^2$ (5,800 sq. miles) plain is covered by the short grasses of the Serengeti National Park, acclaimed as the finest game reserve in Africa. This extraordinary ecosystem is home to enormous populations of mammals. The Serengeti's annual wildebeest migration begins on the southern plateau during the summer rains (December to May) when the herds of 100,000 animals – extending for 40km (25 miles) – begin their 800km (500-mile) trek to the western territories, only to make the gruelling return trip to the southern plains between October and November.

## WALKING THE SERENGETI

The Serengeti is home to some of the most impressive herds of wildlife on the continent; it's also home to valleys, rolling hills and patches of scrubby woodland. The plains are the most memorable and the easiest to cross. One way of avoiding the tourist trap is to explore the land on foot – almost within touching distance of more than a million wildebeest, hundreds of thousands of Thomson's gazelle, and tens of thousands of zebra, impala and topi. The prospect of walking this wild countryside is at once intimidating and enthralling. These herds are stealthily stalked by the great predators of Africa, including lion, cheetah and leopard, but also wild dog, jackal, spotted hyena and bat-eared fox. But even the best roads are poor and the distances vast, so hitchhiking will prove futile! It is best to opt for a tour company and Arusha has plenty of options, but only some hiking tours are based on responsible ecotourism. However, you do not want to end up in the middle of the Serengeti without shelter and without a guide. Reliable operators charge more, but the package includes park fees, camping fees, food and fuel costs, plus they provide drivers, cooks, porters and guides. By choosing to walk, you will be faced with limited facilities such as long-drop toilets and basic camp sites, and will not have at your disposal the luxuries offered by the exclusive lodges and tented camps.

Top to bottom: hot-air balloon over the Serengeti; a 4x4 vehicle tests the shifting sands; the entrance to Ngorongoro National Park; portrait of a Maasai girl.

# The Great Rift Valley

The Great Rift Valley is one of the most spectacular volcanic regions on earth, and the area's geology has given rise to an extraordinary diversity of landscape and faunal life, which reaches its pinnacle on the wild plains of Kenya. At its most dramatic in East Africa, the Great Rift Valley was formed some 20 million years ago when violent subterranean shifts resulted in the collapse of mammoth tracks of land situated along parallel fault lines, causing volcanic eruptions of molten rock. The length of this great scar that has been forged down one-sixth of the earth's circumference is characterised by a succession of great lakes. Today, this massive fissure in the earth's crust stretches 9,500km (6,000 miles) from Lebanon to Mozambique, and no less than 800km (500 miles) between Lake Manyara and the Red Sea. The dramatic inclines of its valley walls cut between 50km (30 miles) and 500km (300 miles) across the width of the African landscape. Apart from Ethiopia on the Horn of Africa, the two countries that are home to the most theatrical inclines of the great valley are Kenya and Tanzania, both of which are characterised by high-lying inland plateaus and fertile coastal belts dotted with tropical islands. The Valley's extraordinarily vertical walls loom up from the wide golden plain below, the cliff-like ramparts broken by cross fractures. In a region perhaps best known for the phenomenon of its wildlife, Kenya and Tanzania have, in the process of capitalising on their extraordinarily rich natural heritage, both achieved an enviable record of conservation.

## NGORONGORO CRATER

The Ngorongoro Crater (see spread 64) is the largest intact volcanic caldera in the world, and the expansive tableland covers the 265km$^2$ (102 sq. miles) of the crater floor and forms the heart of the Ngorongoro Conservation Area. Hedged in by 600m (2,000ft) walls that tower high above the open savanna, the crater is a sweep of untamed wilderness across which herds of zebra and wildebeest (with headcounts numbering in the hundreds) charge. Huge flocks of pink flamingoes wade the seasonal waters.

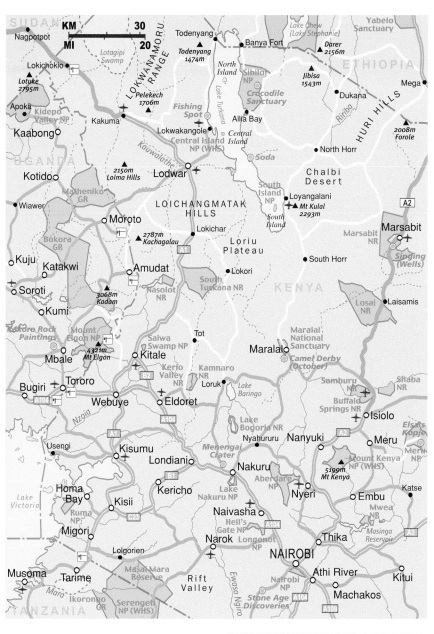

## 65

The plains and montane forest are home to a astounding array of Africa's most recognised wildlife, with no fewer than a quarter million large mammals scattered across the emptiness. The abundance of antelope species means that this is also prime big cat country, with cheetah, leopard and the world's densest population of over 100 lion. The rest of the Big Five have also settled here: elephant bulls, 3,000 head of buffalo, and roughly 20 black rhino.

Opposite page: Ngorongoro crater wall.
Top to bottom: Bagamoyo beach; Ngorongoro crater; Olduvai gorge (Ngorongoro Conservation area).

## NGORONGORO'S WILDLIFE STARS

FLORA Red thorn, *nuxia congesta*, crotons, strangler fig, mosses, orchids, ferns, old man's beard, umbrella trees, lichen, euphorbia, elephant ears, lion's mane, Sodom apple, wild bananas, yellow fever trees, Cape chestnut, a wide range of grassland and the poisonous red-and-yellow leopard lily.
FAUNA Squirrels, baboons, buffalo, cheetah, leopard, lion, elephant, black rhino, antelope such as duiker and bushbuck, genet, serval, African civet, and hundreds of bird species, including masses of flamingo, martial eagles, blacksmith plovers, crested guineafowl, shrikes, weavers, Narina trogon, Livingstone's turaco, kites and marabou storks.

# Kenya

## ADVENTURING THROUGH KENYA (See Contact Details 92-95)

**IN THE AIR**

**BALLOONING**

Countrywide    Balloon Safaris
              Bungiwalla
              Adventures Aloft

## 66

## ON LAND

**GAME VIEWING AND WALKING SAFARIS**
Countrywide — Savage Wilderness Safaris
Hartley's Safaris
Serena Active
Active Kenya
Safaris Unlimited
Lets Go Travel

**HORSERIDING**
Countrywide — Offbeat Safaris
Masai Mara and Chyulu Hills — Safaris Unlimited

**CAMEL SAFARIS**
Great Rift Valley — African Frontiers

**MOUNTAINEERING**
Mount Kenya — Savage Wilderness Safaris
Blue Mountain Adventures
Guided Ascents in Africa

**PHOTOGRAPHIC SAFARIS**
Masai Mara — Safaris Unlimited

**KENYA**
**Capital:** Nairobi
**Area:** 592,747km$^2$ / 228,861mi$^2$
**Population:** 31.1 million
**Main ethnic groups:**
• Kikuyu (21%)
• Luhya (14%)
• Kamba (11%)
**Main languages:**
• Swahili
• English
• Kikuyu
• Luo
• Kamba
**Main religions:**
• Catholic (34%)
• Protestant (32%)
• Traditional beliefs (26%)
• Muslim (6%)
**Currency:** Kenyan shilling
(100 cents)

## ON (OR IN) WATER

**WHITEWATER RAFTING**
Tana and Athi Rivers — Savage Wilderness Safaris

**SCUBA DIVING**
Mombasa — Diani Marine
Buccaneer Dive Centre
Hartley's Oceans and Islands

**SAILING**
Countrywide — Savage Wilderness Safaris

**KITESURFING**
Countrywide — Active Kenya

## ON WHEELS

**4X4 TRAILS**
Rift Valley — Mountain Rock Hotel

**MOUNTAINBIKING**
Rift Valley, Masai Mara — Bike Treks
Laikipia Plateau — Black Mamba Safaris
Amboseli and Masai Mara national parks — Serena Active

**SAND YACHTING**
Countrywide — Active Kenya

**9 GREAT ADVENTURES**
1. Game viewing
2. Scuba diving
3. Hot-air ballooning
4. Mountainbiking
5. Horseriding
6. Birding
7. Mountaineering
8. Whitewater rafting
9. Sailing

# Lake Turkana

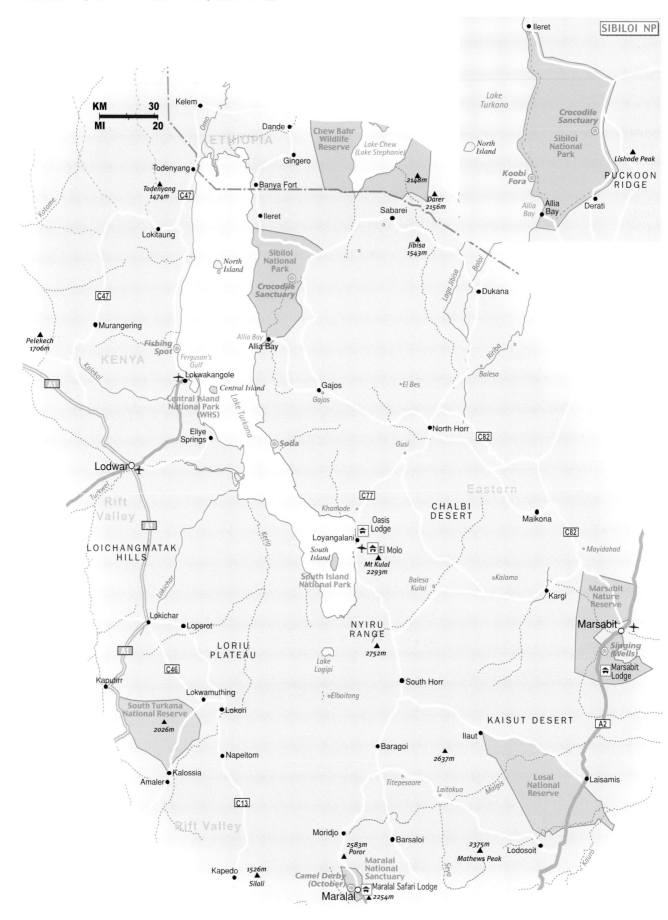

## 67

## LAKE TURKANA

Kenya's long, narrow lake covers 7,104km² (2,743 sq. miles) and is known by many locals as Basso Narok (Black Lake). It forms a ribbon of water 250km (155 miles) long and 56km (35 miles) wide, enclosed by the cliffs of the Rift Valley, and cutting through the parched northern reaches of endless horizons and volcanic outcrops. Fed by Ethiopia's Omo River and, to some degree, by the Turkwel, Lake Turkana is the world's largest desert lake, and one of the largest alkaline lakes. Volcanic islands in the middle of the lake are the territory of hippos and some 22,000 crocodiles, while the waters shelter huge Nile perch. Migrant birds visit in such great numbers that their breeding sites on South and Central Island have been declared national parks.

## THE SOURCE OF THE RIVER

Originating in the forests of the Eastern Mau Escarpment are the Njoro, Makalia and Enderit rivers, which drain into the great body of water that forms the heart of Lake Nakuru National Park, providing sustenance for half a million Kenyans. The lake now flows for only one-third of the year and has been reduced to dust six times in the last decade. The government's Fisheries Department has,

fortunately, taken steps to help preserve the nation's marine life: it declared a short moratorium on trawling, and also established a task force charged with investigating the status of marine resources for future generations.

## AFRICA'S NATIONAL PARK PRIDE

Despite certain conservation problems and concerns, some of the world's finest national parks and reserves exist in Kenya. Parks such as Aberdare, Amboseli, Meru, Tsavo East and West, and Samburu provide, in the most part, an outstanding wildlife experience. Although the tourist trade has its numerous downfalls (Amboseli and Masai Mara are criss-crossed with tracks and trails carved by the caravan of tourists), in most cases a percentage of the revenue generated by safari operations and the entrance fees to government parks and reserves are allocated to local inhabitants and the establishment of wildlife research programmes and conservation education centres. Poaching, an evergrowing population and ever increasing land use create enormous pressure on wild spaces and the Masai Mara's wildebeest population has dropped from 120,000 to 22,000 in 20 years, their seasonal stomping grounds giving way to farmland and cattle pastures. Such situations are exacerbated by seemingly irresponsible and narrow-minded decisions made by non-aligned government officials.

## THE WOOD AND THE TREES

Despite enormous opposition from local, international and non-governmental conservation organisations, the Kenyan government announced that it would excise about 67,000ha (165,500 acres) of the country's unique woodlands, including some 270ha of Nakuru, 1,825ha of Mount Kenya, 2,837ha of Marmanet and 900ha of Molo. Leading environmental groups have lashed out, pointing to the irreparable damage to the immediate environment, as well as the effect on the national economy and the ecology of the broader region. Felling these forests would alter local rainfall, thus affecting the water system and agriculture – not to mention the other industries dependent on hydroelectric power. In fact, Kenya's rivers are already suffering from natural deterioration.

Top to bottom: Lake Turkana at sunset; a local child enjoying some fun in the lake; remnants of Turkana's volcanic past.

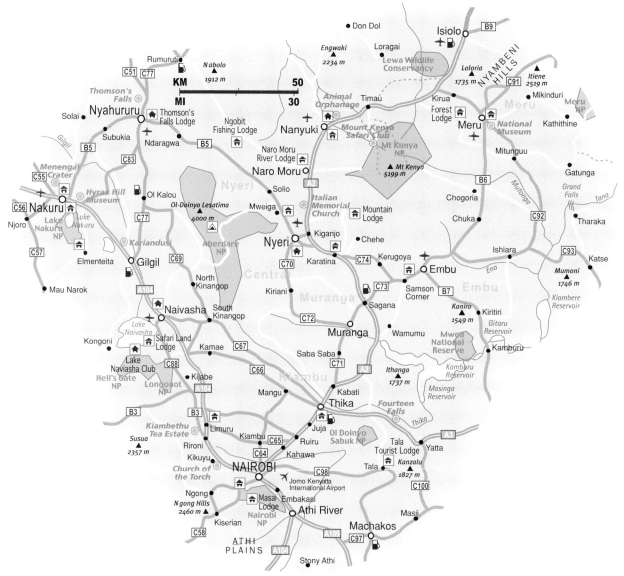

## NAIROBI

One of the most cosmopolitan and certainly one of the youngest of all of Africa's capitals, Nairobi is a metropolis of museums and malls interspersed with boutiques and bars, curios and criminals, market stalls, galleries and even game reserves. The city's two million inhabitants come from a variety of tribal cultures, and the noise, colour and

### NAIROBI'S TO DO LIST

VISIT Nairobi National Park with its wide range of wildlife, as well as the Nairobi Animal Orphanage.
VISIT the Railway Museum with its homage to the 'lunatic line'!
VISIT the Karen Blixen Museum (the author of *Out of Africa*).
ENJOY a night of game viewing at Treetops, The Ark or Mountain Lodge.
PHOTOGRAPH the city's beautiful mosques, notably the Jamia Mosque.

squalor of the older portions contrast greatly with modern structures such as the Kenyatta Conference Centre. Nairobi National Park lies on the city perimeter, with the Aberdare National Park nearby and river rafting on the Athi River.

### NATIONAL PARKS & RESERVES

With nearly 60 separate officially designated conservation areas, including national parks, reserves, marine reserves and wetlands, covering 10 per cent of Kenya's land and waters, Africa's largest, best stocked and most accessible protected areas belong to Kenya. The word 'safari' is taken from the local Swahili language and, appropriately, the safari industry is now one of the nation's most important income producers. Kenya's central plateau is divided by the Great Rift Valley, and the semi-desert stretches south of the equator to

the fertile east coast. The varying geology of the region means that the wildlife areas cover an extraordinary range of landscapes, from open plains to densely wooded forests and marine environments. Sadly, wild Kenya remains under constant threat of numerous scourges.

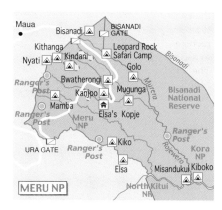

MERU NP

## 68

## AFRICA'S HIGHEST MOUNTAINS

| | | |
|---|---|---|
| Kilimanjaro Tanzania | 5,895m | 19,341ft |
| Mt Kenya Kenya | 5,199m | 17,057ft |
| Stanley Uganda-DRC | 5,110m | 16,765ft |
| Ras Dashen Ethiopia | 4,620m | 15,158ft |
| Meru Tanzania | 4,565m | 14,977ft |
| Karisimbi Rwanda-DRC | 4,507m | 14,787ft |
| Elgon Kenya-Uganda | 4,321m | 14,177ft |
| Toubkal Morocco | 4,165m | 13,655ft |
| Mt Cameroon Cameroon | 4,095m | 13,435ft |
| Thabana Ntlenyana Lesotho | 3,482m | 11,424ft |
| Emi Koussi Chad | 3,415m | 11,204ft |

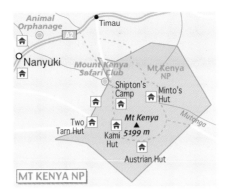

**MT KENYA NP**

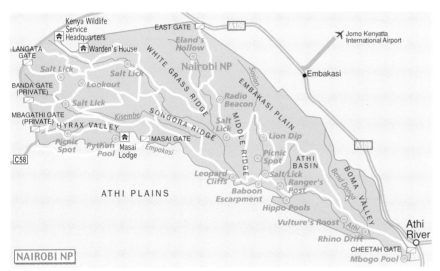

**NAIROBI NP**

## MOUNT KENYA

Sacred Kirinyaga (Mount Kenya) on the central highlands is a playground for hikers, mountaineers and climbers. The snowcapped summit of its three-million-year-old bulk stands at 5,199m (17,058ft), although glaciation has already hacked off 2,000m (6,500ft) from its original height! Topped by three main peaks (Batian, Nelion and Lenana) the slopes of this extinct volcano are covered in snow and ice, with 600km² (230 sq. miles) of protected land above the 3,200m (10,500ft) forest line. The region is the traditional home to the Kikuyu people, and the park is home to birds, elephant, black rhino, buffalo, lion and bushbuck. Mount Kenya NP is one of the country's top safari spots (with more than adequate facilities) and a popular recreation destination for climbers eager to ascend Africa's second-highest peak. The four main hiking routes across Mount Kenya (Naro Muru, Sirimon, Timau and Chogoria) vary in distance and accessibility, demanding various degrees of fitness. Some of the climbs are relatively easy, while others demand all the skills and equipment (ice axes and ropes!) of dedicated mountaineers. Trails, camps and huts on the trail circuit are accompanied by some fine hotels and plush safari lodges that offer excellent game viewing and night drives.

## LAKE VICTORIA

Also known as Victoria Nyanza, Lake Victoria falls within the boundaries of Kenya, Tanzania and Uganda. Covering 69,485km² (26,828 sq. miles), Victoria is Africa's largest and the world's second largest lake. Sitting at an altitude of 1,134m (3,720ft) in the populated highlands of Kenya, it averages a depth of only 78m (255ft), with its waters drained by the Victoria Nile. The lake is dotted with little islands such as Ndere (a national park in the middle of the lake) and Saa Nane (a reserve harbouring island wildlife like rock agamas and hyraxes), while the 240km² (93 sq. miles) Rubondo Island reserve is home to sitatunga, elephant, bushbuck and a variety of chimps. The lake shore is lined with reeds, papyrus and flamingoes, while its banks are settled mostly by the Luo, farmers and fishermen who ply the lake for Nile perch.

Top to bottom: high-rise buildings accentuate Nairobi's development; Mount Kenya National Park; market in Nairobi.

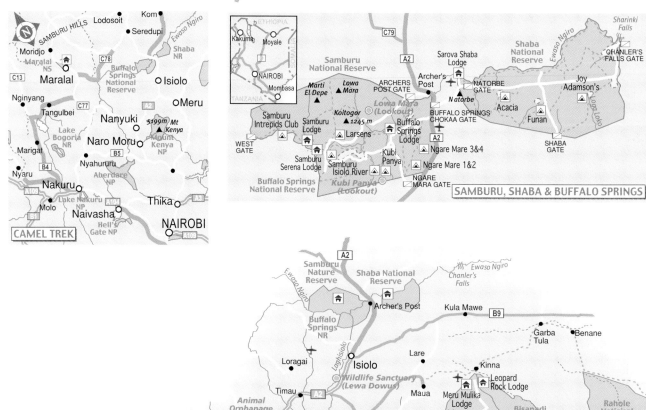

### A MASSIVE RIFT

Cutting through the heart of Kenya and Tanzania is the colossal trench of the Great Rift Valley, one of the world's most spectacular volcanic regions. The area's geology has given rise to an extraordinary diversity of landscape and faunal life, reaching its pinnacle on Kenya's wild plains.

### ABERDARE NATIONAL PARK

Lying 100km (62 miles) north of Nairobi, Aberdare is a fairly small park, weighing in at just 767km² (296 sq. miles), yet it boasts a wide diversity of fauna, partly owing to its mountainous terrain, which includes a highest point of 3,995m (13,100ft) in the form of Ol-Doinyo Satima. Waterfalls are a natural accompaniment to such terrain, and one of the most accessible and widely photographed are the Chania Falls (aka Queen's

Cave Waterfall, as Queen Elizabeth II once lunched here!). The country's highest falls are the Gura Falls, which spill water down from a spectacular height of 457m (1,500ft), although viewing can only be done from the top of the falls, which reduces the 'wow factor' for visitors. The waterfalls and streams are a rich source of trout for those who live for the fly, but the high rainfall in the area makes four-wheel-drive essential. The rains also encourage a proliferation

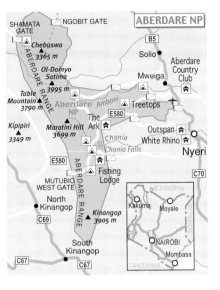

## 69

ABERDARE NP

of wildlife as well as heavy vegetation, which serves to impede game viewing! Sometimes it's best to rise above it all, and a night (or more!) at The Ark or Treetops lodges allows great game viewing after dark.

## SAMBURU, BUFFALO SPRINGS AND SHABA RESERVES

Lying on the Ewaso Ngiro River ('river of brown water'), Samburu and Buffalo Springs create conditions for predators such as lion, cheetah and leopard, as well as the delightful gerenuk ('standing buck'), Gervy's zebra, beisa oryx and the reticulated giraffe. Samburu is also a popular spot for camel safaris. Shaba offers a totally different habitat from the nearby Samburu and Buffalo Springs reserves. Shaba's plains are dotted with springs, small swamps and rocky hills, and it was at Shaba that author and conservationist Joy Adamson lived, rehabilitated a leopard called Penny, and was eventually murdered.

## CAMEL SAFARIS

Camel safaris provide a unique alternative to 4x4. Escorted by an armed guide, you ride and walk alongside the camels throughout the day and get to see scores of wild animals. Although you get to travel through otherwise inaccessible areas, many 'camel safaris' may mean little more than a hike alongside the great beasts as they lumber across the veld, yet this doesn't detract from the experience. Most operators allow trekkers to hitch rides on the backs of the camels, which are constantly tended by expert handlers who are keen to help and are eager to please. Many local safari guides may don traditional dress for the benefit of tourists, but they are

## CAMEL SAFARIS IN A NUTSHELL

Climate: Usually hot and dry throughout the country, and relatively humid along the coastal stretches.

Risk factor: Generally risk-free and, besides stubborn camels and the usual dangers of nights in the bush, safari operators take good care of clients.

Health: Malaria is rife throughout most of Kenya, except at Nairobi and on the highlands where the risk is considerably lower. Dehydration can be an issue, but be sure to drink only bottled water.

Pack: Lightweight clothes, sun hat and sturdy walking boots are essential for trekking safaris.

Facilities: Luxury lodges and very comfortable tented camps cater largely for the upmarket tourist visiting national parks and reserves. A range of more basic – and substantially cheaper! – options may be found throughout the country.

well versed in the lore and the lie of the land, and you would do well to trust their instincts. The pace of the walk is usually brisk, but the guides are able to point out all the wildlife, including countless bird species. At night, the caravan sets up camp on a riverbank or alongside a waterhole … where wildlife tends to congregate after dark.

## A GOOD NIGHT IS HAD BY ALL

Nights are spent under a big, white mosquito net, or in one of the tents carried by the camels. Most camel treks will last at least five days and, although shorter safaris may be available, don't be tempted to take the one- or two-day option, even though it's easier on your body! Apart from the fact that it will give you a far better feel for the land and its people (a glimpse is never enough), the longer the safari, the cheaper the per-day rate. There is plenty of competition among the individual operators, but fees and costs are generally similar and, although there are always chancers, most of the larger, more established safari companies based in Kenya have sound track records and offer a variety of exciting options.

Top to bottom: Mount Kenya; climbers on Point Dutton; Mount Kenya vegetation; Point John on the Naro Moru route.

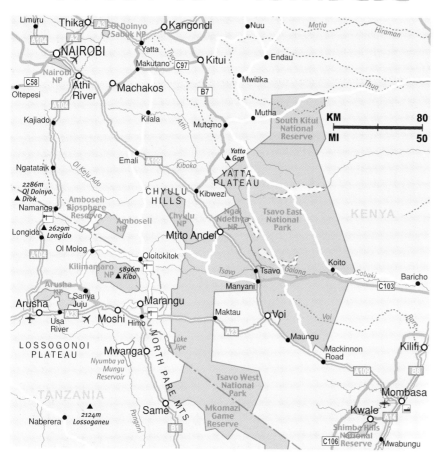

## BALLOONING OVER THE MASAI

The Masai Mara's 1,680km² (650 sq. miles) is little more than an extension of Tanzania's Serengeti. It is also the traditional homeland of the Maasai nation, but much of the land has now been given over to the wildlife that has made the Masai Mara Reserve one of the most highly regarded in the world. Thousands of visitors make their way here every year to witness first-hand the magnificence of Kenya's wildlife in what is acclaimed as the finest game viewing experience in Africa. They cross the great savanna plains on foot, on horseback, via four-wheel-drive and, most memorably, in a hot-air balloon. At the crack of dawn, travellers converge around the deflated balloon and the roaring apparatus that will fill it up. As the sun emerges, the burners are ignited and passengers board for a brief lecture on the etiquette of ballooning, which is essentially a dangerous pastime if rules aren't followed. Looking down from the morning sky, the view is breathtaking – the wilds of the bushveld are stretched out below, dotted with an astonishing number of wild animals.

## TSAVO & AMBOSELI NATIONAL PARKS

Kenya's most-visited wildlife and nature area, Amboseli National Park was reduced to almost one-tenth of its original size following conflict between the Maasai herds and the region's wildlife. Set over 392km² (151 sq. miles), Amboseli is famed for its elephant populations as well as its much-photographed views of Kilimanjaro. The drawcard for tourists is the chance to witness nature's great beasts from close range as they feed and bathe in the swamps. Tsavo West is more scenic than its eastern counterpart, and safaris in the West are a popular attraction, particularly for the famous red elephants. Tsavo is a massive park set on over 20,000km² (8,035 sq. miles), with an altitude ranging from 230m (755ft) to 2,000m (6,562ft)!

## THE MASAI'S FAUNA

Scattered across the veld are the Big Five (elephant, lion, leopard, buffalo and black rhino) as well as big-game species such as cheetah, giraffe and zebra. There are also wildebeest ranging the veld in the thousands, plus impala, hartebeest, bushbuck, waterbuck and reedbuck. Braving the wind-chill factor (even in Africa you'll feel this up in a hot-air balloon) will allow you an unparalleled view of nearly 100 mammal species, at the same time bringing you into close contact with birds that number up to 500 species – among them hawks and falcons, bustards, vultures and sunbirds. Game viewing is outstanding almost all year, but especially good in January and February. The highlight of the year is the migration of wildlife (notably wildebeest) which cross from Tanzania between December

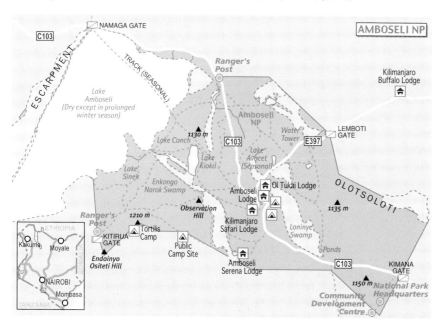

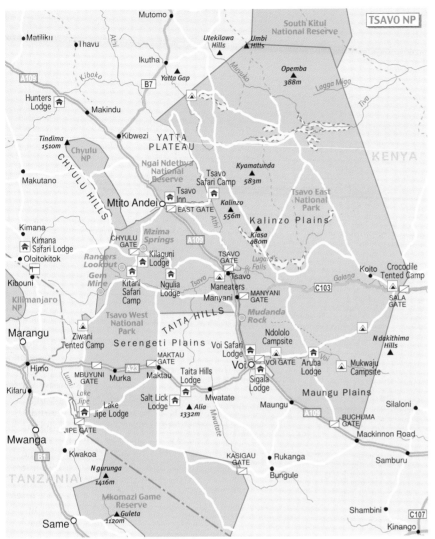

and May in search of pastures. The one-hour aerial flit across the bushveld will inevitably end with a sumptuous champagne breakfast, after which you will be driven back to the lodge on an early-morning game drive. Memorable as the balloon safari is, you should expect to pay a lot for the experience. There is no budget accommodation in the park and, if you do decide to sacrifice the luxury of an upmarket lodge or tented camp in order to rough it at the camp sites, be sure to budget for other expenses such as entry fees, guide fees, porter fees, camping fees, guard fees and firewood. The cheapest way is to tag onto an organized safari led by one of the many competitive private operators working the region.

Top to bottom: maiden of the Samburu tribe; zebra and wildebeest; elephant at Amboseli.

## MASAI MARA IN A BALLOON

Climate: Hot and dry, with heavy rains from December–April.

Risk factor: No more risk than would usually be associated with adventure sports. Nerve-wracking, but safe.

Health: Malaria is rife, except at Nairobi and on the highlands, where risk is lower. Seafood such as shellfish may be a little risky. Drink only bottled water.

Pack: For safaris, light cotton clothes, a sun hat and solid walking boots should be sufficient, but early morning balloon trips can be affected by wind chill.

Facilities: Luxury lodges and comfortable tented camps cater for an extremely upmarket tourist trade. Budget camp sites run by local Maasai (such as Musiara, Talek, Olooloo, Sekenani and Ololaimutiek) are inexpensive but basic.

# The Coast from Mombasa to Lamu

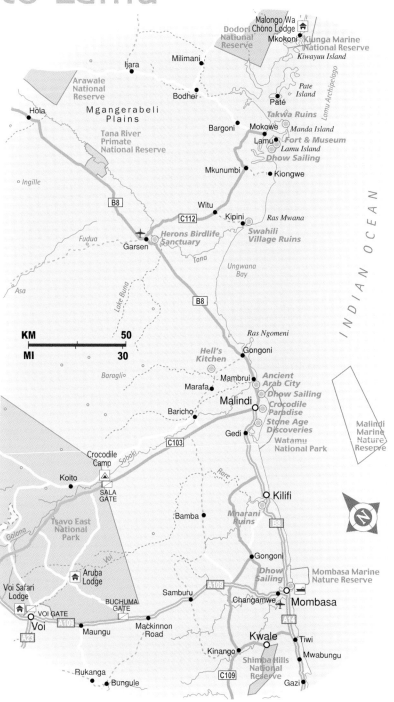

**LAMU & MANDA ISLANDS**

**MOMBASA**

## MOMBASA

A romantic port on a coral island, Mombasa has retained much of its 12,000-year charm. Like Zanzibar, it has remained virtually unchanged for about 100 years, with its floating market skirting the shores of Mombasa Island. With a population of half a million, old Mombasa has a long history of conquerors and colonists. Historic Fort Jesus guards the Old Harbour with spectacular reefs 640m (2,000ft) offshore. These reefs are lined with white, pebble-free beaches such as Tiwi and Diani, circled by dhows and schools of tropical fish, and offer excellent snorkelling and 'scuba'.

## LAMU ARCHIPELAGO

The islands of Lamu, Manda and Pate form the Lamu Archipelago, site of some of the best diving off East Africa. Lesser-known isles include Manda (best known for its Takwa Ruins covering 5 hectares, or 12 acres) and Pate Island, home to the mystical 8 hectares (20 acres) Swahili state of Shanga. Most prominent of the trio is Lamu Island, a 9th-century settlement of cobbled streets and flagstoned courtyards. The island, 19km-long (12 miles), is a mix of traditional Islam and Swahili and offers a fascinating glimpse into old Africa. The lively harbour front is the hunting ground of the island's feral cats.

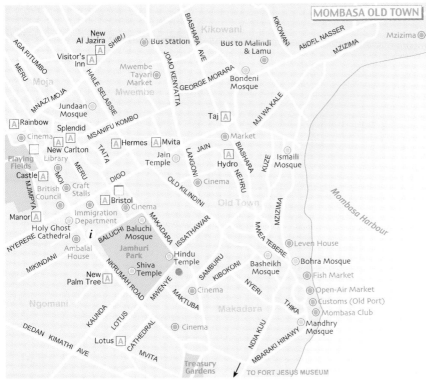

## 71

MOMBASA OLD TOWN

## DHOW SAILING IN A NUTSHELL

Climate: Conditions are usually hot and humid along the tropical coast.
Health: Dehydration can be a risk; drink only bottled water.
Pack: You will need little more than light cotton clothing, sunscreen and a sun hat, as well as some form of cover if you will be cruising at night.
Facilities: Lodges, resorts and upmarket hotels take good care of clients, but dhow taxis and small businesses offer few 'creature comforts'.

## DHOW SAILING ON THE COAST

Most of Kenya's offshore islands offer dhow day trips. The wind-powered craft offer a tempting alternative to the dusty roads of coastal villages. Whether you are taking an extended overnight journey along the Kenyan coast, an afternoon excursion into the bay, a pleasure cruise, or simply using the dhow to get from 'A to B', there will inevitably be plenty of opportunities to weigh anchor anywhere along the shore. Dhow taxis are simple affairs with no frills and they line up for trade along the docks of the main harbour towns, where others from as far afield as Arabia and India may lie at anchor. Impromptu excursions with a party of half a dozen passengers sharing the cost may result in a delay, as skippers often wait until the dhow is full. There are comfortable vessels for more leisurely trips, although these are still quite basic, with few facilities on board.

## CONDITIONS ON BOARD

If you need to sleep, you will be expected to bunk down on the floor of the boat with only the sail and the sky overhead. The only food served may be the fish caught from the dhow en route, and passengers are expected to bring their own water as well as any luxuries they require. Formal tours offer a different experience, and organized cruises usually depart twice a day with lunch and/or dinner included in the fare. Lit either by the midday sun or the silver moon, these trips are lively affairs, with hearty seafood dishes on offer and on-board entertainment in the form of a local band. En route to the islands the dhow will be approached by the many floating markets in dugout canoes that make their way from vessel to vessel, touting and bartering their wares, from brightly coloured kikois and basketware to *objets d'art* and exotic spices. Operators also offer (usually as part of their package) sumptuous meals, live music and guided tours of the historic sites at stopovers such as Mombasa's Old Town, Malindi, and the villages of Shela and Matondoni on Lamu, where builders and sailors practise the timeless skills of building and maintaining these ancient vessels using equipment dating back hundreds of years.

Opposite page: windsurfing at Lamu.
Top to bottom: Lamu's central market; catch of the day; children at the Da Gama monument.

## ADVENTURING THROUGH THE GREAT LAKES REGION
### (See Contact Details 92-95)

## ON (OR IN) WATER

**RAFTING / KAYAKING / RIVERBOARDING**
River Nile, Jinja      Nile River Explorers
     Adrift

**FISHING**
Lake Victoria      GC Tours
Queen Elizabeth & Murchison Falls NP      Uganda Wildlife Authority

**SAILING**
Lake Victoria      Wild Frontiers

**BOATING**
Queen Elizabeth NP      ww.uwa.or.ug/queen.html
Murchison Falls NP      ww.uwa.or.ug/Murchison.html

**SAILING / BOATING**
Lake Kivu, Gisenyi      Kivu Sun hotel

**10 GREAT ADVENTURES**
1. Whitewater rafting
2. Mountaineering
3. Bungee jumping
4. Sailing
5. Gorilla tracking
6. Game viewing
7. Canoeing
8. Fishing
9. Hiking
10. Birding

## IN THE AIR

**BUNGEE JUMPING**
Jinja      Adrift

**SCENIC FLIGHTS**
Countrywide      Aero Club
     Wild Frontiers

## ON WHEELS

**MOUNTAINBIKING & QUADBIKING**
Jinja      Nile River Explorers
     Adrift

## ON LAND

**CLIMBING / TREKKING**
Ruwenzori Mountains      Ruwenzori Mountaineering Services
     Wild Frontiers
     Guided Ascents in Africa
Mount Elgon, Lake Mburo NP & Kibale Forest      Uganda Wildlife Authority
     Wild Frontiers

**GORILLA TRACKING**
Mgahinga & Bwindi NP      Mgahinga Gorilla National Park
     Bwindi National Park

**GAME & CHIMPANZEE VIEWING**
Countrywide      Uganda Wildlife Authority
     Birding & Beyond Safaris

**BIRDING**
Countrywide      Birding & Beyond Safaris
     Tropical Birding
Queen Elizabeth National Park      Uganda Wildlife Authority

**GORILLA TREKKING**
Volcans NP or Nyungwe Forest      ORTPN
     Wild Frontiers

**GAMEVIEWING AND BIRDING**
Akagera NP      GBD Hospitality

**CULTURAL / GENOCIDE SITES VISITS**
Countrywide      ORTPN

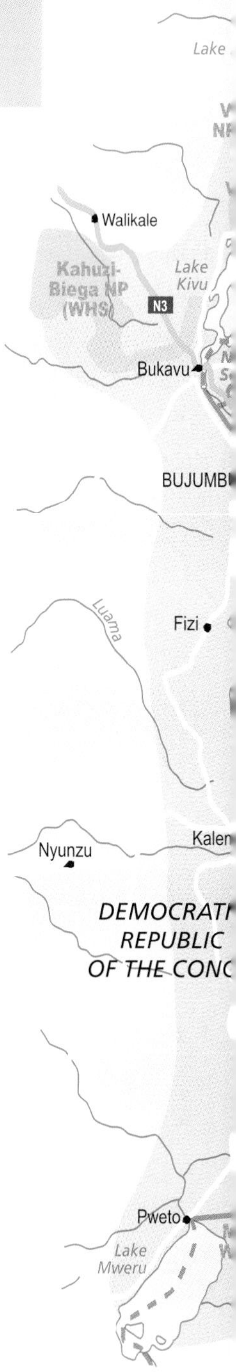

Lake

V
NP

Walikale

Kahuzi-
Biega NP
(WHS)

Lake
Kivu

N3

Bukavu

N
S

BUJUMB

Luama

Fizi

Nyunzu

Kalen

DEMOCRATI
REPUBLIC
OF THE CONG

Pweto

Lake
Mweru

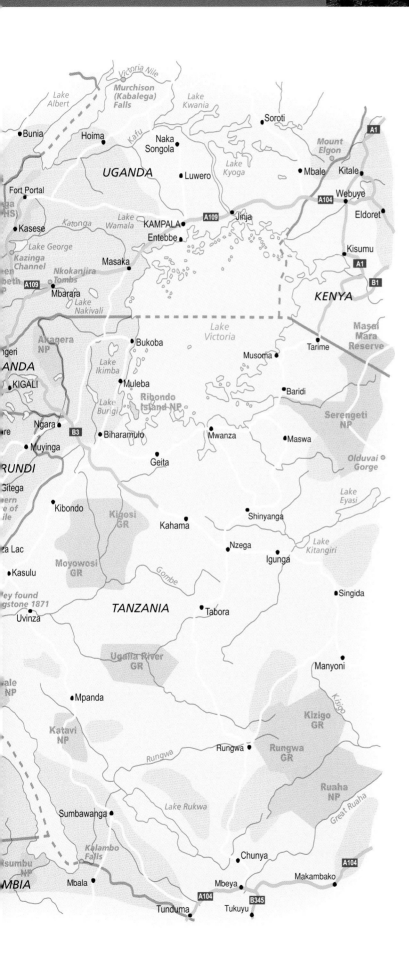

## 73

## RWANDA
Capital: Kigali
Area: 26,340km² / 10,170mi²
Population: 7.4 million
Main ethnic groups:
• Hutu (90%)
• Tutsi (9%)
• Twa pygmy (1%)
Main languages:
• Kinyarwnada
• French
• Kiswahili
Main religions:
• Catholic (65%)
• Traditional beliefs (25%)
• Protestant (7%)
Currency: Rwandan franc (100 centimes)

## BURUNDI
Capital: Bujumbura
Area: 27,830km² / 10,745mi²
Population: 6.7 million
Main ethnic groups:
• Hutu (85%)
• Tutsi (13%)
• Twa pygmy (1%)
Main languages:
• Kirundi
• French
• Swahili
Main religions:
• Catholic (62%)
• Traditional beliefs (32%)
• Protestant (6%)
Currency: Burundi franc (100 centimes)

## UGANDA
Capital: Kampala
Area: 236,036km² / 91,134mi²
Population: 24.7 million
Main ethnic groups:
• Buganda (18%)
• Banyoro (14%)
• Teso (9%)
Main languages:
• English
• Luganda
• Nkole
• Chiga
• Lango
• Acholi
• Teso
Main religions:
• Roman Catholic / Protestant (66%)
• Traditional beliefs (18%)
• Muslim (16%)
Currency: Ugandan shilling (100 cents)

# Lake Victoria

## AFRICA'S AMAZING LAKES
• Africa's largest lake is Lake Victoria, which is also the second-largest freshwater lake in the world. Victoria covers almost 70,000km² (26,830 sq. miles) and sits proudly 1,130m (3,720ft) above sea level. Its deepest known spot lies at a depth of around 82m (270ft).
• The continent's deepest is Lake Tanganyika, stretching down 1,436m (4,710 ft), the world's second-deepest freshwater lake after Lake Baikal in Russia.
• With over 500 species, Lake Malawi boasts the largest number of fish species in the world.

## LAKE VICTORIA
The papyrus-fringed shores and intermittent swamps along Lake Victoria have contributed considerably to its image as one of the most striking in all of Africa. The largest of the continent's great lakes, Lake Victoria is a vast, gentle and tranquil body of water that borders Kenya, Tanzania and Uganda, and is a relatively short distance from Rwanda and Burundi. It is into this great lake that the beginning of the mighty Nile empties, and then leaves again at Jinja as the Victoria Nile.

Together with the Victoria Nile, Lake Victoria is at the heart of some of the best-watered lands on the African continent and is home to an endless variety of wildlife, such as the black-and-white pied kingfishers (at home in the many shoreline bird sanctuaries), and the common Nile perch (which was introduced into the lake). Locals harvest the waters by casting fishing nets from small hand-crafted rowboats to eke out a living: Lake Victoria is a place for the people of Uganda, offering little evidence of the tourist market.

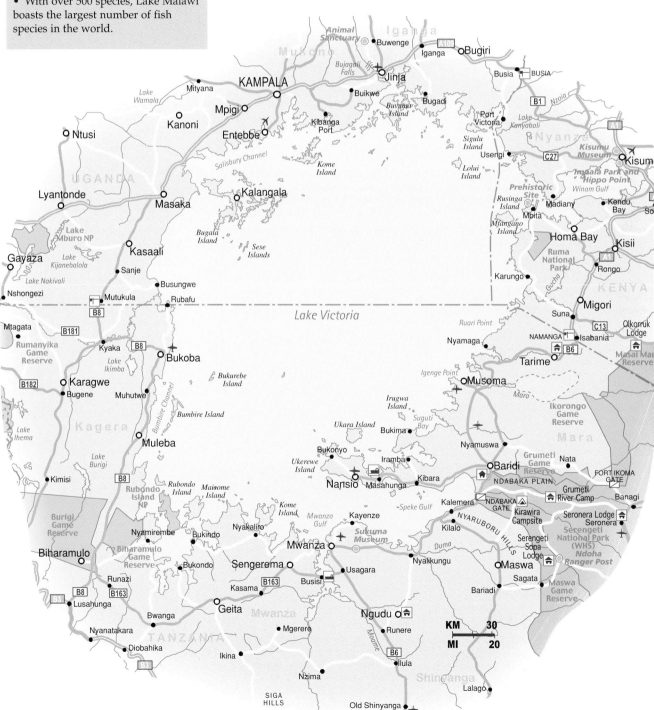

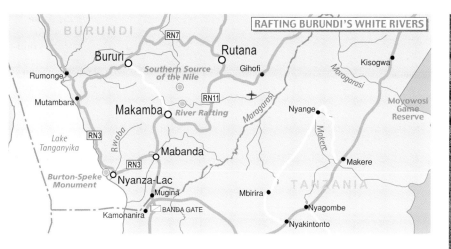

## 74

**RAFTING BURUNDI'S WHITE RIVERS**

## BURUNDI'S WHITE RIVERS

River-rafting in Central Africa (with its abundance of water sources and undulating terrain) is one of the great whitewater experiences. Despite the enormous power of many of the rivers, the section of the Nile that makes its way across the Burundi landscape is far from impressive and, although it does offer at least some opportunity for leisurely exploration, it is not the waters of the Nile that provide thrilling whitewater rafting. Burundi's claim to fame is the Luvironza River in the far south of the country. The lay of the land here is rugged and bumpy, yet it is delightfully green in places and surprisingly hospitable to the traveller, especially given the isolated location. Few operators have established themselves in the region and many of the waterways are largely uncharted, making for some invigorating (but potentially hazardous) rafting that demands careful planning and nerves of steel. While some sections may be misleadingly gentle in appearance, others are clearly the playgrounds of only the most skilled, with one potentially disastrous series of rapids after another, accompanied by masses of frothing water.

## KAMPALA

Despite the crumbling walls of the ghetto areas, what was once considered the Pearl of Africa is re-emerging as one of the gems in Africa's crown. Located on the undulating landscape so typical of Central Africa, the seven hills on which Kampala stands are lush and fertile, and the city is becoming a burgeoning modern centre, with an impressive National Museum and enthralling Kasubi Tombs. The city is peopled with an eclectic mix of colourful characters, a parade of lively vendors and an avian population of marabou storks who consistently alight on every conceivable vantage point.

Top to bottom: Nkusi Falls on Lake Albert; Nile monitor eating a crab; Bismarck's Rock, Lake Victoria.

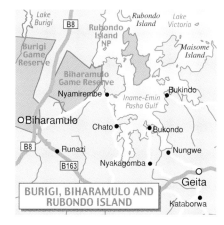

**BURIGI, BIHARAMULO AND RUBONDO ISLAND**

## AFRICA'S GREAT LAKES

| Lake Victoria | Tanzania / Uganda | 26,350 m² | 86,454 ft² |
|---|---|---|---|
| Lake Tanganyika | Tanzania / Burundi / DRC | 13,550 m² | 44,458 ft² |
| Lake Tsad | Chad / Nigeria | 10,430 m² | 34,221 ft² |
| Lake Nyasa | Malawi / Mozambique | 10,230 m² | 33,565 ft² |
| Lake Rudolf | Kenya | 3,960 m² | 12,993 ft² |
| Lake Albert | Uganda / DRC | 1,740 m² | 5,709 ft² |
| Lake Edward | Uganda / DRC | 1,505 m² | 4,938 ft² |

# The Lake Region

## KIGALI

Standing high on a ridge, Kigali lies in the centre of a country surrounded by other nations that have also seen devastating conflict in recent times. With a relatively small citizenship (250,000 – 'serviced' by only 1,000 television sets!) the capital remains the nation's most important cultural, economic and academic centre. Although many of the buildings in the urban hub still bear the scars of the war, there has been a very real attempt to resurrect the beauty of the old city, and a number of small but pretty parks have been established to help enhance the face of Kigali.

## LAKE KIVU

Lake Kivu is a grand body of water covering an impressive 2,698km² (1,042 sq. miles) and plunging to depths of 475m (1,558ft). The lake is navigated by small vessels and shallow barges, and many play a role in the tea and cotton processing industries around Kamembe. The lake shore is equally spectacular and to the south lies the Nyungwe Forest. The surrounds are dotted with Rwanda's natural gems, including the 100m (330ft) Les Chutes (falls) de Ndaba, the waterfalls on the Rusizi River, Nyakabuye's hot springs, and the wildlife of Rugege Forest, with chimpanzee, leopard and even elephant. The shores are studded with a host of pretty towns, from Cyangugu on Kivu's southernmost shore to Gisenyi in the north. Gisenyi is noted for the 3,407m (11,180ft) peaks of Nyiragongo.

## WONDERFUL WATERWAYS

Although the attractions of Volcans National Park in the far north and the Nyungwe Forest in the south remain the most popular, it is the rivers and streams that lead to and from Lake Kivu in the far west, Lake Bulera in the north and Lake Muhazi in the east that provide some of the finest adventure thrills. Only a small section of the mighty Nile falls within the boundaries of Rwanda, and the most eagerly anticipated water rides might be found beyond the country's borders in Uganda on the portion of the Nile known as the Victoria Nile

### GREAT LAKES OF THE REGION
The Great Lakes are:
Lake Malawi (aka Lake Nyasa)
Lake Tanganyika
Lake Victoria
Lake Albert (aka Lake Mobutu Sese Seko)
Lake Edward
Lake Kivu

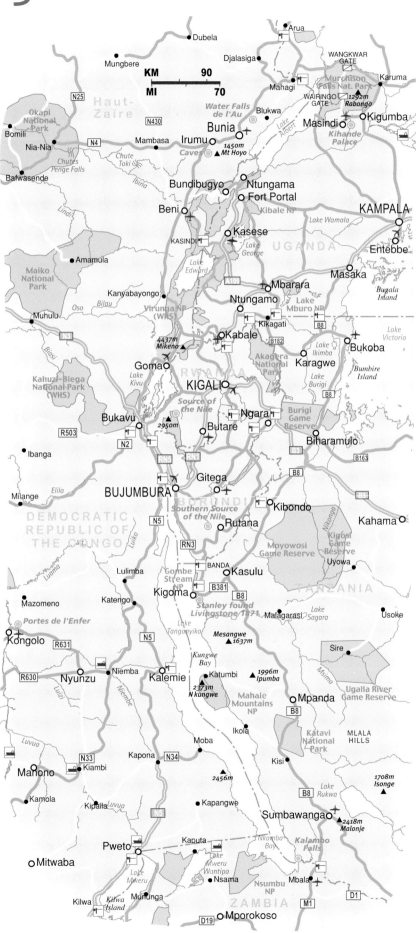

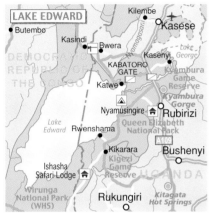

along the river course such as dams is inevitable. Much of the region's landscape comprises undulating mountains and hills, so the land is generally terraced (both naturally and to accommodate plantations), creating a succession of rapids and waterfalls, ranging from a mere step in the river's course to towering (and unrideable) falls. The region's water-based activities tend to focus largely on its lakes, but there are some breathtaking falls on the Rusizi River, and many adventurers establish some sort of base at Kibuye (known for the quality and diversity of its watersport pursuits) on the banks of Lake Kivu.

around Lake Victoria and Lake Mobutu (aka Lake Albert). The Rwandan section has its fair share of thrills and spills – certain sections are relatively gentle in comparison to those in Uganda, while others are hair-raising, with a number of obstacles to be negotiated with considerable skill and perfect timing. Some parts are downright dangerous, and if white-water rafters successfully conquer the steep rapids and avoid the literally thousands of crocodiles lurking on the riverbed or on its banks, a number of sections will demand that you simply get out and walk – portaging some rapids and man-made interruptions

Top to bottom: local girl of the Lake Kivu region; Lake Tanganyika; vendors on Lake Tanganyika.

# National Parks

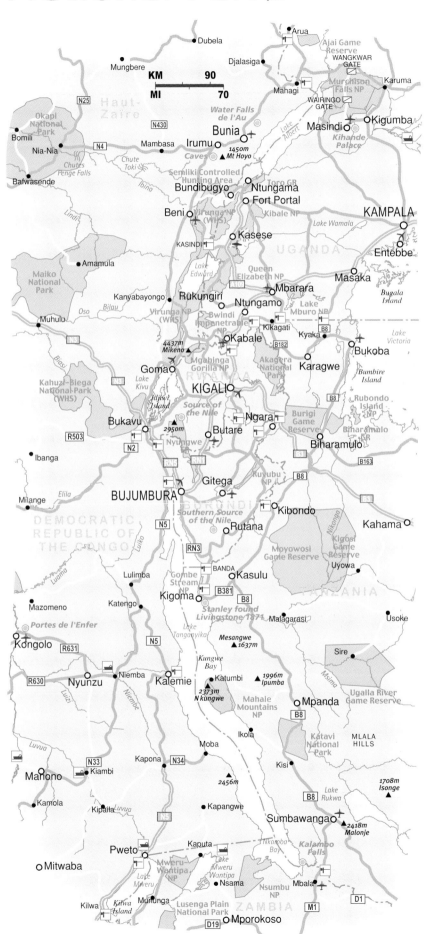

**MURCHISON FALLS NP**

**NYUNGWE FOREST RESERVE**

## MURCHISON FALLS

One of Uganda's greatest icons, the Murchison Falls (or Kabalega Falls) on the Victoria Nile River lie at the heart of 3,900km² (1,500 sq. miles) of natural splendour, neatly divided by the waters of the Victoria Nile as it snakes its way from Lake Kyoga to Lake Albert. The countryside comprises mostly savanna and grassland, but along the banks of the river are stands of densely packed forest, including mahogany, with acacia trees and papyrus reeds filling in the gaps. The terrain is stalked by predators such as lion and leopard, trod by those lanky African giants, the elephant and the giraffe, and grazed by bushbuck and waterbuck, while crocodiles and hippos wallow in the river waters. Waders and other waterfowl are common and it is not unusual to spot shoebills, African skimmers, red-throated bee-eaters, herons and kingfishers among the more than 380 bird species to be found in the national park. The most enduring asset of the park is the spectacular falls, which tumble about 43m (140ft). Even more remarkable is the enormous force of the water of the usually 50m-wide (165ft) Nile as it is thrust through a mere 7m (23ft) gap between the rocks that form the Rift Valley escarpment. A three-hour boat trip from Paraa takes enthralled visitors right up to the foot of the falls. As a diversion, try to catch the restored – yet humble – vessel that carried Katharine Hepburn and Humphrey Bogart to the heights of stardom in the timeless movie *African Queen*. The original vessel was unearthed from the banks of the Victoria Nile during the reclamation of the park and continues to ply the waters of the river.

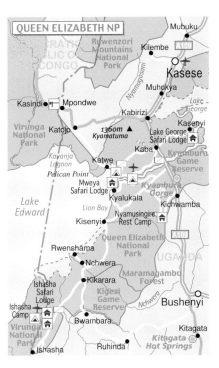

## NYUNGWE IN A NUTSHELL
Climate: Hot and humid year-round. The best (but most uncomfortable) times are in the rains, March–May.
Risk factor: Parts of the country are still considered a security risk and land mines may still be found.
Health: AIDS and malaria are rampant. Tap water is not safe, bilharzia is a problem in slow-moving waters.
Pack: Take all the equipment and gear you need for walks and hikes.
Facilities: Good accommodation is expensive, and few tour operators cater for budget travellers. Forest camps offer simply the basics.

## HIKING THE NYUNGWE RAINFOREST
Nyungwe is a haven for a huge diversity of flora and fauna, from brilliant insects (notably butterflies) to nearly 300 bird species, 50 mammal species and a number of tree varieties. Although the nearly 1,000km² (390 sq. mile) area has not been declared a national park, it remains one of the largest protected rainforests of its kind in Africa. The Nyungwe Forest Conservation Project is already nearly two decades old and, although parts of the forest are still threatened, steady progress is being made. Butare and Cyangugu are fast becoming departure points for hikes, trails and gorilla treks, but offer little beyond basic requirements. Some tours into the forests (such as the one starting from the forest station at Uwinka), take only an hour or two, departing three times a day and covering only the periphery, while others – such as that to the marshes of Kamiranzovu to see the forest elephants – are longer, taking you into the deepest sections. Other guided tours may cover anything from 10km (6 miles) to 25km (15 miles). There are also half a dozen self-guided trails that range in difficulty from a hassle-free stroll to negotiating 10km (6 miles) of forest tracks. The most prominent hiking trails require two or three hours of relatively tiring walking, but there are no steep climbs and few obstacles. Most established routes wind their way through hardwoods and skirt occasional waterfalls, but some may lead through damp swampland – so once you reach the end there may be some cleaning up to do! The rest will, however, be well deserved.

Top to bottom: Murchison Falls National Park; hippos in the Nile below the Murchison Falls; giant eagle owl in the Queen Elizabeth National Park.

## ADVENTURING THROUGH THE INDIAN OCEAN ISLANDS
### (See Contact Details 92-95)

### ON LAND

**MOUNTAINEERING**
| | |
|---|---|
| Mauritius | Vertical World |
| Réunion | Maison de la Montagne de la Réunion |
| | Alpanes |
| | Aquaventure |

**HIKING**
| | |
|---|---|
| Madagascar | Isalo, Ankaran and Antringitra NP |
| | Animaltracks Islandventures |
| Mauritius | Black River Gorges National Park |
| Réunion | GR1 & GR2 |
| | hikes in the cirques de Mafate, Salazie and Cilaos |
| | Department of Nature Central Reservations |
| | Cilaos Aventure |
| Seychelles | Morne Seychellois National Park |

**CANYONING**
| | |
|---|---|
| | Ducrot Daniel |
| | Réunion Sensations |
| | Austral Aventure |

**BIRDING**
| | |
|---|---|
| Mauritius | Casela Bird Park |

**GAME VIEWING AND LEMUR TRACKING**
| | |
|---|---|
| Madagascar | Animaltracks Islandventures |

**HORSERIDING**
| | |
|---|---|
| Réunion | Equi Montagne |

### ON WHEELS

**MOUNTAINBIKING**
| | |
|---|---|
| Mauritius | Yemaya Adventures |
| Réunion | Ducrot Daniel |
| | Austral Aventure |

**4X4 TRAILS**
| | |
|---|---|
| Madagascar | Animaltracks Islandventures |
| Mauritius | Espace Aventure |
| Réunion | Kreolie 4x4 |

**10 GREAT ADVENTURES**
1. Sea kayaking
2. Scuba diving
3. Hiking
4. Canyoning (*kloofing*)
5. Deep-sea fishing
6. Kite surfing
7. Snorkelling with whale sharks
8. Mountainbiking
9. Paragliding
10. Sailing

### IN THE AIR

**PARAGLIDING & HANG-GLIDING**
| | |
|---|---|
| Réunion | Air Lagon Parapente |
| | Parapente Réunion |
| Mauritius | Mauritius Tourism |
| Réunion | Réunion Tourism |
| Seychelles | Seychelles Tourism |

## 77

Silhouette  Praslin

•VICTORIA  La Digue

Mahé

Amirantes
Islands

Agalega Islands
(MAURITIUS)

Tromelin Island
(FRANCE)

INDIAN OCEAN

PORT LOUIS  Port Mathurin

St-Dénis  Mascarene Islands  Rodrigues
Réunion  (MAURITIUS)
(FRANCE)  MAURITIUS

## ON (OR IN) WATER

**SAILING**
| | |
|---|---|
| Madagascar | Classic Sailing Adventures |
| | Island Quest Sailing and Diving |
| Mauritius | Terres Oceanes |
| Réunion | Blue Sail |
| Seychelles | Dream Yacht Seychelles |
| | Island Charters |

**SEA KAYAKING**
| | |
|---|---|
| Madagascar | Kayak Africa |
| Mauritius | www.yemayaadventures.com |

**CANOEING**
| | |
|---|---|
| Countrywide | Mad'Cameleon |

**SCUBA DIVING**
| | |
|---|---|
| Madagascar | Sakatia Passions |
| | Animaltracks Islandventures |
| | Island Quest Sailing and Diving |
| | Classic Sailing Adventures |
| Mauritius/Rodrigues | Sinbad Diving |
| | Sea Fan Diving Centre |
| | Centre De Plongée, Rodrigues |
| Réunion | Abyss Plongée |
| | Bleu Ocean |
| Seychelles | Mahé |
| | Seychelles Underwater Centre |
| | Praslin; Octopus Dive Centre |

**SUBMARINE TOURS**
| | |
|---|---|
| Mauritius | Blue Safari Submarine |

**BIG GAME FISHING**
| | |
|---|---|
| Madagascar | Sakatia Passions |
| | Animaltracks Islandventures |
| Mauritius | Professional Big Game Fishing |
| | Charter Association |
| | Morne Anglers Club |
| Réunion | Réunion Fishing Club |
| Seychelles | Island Charters |
| | Marlin Charters |

**SALTWATER FLYFISHING**
| | |
|---|---|
| Madagascar | Uncharted Safaris |

**SURFING/BODY BOARDING**
| | |
|---|---|
| Réunion | Billabong Surf School |
| | Ecole de surf et body board |
| | des roches noires |

**KITESURFING**
| | |
|---|---|
| Mauritius | Kuxville Kitesurfing |

**SNORKELLING WITH WHALE SHARKS**
| | |
|---|---|
| Seychelles | Seychelles Underwater Centre |

**WHITEWATER RAFTING AND KAYAKING**
| | |
|---|---|
| Réunion | Aquaventure |

# Madagascar

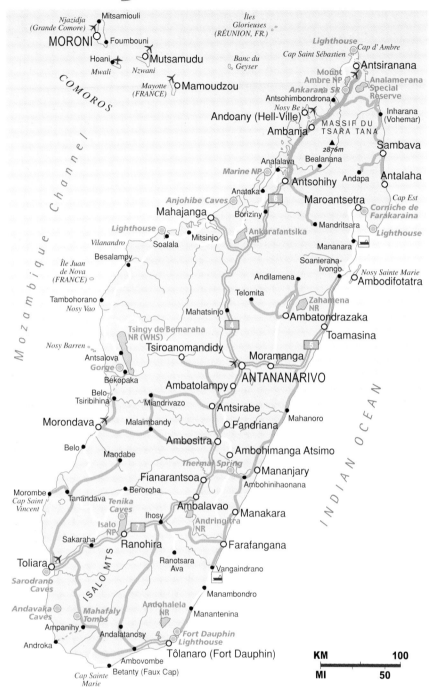

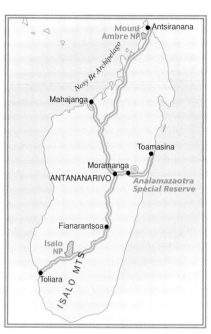

## NOSY BE ARCHIPELAGO

The heart of Madagascar's hospitality industry, the island of Nosy Be is at the centre of the archipelago off the north-west shore that takes its name. Dotted with tourist hotels and amenities, the hilly 280km$^2$ (110 sq. mile) island is easily accessible from the capital and offers open-air markets, a vibrant night-life and boat trips to neighbouring islands. Walking through the luxuriant vegetation that covers much of Nosy Be (or a visit to the fascinating rainforest stand on the Lokobe Peninsula) offers a window into Madagascar's abundant and diverse natural heritage.

## FORT DAUPHIN

Somewhat isolated by unforgiving terrain and an underdeveloped infrastructure, Fort Dauphin was the landing site of the first European travellers in the 16th century and is the centre of Madagascar's lobster industry. The scrubland and relatively high rainfall make it inhospitable to the casual tourist, although naturalists will find the reef-protected beaches a great adventure, most notably at Libanona, the rugged slopes of Pic St Louis and the protected splendour of the nearby Berenty reserve.

## MADAGASCAR'S EXTINCTIONS

The largest island on earth, Madagascar boasts an amazing faunal heritage, yet is sadly tormented by a long list of extinctions: the Dodo, Dutch pigeon, Mascarene coot, Mauritian shelduck, Rodrigues night heron, Broad-billed parrot, Rodrigues ring-necked parakeet and dark flying fox.

## ANTANANARIVO

Charmingly dishevelled in appearance, 'Tana's' cobbled roads are trod by rickety ox-drawn carts and packed with French colonial-style buildings housing anything from souvenir shops to family-owned produce stores. Quaint and laid-back, Tana is the capital of Madagascar. Many visitors are wildlife enthusiasts as it's the uniqueness of the island's indigenous flora and fauna that remains the principal attraction. Tana's zoological gardens provide fascinating insights into the island's wildlife.

## 78

**ANALAMAZAOTRA SPECIAL RESERVE**

**MOUNT AMBRE NP**

## TOURIST TREASURES

The continent-in-miniature is blessed with a unique community of plant and animal life that slowly evolved in a protected environment that was effectively isolated from the world. Perhaps most famed for its chameleons and more than 30 species of lemur, Madagascar is covered with singular habitats spread over numerous parks and conservation areas. Although a regulated tourism industry contributes enormously to conservation, it also tends to put it at risk: take great care when walking this landscape.

## ISALO MOUNTAINS

The sandstone mountains of Isalo offer a different view to the conventional image of lush Madagascar. Small patches of grassland break the rather bleak

**ISALO NP IN A NUTSHELL**
Climate: Tropical Madagascar is hot and humid throughout the year, particularly in forested regions. Sept–Dec provide the best conditions for hikers, but avoid the Jan–March rains.
Risk factor: Malaria is rife, and rabies is common among wild dogs. The water is not drinkable, and bilharzia and giardia are present. AIDS is a risk.
Pack: Comfortable but solid walking boots; lightweight (days) and warm clothing (nights), a flashlight, and waterproof gear for the rainy season.

landscape, and the occasional green belts are interspersed with strange rock configurations. Punctuated with ancient burial sites held sacred by locals, the upgraded network of roads affords access to splendid views of the high-lying landscape. The region is largely the domain of hikers, campers and wildlife enthusiasts.

## HIKING AROUND ISALO

Isalo is one of the best of Madagascar's many great hiking destinations, and is accessed via nearby Ranohira. The superb walks vary from simple one-day excursions to more extended trips. The guides (based at the hotels in Ranohira) are skilled and informed, yet other facilities are simple at best. Isalo is one of the few areas on the island that may be affected by petty crime. Compared to most other parks, animals are generally scarce here, but its Monkey Canyon trail remains popular with hikers, taking in lemur sightings and the gentle pools of l'Oasis and Piscine Naturelle, both of which have pleasant camp sites.

## OTHER HIKING AREAS

Equally untamed, Zombitse has no demarcated trails, camp sites or guides, yet offers a relatively hassle-free stroll through thick woods. The variety of mammals, birds, reptiles and amphibians is unparalleled and, with trained locals acting as guides, the experience is unmatched. Some of the best opportunities are at dusk and nightfall, when nocturnal creatures emerge to hunt and forage. These excursions are best from October to March, when the hibernating inhabitants venture out after the cooler winter months. Some have become quite accustomed to human presence, but direct contact with them is discouraged.

Top to bottom: Avenue du Baobabs; relaxing on Nosy Komba island; the white-footed sportive lemur.

# Seychelles and Mahé

## MAHÉ

The largest of the 40 islands and 75 low-lying atolls that make up the Seychelles, Mahé is home to 90 per cent of the population, the seat of the nation's capital, Victoria, and the nucleus of the vital tourism industry. Visitors are drawn to Mahé by the picturesque environs, most notably exceptional beaches such as Beau Vallon, and the unique plant and animal life. Victoria acts as a base for most excursions into the island wilderness of sea and sand. Blessed with an old-world charm, the capital has rapidly developed a sound infrastructure geared toward the hospitality industry.

## SEYCHELLES

Nearly half of Seychelles' land area has been set aside as national park or protected reserve, with some 40 per cent of its seascape declared marine conservation area. Morne Seychellois National Park, the nation's most impressive, is laced with hiking trails, while Praslin – home to Vallée de Mai, the 18 hectare (45-acre) World Heritage Site – boasts no fewer than six endemic palms, along with numerous other indigenous trees and plants. Even the smaller isles have their treasures, and a number of significant measures have been put into place to help regulate tourist traffic and preserve the balance of unique ecosystems. Despite all these laudable efforts, the Seychelles have seen their fair share of ecological disasters. Tortoise populations have dwindled to alarmingly low numbers, as have fish and bird species, with several species now either endangered or extinct – often because of the competition they face from introduced species. All four of the indigenous turtle species – green, hawksbill, loggerhead and giant leatherback – also remain at risk. At the same time, concerted efforts to protect the Aldabra giant tortoise (both Arnold's

and Marion's tortoises have long been extinct) have meant that further populations have been reintroduced on islands such as Cousin, Frégate and Curieuse. In its favour, the Aldabra Atoll has been declared a World Heritage Site and is thus administered by the Seychelles Islands Foundation, in turn sponsored by the Royal Society at the Smithsonian Institute. Tourism to the 34km-long (21-mile) atoll is extremely limited, and the relatively insignificant human population on islands such as this may account for the fact that the island-specific ecologies have been little influenced by human intervention. Where there is constant human activity on these 'paradise' islands, a number of regulations have been established to help preserve the natural heritage of the region: on no fewer than nine of the islands the sea birds may not be disturbed, while spear-fishing is forbidden throughout the island group, with fishing and the collection of seashells and corals prohibited in the marine parks. At the same time, meticulously planned reforestation schemes have been established on islands already disturbed by indiscriminate plantations.

### GREAT AFRICAN WATERSPORT SPOTS

| | |
|---|---|
| Morocco | West Coast |
| Chad | Lake Chad |
| Guinea-Bissau | Guinea-Bissau Coast |
| Togo | Lac Togo |
| Rwanda | Rwanda's waterways |
| Seychelles | Surfing the Seychelles |
| Zambia | Zambezi River |

## GRAND 'ANSE (MAHÉ) IN A NUTSHELL

**Climate:** Generally warm to hot, with some tropical humidity. Trade winds offer the best surfing conditions from April to October.

**Risk factor:** Virtually no risks, other than the occasional hungry shark and the breakneck speed of the waves.

**Health:** No vaccinations are necessary and malaria poses no threat. The combination of wind and sea can cause severe dehydration and sunburn.

**Pack:** Boardshorts and sunscreen are the most important, but also take a light beach shirt and/or sarong, as well as your own bottled water to the beach.

**Facilities:** Waves are excellent, as are all the visitors' amenities on a group of islands that depends on its tourism income. Even the remotest of beaches has comfortable facilities for tourists.

## 79

MAHÉ

L'Ilot
Machabée
Vista do Mar ▲ Mt Howard
Vista do Mar
458m
Glacis
Sunset Beach ▲
Le Northolme ▲
Carana Beach
Anse Nord-d'Est
North East Point
La Retraite

Saint Anne
Saint
Anne
Old
Whaling
Station
250m
Beacon
Island

Beau Vallon Bay
Auberge Club
des Seychelles ▲
Anse Major
Bel
Ombre
Danzil
Cap
Ternay
Baie aux
Chagrins
Mare
Anglaise
Mt Le N iol
681m
Pascal
Village
Trois
Frères
699m
Union
Vale
Pointe Conan
Victoria
Lighthouse
Market
VICTORIA
Botanical
Gardens
Cemetery
Cerf Passage
Moyenne
St Anne
Marine NP
Long Island
Cerf Island
Round Island
Nature Reserve

Port
Launay
Port
Glaud
L'Embarcadère
Port Glaud
Berjaya
Mahé Beach
Grand 'Anse
Meridien Barbarons ▲
Chateau d' Eau ▲
Port
Launay
Viewpoint
Mission
Tea Factory
and Tea Room
Old Satellite
Tracking
System
Barbarons
216m
Varigault
Cascade
Waterfall
Les Dents
555m
Aero
Club
Cap Ma Georgine
South East
Island
Pointe La Rue
Anse aux Pins
Reef
La Roussette
Anse aux Pins

Anse Polite
Anse Boileau Church
Anse Boileau
Boileau Bay
Chauve Souris
Anse Soleil Beach
Michael Adams
Art Gallery
Plantation Club
Val des Prés
Brulée ▲
501m
Mont
Plaisir
La
Residence
Baie
Lazare
Village
Crafts Village
La Plaine St André
La Marine
Model Boat Centre
Pointe au Sel
(Fairyland)
Anse Royale
Spice Garden
& Museum
Anse Royale
Bay

INDIAN OCEAN

Pointe
Lazare
Pointe
Maravi
Takamaka
Mt Lockyer
378m
Cap Lascars
Allamanda
Quatre Bornes
Collines du Sud ▲
301m
Pointe
Capucins
Pointe Golette
Lighthouse
Pointe
Cocos

KM 4
MI 2

## SURFING THE SEYCHELLES

The waters off the Seychelles are supreme for surfing, and prove most popular during the southeast trade winds. At stretches of unspoiled coastline such as those at Beau Vallon and particularly Grand 'Anse, the wind and waves should be enough to get any surfer pumped. You won't need technical support crews critical in other adrenaline sports; all you need is the wind and the waves. Despite the increasing number of visitors, there are no desperate attempts to find a lift on a wave. Boards most typically seen plying these waters rely on function more than on fashion, and many locals have resigned themselves to the fact that any board is better than none at all. You still see the big, rather ungainly boards that helped pioneer the sport, but the smaller boards (which rely less on volume and more on control and skill) are increasingly common companions to beach users, as they are far easier to carry to and from the beach!

## WATCH OUT FOR SHARKS

Although waters vary from gentle to nerve-wracking (there may be precarious undercurrents off Grand 'Anse), dangers are few. Sharks are virtually impossible to avoid, however; it is in your best interest to steer clear of murky waters during their feeding times. MAKE A NOTE: sharks feed around early morning and evening, so keep that in mind if you do not want to end up as potential shark bait! Given the often neck-breaking speeds reached on these waves, it is best not to take chances in even the least intimidating waves. Generally, if you are surfing in the right places and with the right people who know what they're doing, then these waters are perfectly safe, and you should be able to prevent those injuries that tend to end careers – and lives.

Top to bottom: a typical stretch of white beach;
coco de mer forest; sea turtle.

# Seychelles and Praslin

## SEYCHELLES SUB-WONDERLAND

The reefs off Seychelles teem with fish of every colour and size, and the islands – from the corals and coves that circle Praslin to tiny Dénis, for example – offer opportunities to dive and snorkel among a dazzling diversity of marine life and geological structures. Every one of the islands seems to be entirely different to the next, making for some spectacular diving. The creatures that make the Seychelles such a memorable scuba destination are a diversion from the coral reef's profusion of colour and texture. The fish are entirely familiar with onlookers and pay little attention to divers, allowing easy contact between man and fish. Unfortunately, bleaching has discoloured corals in some areas. In places, powerful sea currents have been known to stir up murky waters … this creates the ideal home for reclusive nurse sharks and feathertail stingrays sheltering in niches, crevices and caves.

| GREAT AFRICAN DIVE SPOTS | |
|---|---|
| Egypt | The Red Sea |
| Sudan | Sudanese coast |
| Eritrea | Dahlek Archipelago |
| Mozambique | Bazaruto Archipelago |
| Tanzania | Zanzibar coastline |
| Mauritius | Mauritius coastline |
| Seychelles | Seychelles coastline |

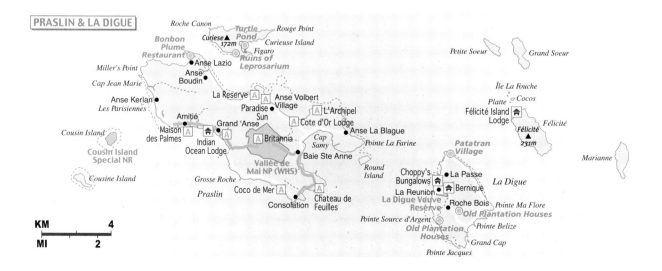

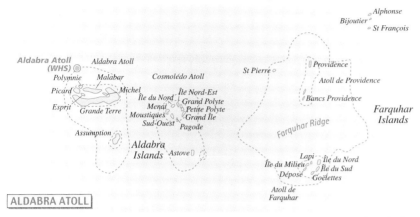

## 80

**ALDABRA ATOLL**

**AMIRANTES & ALPHONSE ISLANDS**

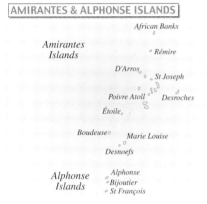

African Banks

*Amirantes Islands*

Rémire

D'Arros

St Joseph

Poivre Atoll    Desroches

Étoile

Boudeuse    Marie Louise

Desnoefs

*Alphonse Islands*    Alphonse
Bijoutier
St François

## SCUBA OFF THE SEYCHELLES

On Aldabra, the world's largest raised coral atoll, schools of black-tipped reef sharks hunt the shallows of the lagoon for small fish, while anemones litter the sea bed, and little angelfish dash in and out of the crevices as the tides recede. In the deeper waters, schools of triggerfish and parrotfish feed placidly as scuba divers skirt the reefs, drifting over some of the most colourful expanses ever to be experienced in the Indian Ocean. The trick here is to take your time as you make your way across the undulating seascape, watching for skittish marine creatures and dodging currents so strong that they can suck you in toward the mouths of small caves that punctuate the rock face.

## SECRETS OF THE DEEP

Off Astove, one of the four islands in the Aldabra group, the steep inclines of the Astove Wall stretch some 5km (3 miles), dropping abruptly to awesome depths to a dark and forbidding realm of rough terrain. The wall itself is pleasantly unblemished by human interference, and this silent world is the home of silver-tipped and hammerhead sharks.

*Top to bottom: yacht moored off Anse Lazio, Praslin; coral reef, Brisarre Rock; a local man preparing a fresh seafood meal.*

Most of the more prominent hotels that dot the islands will provide scuba instruction and are well connected to private operators based here. Even the smaller islands, such as Dénis, boast good diving schools with highly qualified dive masters and reliable equipment. There's no excuse for not enjoying the natural diving facilities!

## ALDABRA ATOLL

Aldabra is the most removed atoll, situated 1,200km (750 miles) from the frenetic activity of Mahé and the capital. This small collection of 14 islets is best accessed via a three-hour boat trip from the nearest airstrip on Assumption. The large coral lagoon and the immediate environs of mangrove are a sanctuary for flora and fauna, including pemphis scrub and giant land tortoises. The crystal waters and well-preserved corals around the 100km (62-mile) coast of Aldabra's islands are a much admired haven for water adventurers, who consider the atoll to be the most pristine in all Seychelles.

## SEYCHELLES IN A NUTSHELL

**Climate:** Weather is pleasantly hot all year, with sea temperatures seldom less than 18°C (64°F); Nov-Feb is humid, with heavy monsoon rains occasionally affecting water clarity. Diving is good year-round, but is definitely best in October.
**Risk factor:** The only risk is of individual inexperience! Minimal dangers from marine life, but brush up on the threat of stone fish and the like.
**Pack:** Swimwear and beach clothing should be enough, but pack your own scuba gear to avoid high hiring costs.
**Facilities:** Scuba facilities are of a high standard and are available through the main hotels and specialist operators. Dive schools cater for novices as well as advanced dives for certified divers (remember to take proof).

# Réunion, Comoros and Rodrigues

**MORONI**

Capital of the Comoros, Moroni can be found on the island of Grande Comore, the most prominent of the three main volcanic islands that are surrounded by a number of picturesque coral atolls. These atolls are best known for the fantastic diving opportunities offered by their unusual geological formations. Moroni is scenically beautiful, as are the surrounding islands – heavily wooded and cultivated with aromatic crops such as cloves and vanilla, which perfume Comoros. Although tourism is a burgeoning industry – as well as a vital earner of foreign exchange – most of the 25,000 impoverished citizens of Moroni are in some way involved with the farming of cash crops. The capital is rustic in appearance and there is little

urban lifestyle, yet it is lively and colourful. Moroni's primary attractions make it a true 'island paradise', with magnificent scenery and an unspoiled island wilderness.

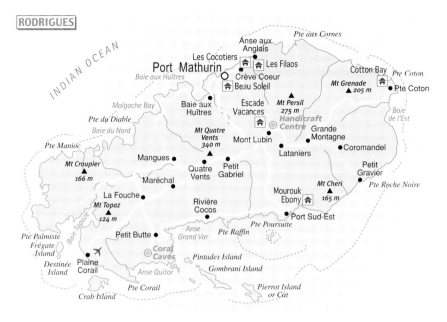

## 81

RODRIGUES

## RÉUNION BY AIR

This tiny island is surprisingly sophisticated in its infrastructure, and the knowledge and skill of the few adventure spe-
cialists based on Réunion has resulted in
a plethora of top-flight outdoor pursuits.
Yet, the most memorable is what you see
from the air: gloriously rugged mountain faces cracking through the highlands, dormant or extinct volcanoes
brooding alongside massive amphitheatres, and cirques carved into the
magnificent landscape. The land is pinpointed by the 3,069m (10,069ft) peak of
Piton des Neiges, highest in the Indian
Ocean, and the 2,632m (8,635ft) Piton de
la Fournaise, one of the world's most
active volcanoes. The hardy interior of
plains and gorges is crowned by cirques
and mountains, and Réunion's natural
heritage is that much more fascinating
from an adrenaline-pumping helicopter
flip which takes in the magical beauty
from a bird's-eye view. Virtually all the
natural arenas and other out-of-the-way
spots sprinkled across the land are inaccessible by vehicle, and may only be
reached on foot – often arduous and
time-consuming. Helicopters and other
aircraft excursions take off at St Gilles
les Bains. The skill (and daring!) of your
pilot will take your breath away as you

flit across this remote part of the Indian
Ocean, accompanied by the pilot's running commentary: skimming the waters,
flipping across vast amphitheatres, diving from dizzying heights, or gently
drifting on the sea breeze. Light aircrafts
in particular can cruise at low speeds.
The flip across the entire island lasts less
than an hour, but takes in everything
there is to see: waterfalls and rivers,
cirques and mountains, beaches and sea,
the gorges of Maïdo as well as the
craters of the Plaine des Sables. You can
even lunch in the heart of the great
Mafate Cirque.

## ST-DÉNIS

Located on the scenic north coast of the
island, Réunion's capital is most admired for its mountain and volatile volcano,
yet boasts picturesque beaches and is a
lively centre of social activity. The Indian
Ocean's highest mountain is Piton des
Neiges (3,069m / 10,068ft) separating
St-Dénis from the urban hub of south-
coast St-Pierre. A trendy resort town
bordering foothills of rugged hinterland
and skirted by cultivated lands of grape-
vines and crops, St-Dénis' varied climate
lends itself to a diverse landscape, from
tropical lushness to more temperate
vegetation. Most travellers visit the three
cirques, the natural amphitheatres that
form the island's heart.

### ST GILLES LES BAINS IN A NUTSHELL

Climate: Balmy to hot with seasonal
rains and warm sea temperatures.
Best time to visit: May to October.
Risk factor: Buckle up and avoid the
cyclone season (January to March).
Pack: Light summer clothing; some
rain gear if travelling in the warm wet
period (November to April).

Opposite page: bread for sale, Moroni market.
Top to bottom: Réunion's rocky coast; Moroni
city; waterfall in Langevin River Valley.

# Mauritius

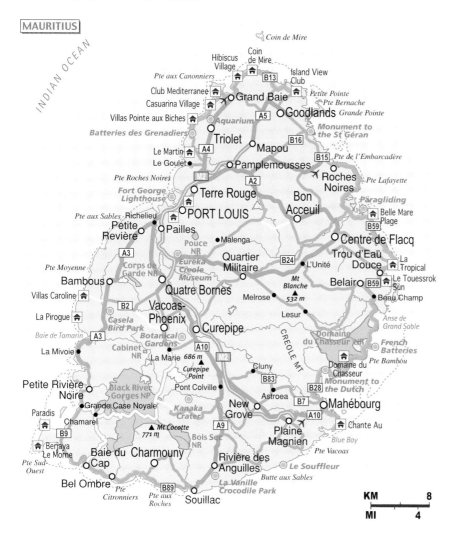

MAURITIUS

INDIAN OCEAN

Coin de Mire

Pte aux Canonniers
Hibiscus Village
Coin de Mire
B13
Island View Club
Club Mediterranee
Grand Baie
Petite Pointe
Pte Bernache
Grande Pointe
Casuarina Village
Goodlands
Villas Pointe aux Biches
A5
Monument to the St Géran
Aquarium
Batteries des Grenadiers
Triolet
B16
Le Martin
A4
Mapou
Pte de l'Embarcadère
Le Goulet
Pamplemousses
B15
Pte Roches Noires
A2
Roches Noires
Pte Lafayette
Fort George Lighthouse
M2
Terre Rouge
Bon Acceuil
Paragliding
Pte aux Sables
Richelieu
PORT LOUIS
Belle Mare Plage
B59
Petite Revière
Pailles
Malenga
Centre de Flacq
A3
Pouce NR
Quartier Militaire
B24
Trou d'Eau Douce
La Tropical
Pte Moyenne
Corps de Garde NR
Eureka Creole Museum
L'Unité
Le Touessrok
Bambous
Quatre Bornes
Mt Blanche 532 m
Belair
B59
Sun
Villas Caroline
B2
Melrose
Beau Champ
La Pirogue
Vacoas-Phoenix
Lesur
Anse de Grand Sable
Casela Bird Park
Botanical Gardens
Curepipe
CREOLE MT
Domaine du Chasseur NR
French Batteries
Baie de Tamarin
A3
Cabinet NR
A10
Pte Bambou
La Mivoie
La Marie 686 m
M2
Cluny
Domaine du Chasseur
Curepipe Point
B83
Monument to the Dutch
Petite Rivière Noire
Black River Gorges NP
Pont Colville
Astroea
B28
B7
Mahébourg
Paradis
Grande Case Noyale
Kanaka Crater
New Grove
A10
Chamarel
Mt Cocotte 771 m
A9
Chante Au
B9
Bois Sec NR
Plaine Magnien
Blue Bay
Benjaya
Le Morne
Baie du Cap
Charmouny
Rivière des Anguilles
Pte Vacoas
Pte Sud-Ouest
Le Souffleur
Bel Ombre
Pte Citronniers
B89
Pte aux Roches
Souillac
La Vanille Crocodile Park
Butte aux Sables

KM 8
MI 4

## PORT LOUIS

As the heart of idyllic Mauritius, Port Louis is an amalgamation of old and new, wild and sedate. Encircled by the craggy volcanic peaks of the Moka Mountains and overlooked by the 19th-century ramparts of La Citadelle, the few remaining clearings and gardens are lined with banyan trees and old colonial buildings, legacy of Victoria's empire. The city has retained a village atmosphere, yet the increasingly modern skyline is dotted with ever-popular fast-food and souvenir shops. Caudan Waterfront is a thoroughly contemporary and impressive tourist hotspot.

## TAMARIND FALLS

The hot and dry Sunset Coast is pummelled on occasion by tropical storms and lashed by waves that lure surfers of all abilities. Inland lie the decidedly more tranquil environs of Mare aux Vacoas, a mountain lake encircled by forests of pine and palm, green woods and tea plantations, with stunning views of the Black River Gorges. The sometimes demanding forest trails are the domain of deer and monkey, and many visitors hike to the spectacular 295m (968ft) Tamarind Falls, the island's biggest and most impressive waterfall.

## LE MORNE PENINSULA

A former haven for runaway slaves, the scenic peninsula is widely considered the last remaining outpost of African-Creole culture. The rocky landscape, pinpointed by the 556m (1,824ft) Le Morne Brabant, offers spectacular views of the 14km (9-mile) coast and is a popular tourist drawcard.

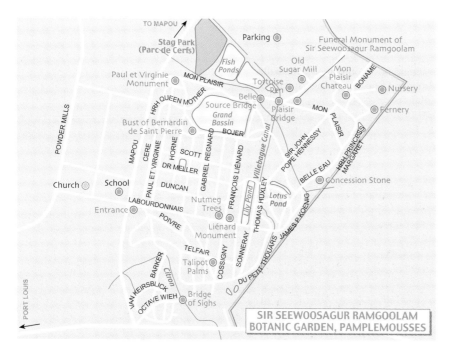

TO MAPOU

Stag Park (Parc de Cerfs)
Parking
Funeral Monument of Sir Seewoosagur Ramgoolam
Fish Ponds
Old Sugar Mill
Mon Plaisir Chateau
BONAME
Paul et Virginie Monument
MON PLAISIR
Tortoise Pen
Nursery
HRH QUEEN MOTHER
Belle
Plaisir Bridge
MON PLAISIR
Fernery
Source Bridge
Bust of Bernardin de Saint Pierre
Grand Bassin
BOJER
POWDER MILLS
MAPOU
CERE
HORNE
SCOTT
GABRIEL REGNARD
FRANÇOIS LIÉNARD
Tilly Pond
Villebague Canal
SIR JOHN POPE HENNESSY
BELLE EAU
HRH PRINCESS MARGARET
PAUL ET VIRGINIE
DR MELLER
DUNCAN
Concession Stone
Church
School
LABOURDONNAIS
Nutmeg Trees
THOMAS HUXLEY
Lotus Pond
Entrance
POIVRE
Liénard Monument
TELFAIR
COSSIGNY
SONNERAY
DU PETIT THOUARS
JAMES P. KOENIG
Talipot Palms
VAN KEIRSBLICK
Clifton
BARKER
OCTAVE WIEH
Bridge of Sighs
PORT LOUIS

SIR SEEWOOSAGUR RAMGOOLAM BOTANIC GARDEN, PAMPLEMOUSSES

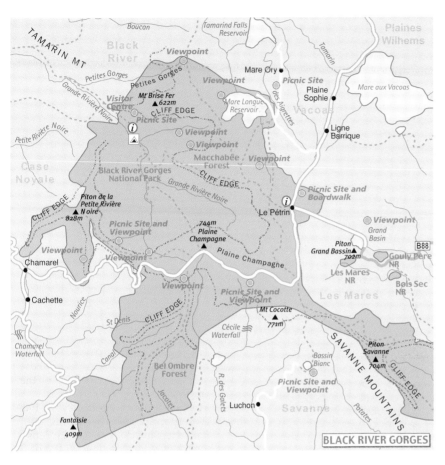

## 82

BLACK RIVER GORGES

## BIG GAME FISHING IN MAURITIUS

The waters off Mauritius are home to an endless stream of sailfish, tuna, kingfish, barracuda and marlin, most of which are caught in huge numbers. The deep-sea fishing here is some of the best in the world, and the season extends throughout the year. La Pirogue hosts the annual 555 Big Game Fishing World Cup, and many world records have been set in waters less than a kilometre (half a mile) off the west coast.

## DIVING OFF MAURITIUS

Mauritius provides a varied diving experience off the African coast: wreck dives, shelf dives, night dives as well as diving excursions to nearby island dive sites. The seabed and even wrecks are covered with sponges and corals, and are home to fan worms, sea urchins and anemones. Visibility is best in winter, but the summer months attract the fish and marine life. Nowhere in Mauritius are spear guns permitted, and the removal of shells and corals is forbidden.

Top to bottom: aerial view of Ile Aux Cerfs; local hawker on the beach; sugar cane fields.

## MAURITIUS IN A NUTSHELL

Climate: Weather is generally good all year. The west coast fishing grounds are dry and hot, especially from Jan–March (Feb–March the wettest).
Risk factor: Big game fishing is a specialised activity that demands both expertise and strength – novices should be accompanied by a skilled angler. Deep-sea diving can be a very dangerous pastime; obey the rules of safety and etiquette – even in Mauritius' idyllic waters – and employ the services of professional dive masters.
Health: Sunburn can cause considerable discomfort.
Pack: If travelling on a deep-sea fishing trip in a private capacity, make sure you are fully prepared and well equipped, although such diving trips are not recommended. The services of a professional operator are highly recommended and they will provide all the gear you need. All diving equipment and accessories are provided by the more established dive schools and dive operators, especially for those who are not seasoned divers.

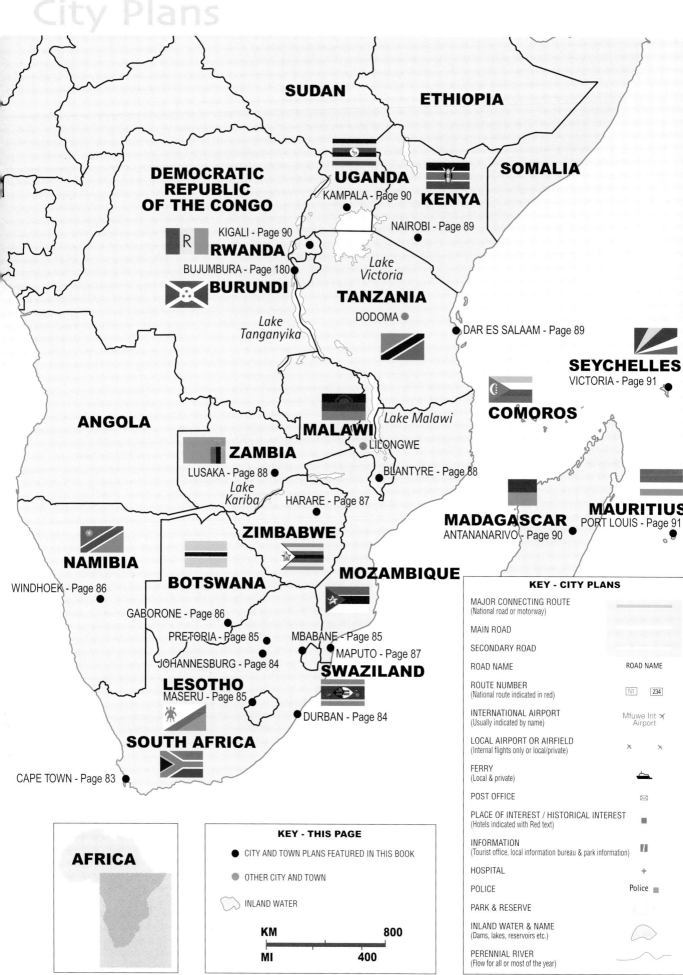

# City Plans

**SUDAN**

**ETHIOPIA**

**DEMOCRATIC REPUBLIC OF THE CONGO**

**UGANDA**
KAMPALA - Page 90

**SOMALIA**

**KENYA**
NAIROBI - Page 89

KIGALI - Page 90
**RWANDA**

BUJUMBURA - Page 180
**BURUNDI**

*Lake Victoria*

**TANZANIA**
DODOMA

*Lake Tanganyika*

DAR ES SALAAM - Page 89

**SEYCHELLES**
VICTORIA - Page 91

**ANGOLA**

*Lake Malawi*

**MALAWI**
LILONGWE

**COMOROS**

**ZAMBIA**
LUSAKA - Page 88

BLANTYRE - Page 88

**MAURITIUS**
PORT LOUIS - Page 91

*Lake Kariba*

HARARE - Page 87

**MADAGASCAR**
ANTANANARIVO - Page 90

**ZIMBABWE**

**NAMIBIA**

**MOZAMBIQUE**

WINDHOEK - Page 86

**BOTSWANA**

GABORONE - Page 86

PRETORIA - Page 85

MBABANE - Page 85

MAPUTO - Page 87

JOHANNESBURG - Page 84

**SWAZILAND**

**LESOTHO**
MASERU - Page 85

DURBAN - Page 84

**SOUTH AFRICA**

CAPE TOWN - Page 83

---

**KEY - CITY PLANS**

| | |
|---|---|
| MAJOR CONNECTING ROUTE (National road or motorway) | |
| MAIN ROAD | |
| SECONDARY ROAD | |
| ROAD NAME | ROAD NAME |
| ROUTE NUMBER (National route indicated in red) | N1  234 |
| INTERNATIONAL AIRPORT (Usually indicated by name) | Mfuwe Int ✈ Airport |
| LOCAL AIRPORT OR AIRFIELD (Internal flights only or local/private) | ✕  ✕ |
| FERRY (Local & private) | 🛥 |
| POST OFFICE | ✉ |
| PLACE OF INTEREST / HISTORICAL INTEREST (Hotels indicated with Red text) | ■ |
| INFORMATION (Tourist office, local information bureau & park information) | 🅸 |
| HOSPITAL | + |
| POLICE | Police ■ |
| PARK & RESERVE | |
| INLAND WATER & NAME (Dams, lakes, reservoirs etc.) | |
| PERENNIAL RIVER (Flow for all or most of the year) | |

---

**AFRICA**

**KEY - THIS PAGE**

● CITY AND TOWN PLANS FEATURED IN THIS BOOK

● OTHER CITY AND TOWN

INLAND WATER

| KM | | 800 |
|---|---|---|
| MI | | 400 |

ATLANTIC OCEAN

Mouille Point
Mouille Point

Granger Bay
Granger Bay

Breakwater

Metropolitan Golf Course

Green Point Sports Ground

Green Point Common

Green Point Stadium

Three Anchor Bay Sports Ground

Green Point

Green Point Track

Weekend Market

WESTERN BOULEVARD

Fort Wynyard

Fort Wynyard

BMW Pavilion & IMAX Cinema
New Somerset

Telkom Exploratorium
Portswood Lodge
Commodore

Breakwater Lodge

UCT Graduate School of Business

Robinson Dock

Art & Craft Market

Two Oceans Aquarium

Waterfront Residential Marina

Kings Warehouse
Ferryman's Tavern

Agfa Amphitheatre
Quay Four

Alfred Mall

Victoria & Alfred

Buses to City

Victoria Wharf

Table Bay

Parking

EAST PIER

Helicopter Flights

Breakwater

Victoria Basin

NO 7 QUAY
NO 6 QUAY
NO 2 QUAY

Trips to Robben Island
Nelson Mandela Gateway to Robben Island
Waterfront Clocktower Precinct

SOUTH ARM

Victoria & Alfred Waterfront

Cape Grace
Yacht Marina

FISH MARKET

WEST QUAY

Cruise Ship Berths

Duncan Dock

Waterfront Theatre School

City Lodge

Roggebaai Canal Tourism Precinct [Under construction]

Indoor Karting Track

Cape Town International Convention Centre

The Cullinan

Holiday Inn Crowne Plaza Waterfront

Tulbagh Square

Capetonian

Diaz Statue

Tulbagh

Medipark

Van Riebeeck Statue

Artscape (Nico Theatre Centre)

Formule 1

Foreshore

TABLE BAY BOULEVARD

De Waterkant

Noon Gun

Schotsche Kloof

Signal Hill 350m

Lion's Rump

Malay Quarter

Martin Melck House
Lutheran Church

Tulip Inn

Heritage Square

Riebeeck Square

Bo-Kaap Museum

City Park

Holiday Inn Garden Court Greenmarket Square

Greenmarket Square

Old Town House

Provincial Building

Supreme Court

St George's Cathedral

Cultural History Museum (Old Slave Lodge)

Houses of Parliament

City Hall

City Library

Castle of Good Hope

The Grand Parade

Fruit & Vegetable Market

Flower Market

Golden Acre

Cape Town Railway Station

Inter-City Bus Terminus & Information

'Minibus' Terminus

Long-Distance 'Minibus' Terminus

Thibault Square

Fountain

Civic Centre

CIVIC

Tamboerskloof

Labia Gallery

Long Street Turkish Baths

De Tuynhuys

Company's Garden

SA Museum
Planetarium

National Art Gallery

Jewish Museum

Cape Town High School

Library

Mount Nelson

Lady Hamilton
Cape Swiss

Don Apartments

Holiday Inn Garden Court De Waal

Gardens Shopping Centre

New Holland Publishing

Cape Town Fire Station

Botha Statue

SARS

Town House

Magistrates' Court

District Six Museum

Police

Good Hope Centre

Automobile Association

Sir Lowry

SELKIRK

Cape Technikon

Zonnebloem

District Six

Best Western

State Archives

Zonnebloem College

Walmer Estate

Hof Street Medi-Clinic

De Waal Park

Vredehoek

Devil's Peak Estate

M
Yd
500
500

# Durban

INDIAN

OCEAN

Windermere

GORDON

Durban Preparatory School

MILLAR

King's Park Sport Ground

M4

Water World

Village Green

Oasis Beach

CHURCHILL

TENTH AVE NORTH

MCKENZIE

HARVEY

LINKWAY

NINTH AVE NORTH

CLARIBELL

MADELINE

EIGHTH AVE NORTH

California

BISHOP

ROADKNIGHT

UMGENI

NMR AVE

King's Park Olympic Swimming Pool

Windermere Shopping Centre

SEVENTH AVE NORTH

BATTERY BEACH

NORTHERN FREEWAY

M12

SNELL PARADE

Animal Farm

BATTERY BEACH

M17

ARGYLE

SIXTH AVE NORTH

SILVER

STEEL

HENWOOD

STAMFORD HILL

OLDHAM

IVY

WALLS

MONTPELIER PL

FIFTH AVE

ARGYLE

M17

Battery Beach II

SIXTH AVE

FIFTH AVE

FOURTH AVE

FLORIDA

Little Chelsea

LENNOX

FINDLAY

German School

OBLATE

LINZE

STANGER

Durban Drive-In

Blue Waters

Battery Beach I

THIRD AVE

ST MARYS

R102

SANDOWN

Clarence Primary School

FIR

SECOND

WALKERS

KENT

BRICKHILL

SOL HARRIS

Snake Park

Snake Park Beach

MITCHELL CRES

Durban Bowling Club

FIRST AVE

Queen's Tavern

Game City Shopping Centre

Parking

PLAYFAIR

Parking

Somtseu Road Pier

Royal Durban Golf Course

DALY

Bechet Training College

KOLLING

OSBORNE

R102

Durban Railway Station

SOMTSEU

Magistrates' Court

STANGER

Mangrove Beach Shopping Centre

Minitown

Parking

Bay of Plenty

AVONDALE

DLI

FIRST

FYNN

Parking

Durban Fire Station

SOMTSEU

M4

Baseball Park

BRICKHILL

Holiday Inn Garden Court North Beach

PEDESTRIAN WALK

Amphitheatre

Beachfront

Greyville

MITCHELL

MAY

NEWMARKET

JEFF TAYLOR

M12

Hoy Park

Holiday Inn Crowne Plaza

Bay of Plenty Pie

SYDENHAM

Greyville Race Course

UMGENI

ASCOT

EPSOM

Traffic Department

KINGSMEAD

MOLYNEUX

SNELL PARADE

Superior College of Education

DLI Hall

St Augustine Primary School

PRINCE ALFRED

Parking

PAVILION TCE

Durban Jewish Club

PLAYFAIR

Exhibition Hall

Parking

Futura Secondary School

M15

ML Sultan Technikon

Old Fort Clinic

Kingsmead Cricket Ground

OLD FORT

Old Fort & Warrior's Gate

Kingsmead

SABC

M4

STANGER

OLD FORT

City Lodge

Pavilion

Parking

Police

North Beach Pie

Orient Islamic Educational Institution

St Anthony's Catholic Private Aided School

DARTNELL

DERBY

Church

ALBERT

Berkeley

Durban Indoor Sports Centre

FROBISHER

BOSCOMBE

FOSTER

SERRIDGE

Durban Girls' School

CARLISLE

M15

M15

LORNE

DUNFORD

NORTH

MORRISON

BAUMANN

BRICKHILL

Parade

Holiday Inn Garden Court Marine Parade

Dairy Beach Pier

St Aidans

Himalaya

MAUDE

OLD FORT

WEST

JOHN MILNE

HUNTER

EAST

Library

Paddling Pools

Central Fire Station

Department of Transport

BEATRICE

FOUNTAIN

DURNFORD

WYATT

PRIOR

M4

The Durban Hilton International

MILNE

SOUTH

SEA VIEW

Victoria Park

The Edward

Dairy Beach

Amusement Park

MARINE PARADE

CROSS

Road Lodge

Kwa Muhle Museum

ALIWAL

WALNUT

Conservation Centre

Killarney

Wedge Bea

M13

MARKET

ALICE

Stable Theatre

LEOPOLD

SHORT

FIELD

SOLDIERS' WAY

Parking

Parking

Durban Exhibition Centre

Durban International Convention Centre

KEARSNEY

West St Jet

M4

Surat Hindoo School Primary

PRINCE EDWARD

Library

Parking

VICTORIA

Buses

Central Park

South Plaza Market

Varsity School

PINE

PALMER

FAREWELL

PALMER

Beach

Palm Beach

POINT

Parking

ACORN

BOND

RUSSELL

BROOK

GREY

QUEEN

ALBERT

The Workshop Shopping Centre

COMMERCIAL

UNION

WEST

PECK

Seaboard

Tropicana

Sea World Dolphinariu and Aquarium

Holiday Inn Garden Court South Beach

WARWICK

MARKET

Victoria Street Market

Juma Musjid Mosque

PINE

African Art Centre

Medwood Gardens

Parking

Tudor House

New Rand

SMITH

GULL

MULBERRY

Four Seasons

BRIGHTON

Lido

Muthi Market

Berea Rd Railway Station

West Street Cemetery

Parking

Durban Academy of Learning

CHURCH

History Museum

Francis Farewell Gardens

City Hall

Central

TIMBER

MAZEPPA

ROY

KEELER

FISHER

The Wheel Shopping Complex

BEATTY

GRENVILLE

NIVERSITY

THEATRE

DAVIS

WEST

FIELD

Cambridge College

Natal Playhouse Theatre

Albany

MONA

JONSSON

MILLS

CREEK

PICKERING

STURDEE

RICHARDS

City Market

PARK

CONVENT

St James College

Damelin College

BAY

Royal

GARDINER

BEACH

ALBANY

ALIWAL

Parking

KITCHENER

WINDER

ROCHESTER

Parking

Trampolines

Botha ardens

Natal Technikon

BROOK

SMITH

ALEXANDRA

Durdoc Clinic

GA Riches Building

HERMITAGE

FENTON

PARRY

Quadrant House

Natal

VICTORIA EMBANKMENT

Da Gama Clock

Department of Customs & Excise

BAY TERRACE

OCEAN

SHEARER

Police

Addington

COLLEGE

Belgica

BENNINGFIELD

BAKER

SALMON

Dick King Statue

Maritime Museum

SHEPSTONE

MASONIC

PRINCE

ST GEORGES

Parking

Police

Pleasure Cruises

BAT Centre Museum

Point Clinic

JEWITTS

102

MCARTHUR

ST ANDREWS

Supreme Court

Point Yacht Club

Gardiner St Jetty

Small Craft Harbour

R Berth

Addingto Children'

RUSSELL

Le Plaza

Old House Museum

Royal Natal Yacht Club

YACHT MOLE

Q Berth

HOSPITAL

RIPLEY

Albert Park

LLOYD

BOATMAN'S

P Berth

QUAYSIDE

BEACH

CANAL

MAYDON WHARF

Fish Wharf

Bay of Natal

T Jetty

SOUTH

POINT

Point

Sugar Terminal

Fishing Boat Jetty

Ocean Terminal

H Berth

BEL

M

Yd

50

500

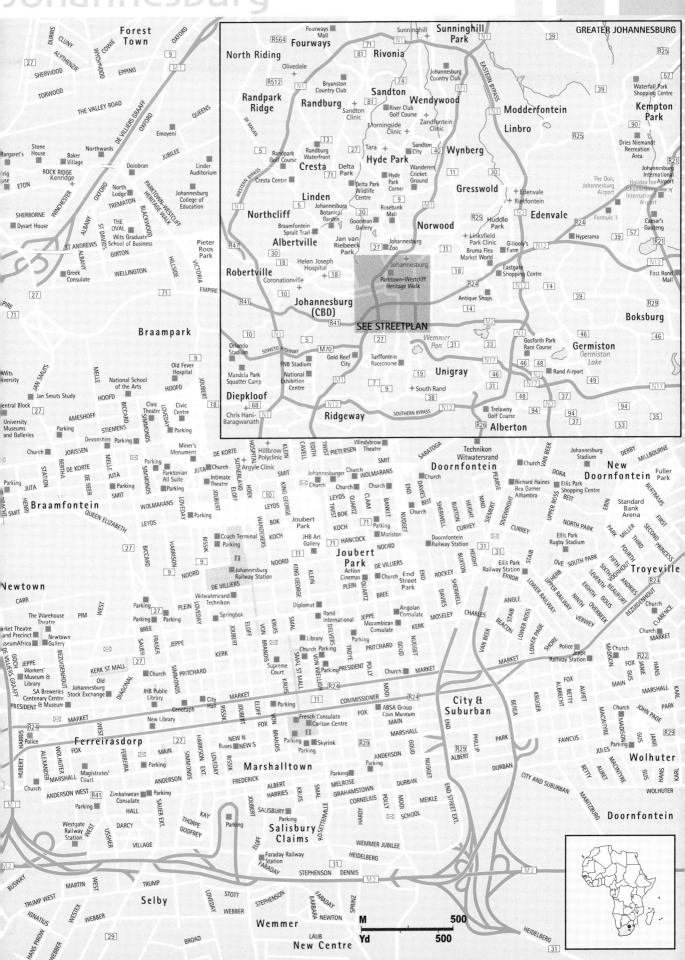

# Pretoria

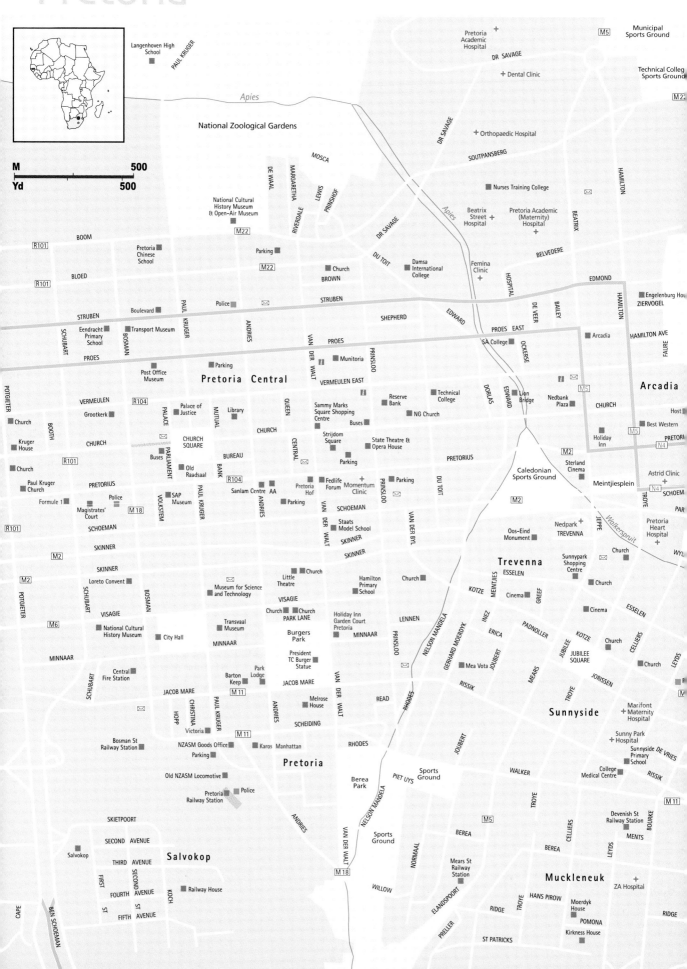

M ———— 500
Yd ———— 500

**National Zoological Gardens**

Langenhoven High School
PAUL KRUGER

*Apies*

Pretoria Academic Hospital
DR SAVAGE
M5
Municipal Sports Ground

Dental Clinic
Technical Colleg Sports Ground
M22

MOSCA

National Cultural History Museum & Open-Air Museum
DE WAAL
MARGARETHA
LEWIS
PRINSHOF
RIVERDALE
M22

Orthopaedic Hospital
SOUTPANSBERG
HAMILTON

Nurses Training College

DR SAVAGE
DU TOIT
Beatrix Street Hospital
Pretoria Academic (Maternity) Hospital
BEATRIX

BOOM
R101
Pretoria Chinese School
Parking
M22
Church
BROWN
Damsa International College
Femina Clinic
BELVEDERE

BLOED
R101
Police
STRUBEN
SHEPHERD
EDWARD
PROES EAST
EDMOND
HAMILTON

STRUBEN
Boulevard
PAUL KRUGER
ANDRIES
PROES
SA College
OCKERSE
DE VEER
BAILEY
Engelenburg Hou
ZIERVOGEL

Eendracht Primary School
Transport Museum
BOSMAN
VAN DER WALT
Munitoria
PRINSLOO
VERMEULEN EAST
DORLAS
EDWARD
Lion Bridge
Nedbank Plaza
M5
Arcadia
HAMILTON AVE
FAURE

PROES
SCHUBART
Post Office Museum
**Pretoria Central**
Reserve Bank
Technical College
NG Church
**Arcadia**
CHURCH
Host

POTGIETER
VERMEULEN
Grootkerk
Palace of Justice
Library
QUEEN
CHURCH
Sammy Marks Square Shopping Centre
Buses
Strijdom Square
State Theatre & Opera House
PRETORIUS
Holiday Inn
M5
Best Western
PRETORI
N4

Church
BOOTH
Kruger House
CHURCH
MUTUAL
PALACE
CHURCH SQUARE
CENTRAL
Parking
Caledonian Sports Ground
Sterland Cinema
Meintjiesplein
Astrid Clinic
SCHOEM
N4
PAR

Church
PARLIAMENT
Buses
BUREAU
BANK
Old Raadsaal
Fedlife Forum
Momentum Clinic
PRINSLOO
Parking
M2
Nedpark
TREVENNA
JEPPE
Walkerspruit
Pretoria Heart Hospital
WYL

Paul Kruger Church
PRETORIUS
Sanlam Centre
AA
R104
Pretoria Hof
Parking
SCHOEMAN
DU TOIT
Oos-Eind Monument
**Trevenna**
ESSELEN
Church

Formule 1
Police
VOLKSTEM
SAP Museum
PAUL KRUGER
Staats Model School
SKINNER
VAN DER BYL
M2
KOTZE
MEINTJIES
Cinema
GREEF
Sunnypark Shopping Centre
Church
ESSELEN

Magistrates' Court
M 18
SCHOEMAN
VAN DER WALT
SKINNER
KOTZE
Cinema
Church

SCHOEMAN
SKINNER
Church
Little Theatre
Hamilton Primary School
Church
PADNOLLER
JUBILEE
KOTZE
CELLIERS
Church

SKINNER
Loreto Convent
SCHUBART
BOSMAN
Museum for Science and Technology
VISAGIE
Church Church
PARK LANE
INEZ
JOUBERT
MEARS
JUBILEE SQUARE
LEYDS

M6
VISAGIE
National Cultural History Museum
Transvaal Museum
Holiday Inn Garden Court Pretoria
LENNEN
ERICA
Mea Vota
Church
**Sunnyside**

POTGIETER
City Hall
MINNAAR
**Burgers Park**
MINNAAR
NELSON MANDELA
RISSIK
TROYE
JORISSEN

MINNAAR
Central Fire Station
President TC Burger Statue
Marifont Maternity Hospital
M

SCHUBART
Barton Keep
Park Lodge
JACOB MARE
READ
Sunny Park Hospital
Sunnyside Primary School
DE VRIES

JACOB MARE
PAUL KRUGER
M 11
ANDRIES
Melrose House
VAN DER WALT
RHODES
JOUBERT
College Medical Centre
RISSIK

CHRISTINA
HOPP
Victoria
SCHEIDING
WALKER
M11

Bosman St Railway Station
NZASM Goods Office
Karos Manhattan
RHODES
TROYE
Devenish St Railway Station
BOURKE
MENTS

Parking
**Pretoria**
Berea Park
PIET UYS
Sports Ground
CELLIERS
BEREA
LEYDS

Old NZASM Locomotive
Police
NELSON MANDELA
Mears St Railway Station
BEREA
ZA Hospital

Pretoria Railway Station
SKIETPOORT
M5

SECOND AVENUE
Salvokop
THIRD AVENUE
**Salvokop**
Sports Ground
NORMAAL
TROYE
HANS PIROW
Moerdyk House
**Muckleneuk**

FIRST ST
SECOND ST
FOURTH AVENUE
FIFTH AVENUE
KOCH
Railway House
VAN DER WALT
M 18
WILLOW
ANDRIES
ELANDSPOORT
POMONA
Kirkness House

CAPE
BEN SCHOEMAN
PREILER
ST PATRICKS
RIDGE
TROYE
RIDGE

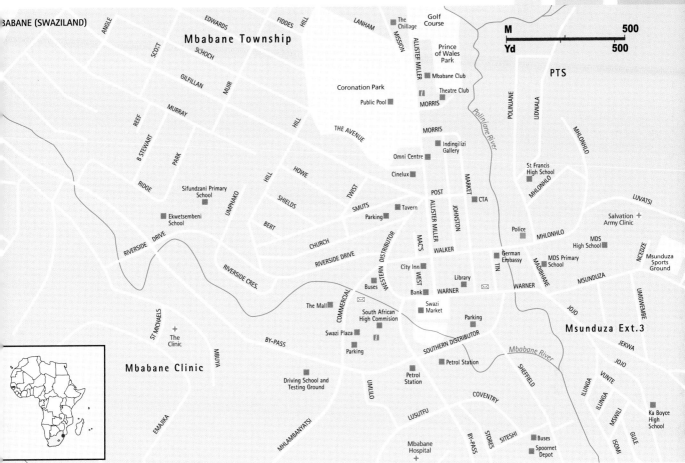

## Mbabane (Swaziland)

Mbabane Township

Coronation Park
Public Pool
The Chillage
Golf Course
Mbabane Club
Theatre Club
Prince of Wales Park
PTS

EDWARDS
FIDDES
HILL
LANHAM
MISSION
ANGLE
SCOTT
SLHOCH
GILFILLAN
MUIR
MURRAY
REEF
B STEWART
PARK
RIDGE
UMPHAKO
HILL
HOWE
BERT
SHIELDS
TWIST
SMUTS
THE AVENUE
CHURCH
RIVERSIDE DRIVE
RIVERSIDE CRES.
RIVERSIDE DRIVE
ALLISTER MILLER
MORRIS
MORRIS
Indingilizi Gallery
Omni Centre
Cinelux
POST
MARKET
JOHNSTON
MAC'S
WALKER
WEST
WARNER
Tavern
Parking
City Inn
Buses
Bank
Library
Swazi Market
TIN
German Embassy
Police
MHLONHLO
St Francis High School
MDS High School
MDS Primary School
CTA
Salvation Army Clinic
LUVATSI
NCEDZE
Msunduza Sports Ground
UMGWEMBE
MSUNDUZA
JOJO
JEKWA
JOJO
VUNTE
ILUNGA
MSWILI
ISOMI
GULE
Ka Boyce High School
POLINJANE
LIDWALA
MHLONHLO
MADINBHANE
MHLONHLO

Polinjane River

Sifundzani Primary School
Ekwetsembeni School

ST MICHAELS
The Clinic

Mbabane Clinic

MBUYA
BY-PASS
COMMERCIAL
WESTERN DISTRIBUTOR
The Mall
Swazi Plaza
Parking
South African High Commision
Parking
SOUTHERN DISTRIBUTOR
Mbabane River
Msunduza Ext.3
SHEFFIELD
Petrol Station
Petrol Station

EMAJIKA
MHLAMBANYATSI
UMILLO
Driving School and Testing Ground
LUSUTFU
COVENTRY
BY-PASS
STORES
SITESHI
Mbabane Hospital
Buses
Spoornet Depot

M 500
Yd 500

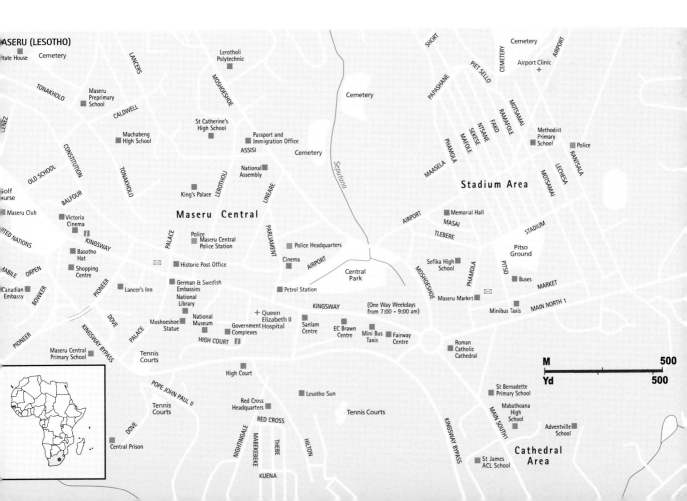

## Maseru (Lesotho)

State House
Cemetery
Lerotholi Polytechnic
SHORT
Cemetery
Airport Clinic
AIRPORT
CEMETERY
PIET SELLO
PAPASHANE
MOTSAMAI
RAMAFOLE
FAKO
NTSANE
SEKESE
MAFOLE
PHAMOLA
MAASELA
Methodist Primary School
Police
RANTSALA
LECHESA
MOTSAMAI

TONAKHOLO
LANCERS
MOSHOESHOE
Maseru Preprimary School
CALDWELL
Machabeng High School
St Catherine's High School
Passport and Immigration Office
ASSISI
National Assembly
Cemetery
Seputona
Stadium Area
STADIUM
PHAMOLA

ENEZ
OLD SCHOOL
CONSTITUTION
BALFOUR
TONAKHOLO
LEROTHOLI
LINEARE
King's Palace
Maseru Central
AIRPORT
Memorial Hall
MASAI
TLEBERE
Pitso Ground
Golf Course
Maseru Club
Victoria Cinema
KINGSWAY
Basotho Hat
Shopping Centre
Police
Maseru Central Police Station
Historic Post Office
PALACE
PARLIAMENT
Police Headquarters
Cinema
AIRPORT
Central Park
MOSHOESHOE
Sefika High School
PHAMOLA
PITSO
Buses
MARKET

MABILE
ORPEN
Canadian Embassy
BOWKER
PIONEER
DOVE
PIONEER
Lancer's Inn
German & Swedish Embassies
National Library
Moshoeshoe Statue
National Museum
HIGH COURT
Government Complexes
Queen Elizabeth II Hospital
KINGSWAY
Petrol Station
Sanlam Centre
EC Brawn Centre
Mini Bus Taxis
Fairway Centre
(One Way Weekdays from 7:00 – 9:00 am)
Maseru Market
Minibus Taxis
MAIN NORTH 1

KINGSWAY BYPASS
Maseru Central Primary School
PALACE
Tennis Courts
High Court
Roman Catholic Cathedral

POPE JOHN PAUL II
DOVE
Tennis Courts
Red Cross Headquarters
RED CROSS
Lesotho Sun
Tennis Courts
St Bernadette Primary School
Mabathoana High School
Adventville School

NIGHTINGALE
MABEKEBEKE
THEBE
HILTON
KUENA
KINGSWAY BYPASS
MAIN SOUTH1
St James ACL School
Cathedral Area
Central Prison

M 500
Yd 500

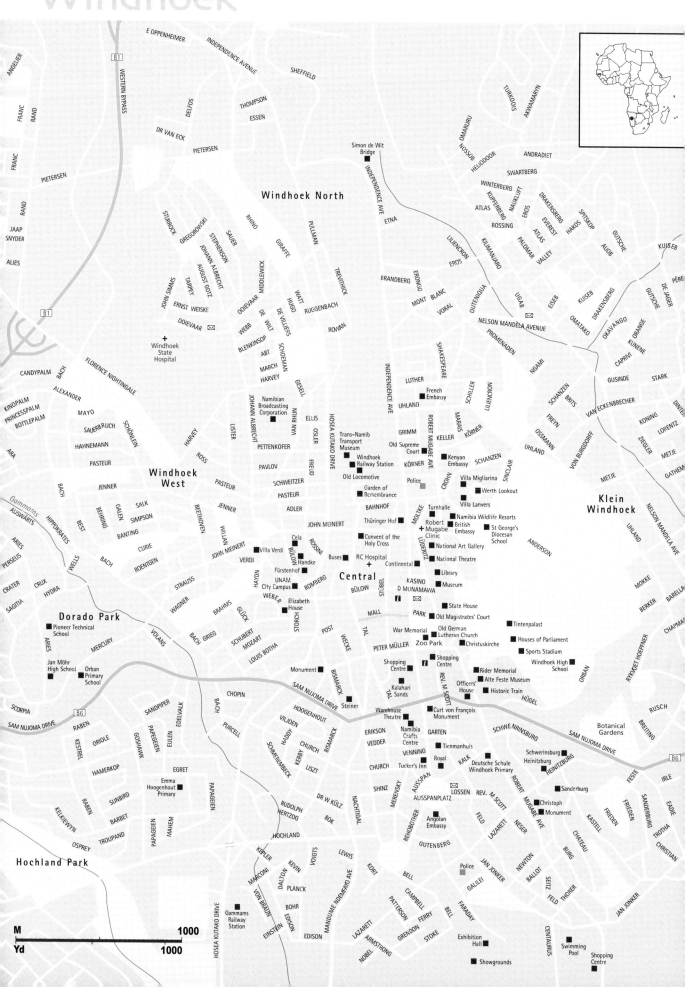

# Windhoek

**Windhoek North**

**Windhoek West**

**Windhoek State Hospital**

**Dorado Park**

**Central**

**Klein Windhoek**

**Hochland Park**

ANGELIER
FRANC
RAND
FRANC
RAND
JAAP SNYDER
ALIES

E OPPENHEIMER
INDEPENDENCE AVENUE
SHEFFIELD
THOMPSON
ESSEN

WESTERN BYPASS
B1
DR VAN ECK
PIETERSEN
DELFOS
PIETERSEN

Simon de Wit Bridge

TURKOOIS
AKWAMARYN
OMARURU
OMARURU
NOSSOB
HELIODOOR
ANDRADIET
SWARTBERG
WINTERBERG
NAUKLUFT
DRAKENSBERG
SPITSKOP
HAKOS
EROS
EVEREST
GUTSCHE
KUPFERBERG
ATLAS
ROSSING
ATLAS
PALOMAR VALLEY
AUOB
KUISEB
KILIMANJARO
UGAB
EISEB
DRAKENSBERG
GUTSCHE
DE JAGER
NELSON MANDELA AVENUE
KUISEB
OMATAKO
OKAVANGO
CAPRIVI
KUNENE
PÈRE

STURROCK
GREGOROWSKI
SAUER
STEPHENSON
JOHANN ALBRECHT
RHINO
GIRAFFE
PULLMAN
TREVITHICK
BRANDBERG
ERONGO
MONT BLANC
VORAL
OUTENIQUA
PROMENADEN
NGAMI
SCHANZEN
BRITS
FREYN
VON ECKENBRECHER
GUSINDE
STARK
DINTE
KONING
LORENTZ
METJE
GATHEM

JOHN SIMMS
ERNST WEISKE
TARPEY
AUGUST GOTZ
OOIEVAAR
OOIEVAAR
WEBB
DE WILT
MIDDLEWICK
HUGO
WATT
RUGGENBACH
ROMAN

Windhoek State Hospital

FLORENCE NIGHTINGALE
CANDYPALM
BACH
ALEXANDER
KINOPALM
PRINCESSPALM
MAYO
BOTTLEPALM
SAUERBRUCH
SCHÖNLEIN
ARA
HAHNEMANN
PASTEUR
JENNER

BLENKINSOP
ABT
MARCH
HARVEY
SCHOEMAN
GESELL
JOHANN ALBRECHT
LISTER
HARVEY
ROSS
PASTEUR
PETTENKOFER
PAVLOV
SCHWEITZER
PASTEUR
ADLER

Namibian Broadcasting Corporation

VAN RHIJN
ELLIS
OSLER
HOSEA KUTAKO DRIVE
FREUD

SHAKESPEARE
LUTHER
SCHILLER
UHLAND
French Embassy
GRIMM
KELLER
KÖRNER
MARAIS
LILIENCRON
Kenyan Embassy
SCHANZEN
SINCLAIR
UHLAND
OSSMANN
VON BURGDORFF
METJE
METJE
MOKKE
BERKER
BARELLA
CHAPMAN

INDEPENDENCE AVE
ROBERT MUGABE AVE

Old Supreme Court
KÖRNER
Police
CROHN
Villa Migliarina
Werth Lookout
Villa Lanvers
Turnhalle
Namibia Wildlife Resorts
Robert British Embassy
St George's Diocesan School
Mugabe Clinic
National Art Gallery
ANDERSON
National Theatre
Library
Museum

Trans-Namib Transport Museum
Windhoek Railway Station
Old Locomotive
Garden of Remembrance
BAHNHOF
Thüringer Hof
Convent of the Holy Cross
Buses
RC Hospital
Continental

BEST
BEHRING
GALEN
SALK
BANTING
CURIE
ROENTGEN
BACH
BACH
HIPPOKRATES
AUSWARTS
Gammoms
WELLS
ARIES
PERSEUS
CRATER
CRUX
HYDRA
SAGITIA

JENNER
SIMPSON
BEETHOVEN
PASTEUR
STRAUSS
WAGNER
BRAHMS
GLÜCK
SCHUBERT
MOZART
LOUIS BOTHA
BACH
GRIEG
CHOPIN

WILLAN
JOHN MEINERT
JOHN MEINERT
HAYDN
VERDI
WEBER
STORCH

Villa Verdi
Cela
BÜLOW
Handke
ROSSINI
Fürstenhof
UNAM City Campus
ROMBERG
Elizabeth House
BÜLOW
MOLTKE
LÜDERITZ
STÜBEL
KASINO
D MUNAMAWA
State House
Old Magistrates' Court
PARK
Tintenpalast
War Memorial
Old German Lutheran Church
Houses of Parliament
Zoo Park
Christuskirche
Sports Stadium
Windhoek High School
Rider Memorial
Alte Feste Museum
Historic Train
HÜGEL

MALL
TAL
POST
WECKE
PETER MÜLLER
BISMARCK
Monument
Shopping Centre
Shopping Centre
Kalahari Sands
Officers' House
ORBAN
RUSCH

Pioneer Technical School
MERCURY
ARIES
Jan Möhr High School
Orban Primary School
SCORPIA
SAM NUJOMA DRIVE
B6
RABEN
KESTREL
ORIOLE
SANDPIPER
EULEN
EDELVALK
PAPAGEIEN
GOSHAWK
HAMERKOP
EGRET
Emma Hoogenhout Primary
SUNBIRD
BARBET
RABEN
KELKIEWYN
OSPREY
MAHEM
TROUPAND
PAPAGEIEN

VOLANS
BACH
VILJOEN
HOOGENHOUT
HADDY
CHURCH
KERBY
LISZT
SCHMEREMBECK
PURCELL
SAM NUJOMA DRIVE
Steiner
SCHWERINSBURG
SAM NUJOMA DRIVE
B6
Botanical Gardens
BREITING
IRLE

ERIKSON
VEDDER
VENNING
CHURCH
SHINZ
MERENSKY
REHOBOTHER
Warehouse Theatre
Namibia Crafts Centre
GARTEN
Tienmanhuis
Royal
KALK
Tucker's Inn
Deutsche Schule Windhoek Primary
AUSSPAN
AUSSPANPLATZ
LOSSEN
REV. M SCOTT
Curt von François Monument
Schwerinsburg
Heinitzburg
Heinitzburg
Sanderburg
SCHNEE
FFANE
FELD
LAZARETT
NESER
ROBERT MUGABE AVE
Christoph Monument
KASTELL
FRIEDEN
SANDERBURG
TROTHA
CHRISTIAN

DR W. KÜLZ
BOK
NACHTIGAL
Angolan Embassy
GUTENBERG
BELL
CAMPBELL
PATTERSON
FERRY
STOKE
Police
JAN JONKER
GALILEI
NEWTON
BALLOT
SEITZ
FELD
THORER
JAN JONKER
EADIE

MANDUME NDEMFAYO AVE
KORT
LEWIS
BELL
BELL
FARADAY
CENTAURUS

HOCHLAND
KEPLER
MARCONI
DALTON
KEVIN
VOIGTS
PLANCK
BOHR
EINSTEIN
EDISON
VON BRAUN
RUDOLPH HERTZOG
HOSEA KUTAKO DRIVE

Gammams Railway Station
LAZARETT
ARMSTRONG
NOBEL
GRENDON
Exhibition Hall
Showgrounds
Swimming Pool
Shopping Centre

B1

M 1000
Yd 1000

# Harare

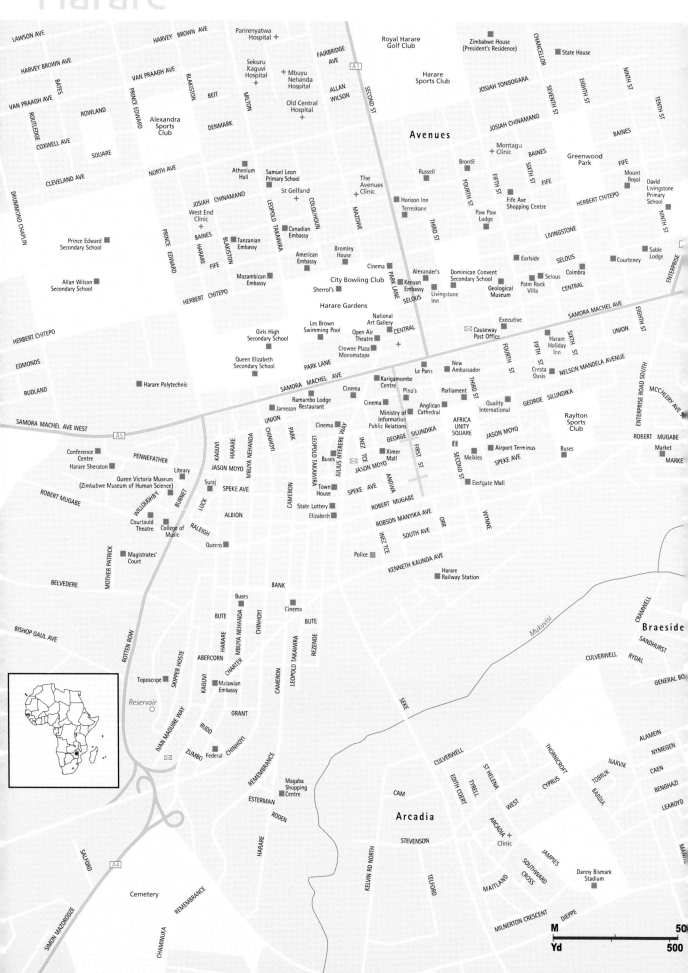

LAWSON AVE
HARVEY BROWN AVE
HARVEY BROWN AVE
VAN PRAAGH AVE
BATES
VAN PRAAGH AVE
ROUTLEDGE
ROWLAND
COXWELL AVE
SQUARE
CLEVELAND AVE
PRINCE EDWARD
BLAKISTON
BEIT
DENMARK
MILTON

Parirenyatwa Hospital +
Sekuru Kaguvi Hospital
+ Mbuyu Nehanda Hospital
Old Central Hospital
FAIRBRIDGE AVE
A1
ALLAN WILSON
SECOND ST

Royal Harare Golf Club
Zimbabwe House (President's Residence)
CHANCELLOR
State House
Harare Sports Club
JOSIAH TONGOGARA
SEVENTH ST
EIGHTH ST
NINTH ST
TENTH ST
JOSIAH CHINAMANO
BAINES

Avenues

Alexandra Sports Club
NORTH AVE
Montagu + Clinic
Greenwood Park
FIFE
Mount Royal
David Livingstone Primary School
NINTH ST

Athenium Hall
Samuel Leon Primary School
St Gelfand
The Avenues + Clinic
Brontë
Russell
BAINES
SIXTH ST
FIFE
HERBERT CHITEPO

JOSIAH CHINAMANO
West End Clinic +
BAINES
LEOPOLD TAKAWIRA
COLQUHOUN
MAZOWE
Horizon Inn
Terreskane
THIRD ST
FOURTH ST
FIFTH ST
Fife Ave Shopping Centre
Paw Paw Lodge
LIVINGSTONE

DRUMMOND CHAPLIN
Prince Edward Secondary School
PRINCE EDWARD
HARARE
FIFE
BLAKISTON
Tanzanian Embassy
Canadian Embassy
Bromley House
Earlside
SELOUS
Courteney
Sable Lodge
ENTERPRISE

HERBERT CHITEPO
Allan Wilson Secondary School
Mozambican Embassy
American Embassy
Cinema
City Bowling Club
Sherrol's
Harare Gardens
Kenyan Embassy
Alexander's
Livingstone Inn
SELOUS
Dominican Convent Secondary School
Geological Museum
Selous
Palm Rock Villa
Coimbra
CENTRAL

HERBERT CHITEPO
EDMONDS
RUDLAND
Harare Polytechnic
Girls High Secondary School
Queen Elizabeth Secondary School
PARK LANE
Les Brown Swimming Pool
National Art Gallery
Open Air Theatre
Crowne Plaza Monomatapa
CENTRAL
SAMORA MACHEL AVE
Executive
Causeway Post Office
Harare Holiday Inn
UNION
SIXTH ST
EIGHTH ST

SAMORA MACHEL AVE WEST
A5
PARK LANE
SAMORA MACHEL AVE
Cinema
Ramambo Lodge
Jameson Restaurant
UNION
CHINHOYI
PARK
Le Paris
Karigamombe Centre
Pino's
New Ambassador
Parliament
FOURTH ST
FIFTH ST
Cresta Oasis
THIRD ST
NELSON MANDELA AVENUE
GEORGE SILUNDIKA
Raylton Sports Club
ENTERPRISE ROAD SOUTH
MCCHLERY AVE

PENNEFATHER
Conference Centre
Harare Sheraton
Library
KAGUVI
HARARE
MBUYA NEHANDA
LEOPOLD TAKAWIRA
Cinema
Buses
JULIUS NYERERE WAY
INEZ TCE
JASON MOYO
GEORGE SILUNDIKA
Anglican Cathedral
Ministry of Information Public Relations
AFRICA UNITY SQUARE
Quality International
JASON MOYO
Ximer Mall
Airport Terminus
Meikles
SPEKE AVE
Buses
ROBERT MUGABE
Market
MARKE

ROBERT MUGABE
Queen Victoria Museum (Zimbabwe Museum of Human Science)
JASON MOYO
Suraj
SPEKE AVE
Town House
State Lottery
Elizabeth
SPEKE AVE
ANGWA
ROBERT MUGABE
Eastgate Mall

Courtauld Theatre
College of Music
WILLOUGHBY
BURNET
LUCK
RALEIGH
ALBION
Queens
CAMERON
FIRST ST
SECOND ST
WYNNE
ROBSON MANYIKA AVE
ORR
SOUTH AVE
INEZ TCE
Police
KENNETH KAUNDA AVE
Harare Railway Station

MOTHER PATRICK
Magistrates' Court
BELVEDERE
BISHOP GAUL AVE
Toposcope
ROTTEN ROW
SKIPPER HOSTE
BUTE
BUTE
Buses
HARARE
MBUYA NEHANDA
CHINHOYI
Cinema
BANK
BUTE
REZENDE
LEOPOLD TAKAWIRA
CAMERON
Mukuvisi
CRAMWELL
Braeside
SANDHURST
CULVERWELL
RYDAL
GENERAL BO

Reservoir
IVAN MAGUIRE WAY
CHARTER
ABERCORN
KAGUVI
Malawian Embassy
GRANT
RUDD
ZUMBO
Federal
CHINHOYI
REMEMBRANCE
Magaba Shopping Centre
ESTERMAN
RODEN
HARARE
SEKE
CAM
Arcadia
CULVERWELL
STEVENSON
ST HELENA
TYRELL
WEST
EDITH COERT
ARCADIA + Clinic
THORNCROFT
CYPRUS
ALAMEIN
NYMEGEN
NARVIK
CAEN
TOBRUK
BARDIA
BENGHAZI
LEAROYD

SALFORD
A4
Cemetery
REMEMBRANCE
CHAMINUKA
SIMON MAZORODZE
KELVIN RD NORTH
TELFORD
JAMPIES
SOUTHWARD CROSS
MAITLAND
Danny Bismark Stadium
MILNERTON CRESCENT
DIEPPE
MARI

M
Yd
50
500

**Malhangalene**

Police

Mercado

AVENIDA ALBERT LUTHULI

AVENIDA DA MAGUIGUANA

Cinema

AVENIDA EDUARDO MONDLANE

Moçambicano

Cemetery

AVENIDA DA GUERRA POPULAR

Universo

AVENIDA FILIPE SAMUEL MAGAIA

AVENIDA EDUARDO MONDLANE

AVENIDA KARL MARX

AVENIDA AHMED SEKOU TOURÉ

Cinema

Museu de Arte

Bazar do Povo

OLOF PALME

City Hall/ Civic Centre

AVENIDA JOSINA MACHEL

DA SÉ

PRAÇA DA INDEPENDÊNCIA

Cathedral

Rovuma

Samora Machel Statue

French Cultural Centre

AVENIDA VLADIMIR I LENINE

AVENIDA SAMORA MACHEL

Casa do Ferro (Eiffel's 'House of Steel')

Cinema

Bank

British High Commission

AVENIDA 24 DE JULHO

VIANA DE MOTA

AVENIDA HO CHI MIN

AVENIDA ZEDEQUIAS MANGANHELA

Jardim Tunduru Botanical Gardens

AVENIDA PATRICE LUMUMBA

Santa Cruz

JOSÉ SIDUMO

E INSET

Supreme Court

JOHN ISSA

Pensão Alegre

AVENIDA AMILCAR CABRAL

AVENIDA AHMED SEKOU TOURÉ

Andalucia

DO D ALMEIDA RIBEIRO

Library

Tivoli

JOAQUIM LAPA

ENT

DE TIMOR LESTE

Theatre

Stadium

Feira Popular

AVENIDA DO PRESIDENTE CARMONA

Girassol

Aviz

AVENIDA SALVADOR ALLENDE

DA IMPRENSA

MARQUES DE POMBAL

Sports Ground

Maputo

BELMIRO OBADIAS MUIANGA

AVENIDA 25 DE SETEMBRO

Feira Popular

DE ANTÓNIO FERNANDES

AVENIDA 10 DE NOVEMBRO

FACIM Complex

PRAÇA ROBERT MUGABE

DA GUARDA

AVENIDA VLADIMIR I LENINE

AVENIDA DA RESISTÊNCIA

Cooperativa De Arte Maconde

RUA DA MALHANGALENE

AVENIDA MILAGRE MABOTE

AVENIDA PAULO SAMUEL KANKHOMBA

AVENIDA AGOSTINHO NETO

AVENIDA EMILIA DAUSSE

AVENIDA DA MAGUIGUANA

PRAÇA DO MERCADO

OLIVENÇA

ESPERANCA

Mercado Janet

Police

Cinema

AVENIDA AMILCAR CABRAL

Fatima's

VALENTIM SITI

Police

**Central**

AVENIDA EMILIA DAUSSE

AVENIDA DA MAGUIGUANA

DO COM. JOÃO BELO

AVENIDA SALVADOR ALLENDE

Club Desportivo de Maxaquene (Swimming Pool)

Pensão Martins

Intercape Bus Terminus

FRANCISCO MALANGE

AVENIDA AUGUSTO CARDOSO

AVENIDA SALVADOR ALLENDE

DO COM. AUGUSTO CARDOSO

The Base Backpackers

AVENIDA DA BASE N'TCHINGA

AVENIDA VLADIMIR I LENINE

AVENIDA DA GUARDA

AVENIDA GENERAL TEXEIRA BOTELHO

PÉRO DE ANAYA

KWAME NKRUMAH

MAIA E VASCONCELOS

Extravanância Crafts

AVENIDA MAO TSE TUNG

GEN. PEREIRA D'EÇA

AVENIDA PAULO SAMUEL KANKHOMBA

AVENIDA AGOSTINHO NETO

DE TCHAMBA

AVENIDA EDUARDO MONDLANE

DOS MÁRTIRES DA MACHAVA

AVENIDA TOMÁS NDUDA

MUKUMBURA

DE KASSUENDA

Instituicão de Siencias

Maputo Central

Dutch Embassy

Tanzanian High Commission

Hoyo-Hoyo

**Polana Cimento**

Bureau de Informação Público

AVENIDA TOMÁS NDUDA

DOS LUZíADAS

Museu de Geologia

AVENIDA DOS MÁRTIRES DA MACHAVA

AVENIDA FRANCISCO ORLANDO MAGUMBWE

Museu de Historia Natural

DE ARGÉLIA

PRAÇA DA TRAVESSIA DO ZAMBEZE

MATEUS SANSÃO MUTHEMBA

Cardoso

JOSÉ MATEUS

Núcelo de Arte

Associação Cultural Tchova Xitaduma

DE NACHINWEA

AVENIDA DOS MÁRTIRES DA MUEDA

JOSÉ MACAMO

UDAQUIM MARA

AVENIDA CAHORA BASSA

Zambian High Commission

DF BARRETO

DAMIÃO DE GIÙS

Police

AVENIDA LUCAS ELIAS KUMATO

JOÃO DE BARROS

DA GARCIA DE RESENDE

KWAME NKRUMAH

Santo Antonio Da Polana Church

AVENIDA KIM II SUNG

Zimbabwean High Commission

Parque José Cabral

Instituto Nacional de Metéorologia

Observatorio

AVENIDA JULIUS NYERERE

AVENIDA ARMANDO TIVANE

Buses

Polana

Canadian High Commision

Cinema

Terminus

SA Embassy

AVENIDA ARMANDO TIVANE

Avenida

Villa Itália

AVENIDA FRIEDRICH ENGELS

Clube Naval

Police

Escola Nautica

AVENIDA DOS MÁRTIRES DA MUEDA

AVENIDA DA MARGINAL

*Rio Espírito Santo*

**E INSET**

AVENIDA 25 DE SETEMBRO

AVENIDA ZEDEQUIAS MANGANHELA

Railway Station

Mercado Central

CONSIGLIERI PEDROSO

PRAÇA DOS TRABALHADORES

Tamariz

DA MESQUITA

Archives

Central

Hotel Carlton

AVENIDA SAMODA MACHEL

JOAQUIM LAPA

DE TIMOR LESTE

Turismo

DO BAGAMOIO

Museu da Moeda

Saturday Craft Market

Buses

PRAÇA 25 DE JÚNHO

AVENIDA MÁRTIRES DE INHAMINGA

Fortaleza da Nossa Senhora da Conceição

Ferry to Catembe and Ponta do Ouro

0       500

0       500

*Baía de Maputo*

*(Maputo Bay)*

# Lusaka

**VUBU**
**KAPOCHE**
**NSEMBE**
**BWEMBELELO**
KATIMA MULILU
**MULULU**

Emmasdale Primary School

Ngwerare Primary School

KATIMA MULILO

CHAINAMA
NJOKA
MAPEPE
KATIMA MULILO
LUKUSUZ
LUBANGSENSH

Olympia Park Primary School

**Chiwala Mabwe (Olympia Park)**

MWANSABOMBWA
CHAKELIKA
KWACHA
LUBANGSENSH

CONAKRY
CHAPITA

CHIWAYA

MWALESHI
CHAKELIKA

Political Museum

ZUNGULU

Police

PARLIAMENT

National Assembly

MPULUNGU
MANDA HILL
MARTIN
MWAMBA
KWACHA

Agricultural Society Showgrounds

Muleya Primary School

MANCHICHI

MANDA HILL
MULOREZI
NGWEREMA

MULULU

WAMALUNGA
VIMBE
UNDI MUKOSA
LOUMOE
MAKSHI
BAKAVU
BUWA
DOKO CHILEBE
WAMULUWA

CHANDE

MANCHICHI

Northmead Primary School

**Chikonkoto (Northmead)**

AZIKIWI
KALUNGU
PASELI
NANYAKATOLO
CHITULI
SIBWENI
CHISOKONE
MUKONTEKA
TWIKATANE

NANGWENYA

International School

BUCHI
NCHENJA
WUSKILI
KACHA
PASELI
BENAKALE
CHITEMENE
KATOPOLA
KALEMBWE

LUNZUA

MWALULE
CHALA
MALILA
LUBAMBE
CHOZI

CHIKUNI
MWAMBESHI
LANDA

Mozambican Embassy

ALEX MASALA
CHAHOLI

MOTH Club
LUBU

Public Swimming Pool

LUZI
CHIYANGA
LUMBE
MBYA

Northmead Shopping Centre & Market

GREAT EAST

EULIWE
LUBUTO
TEAK
NYATI

Lusaka Municipal Sports Club

LUANSHYA

Fairview Medical Centre

MTANDANI
LUNGWEBUNGU
NKAN CHIBAYA
ENOCK KAVU

NAMBALA
JOSEPH
OMELO
Lagos Road Cemetery
LAGOS
MACHA ZIMBABWE
FREETOWN
CHIPOVU
NALUBUTU

**Luneta (Thorn Park)**

TULETEKA
MANSANSA
CHINGALIKA
KATEMO
LAGOS
ADDIS ABABA DRIVE
SAISE

Lusaka Central Sports Club

KABELENGA
LONGOLONGO
MAKISHI
BROADS
MWILWA
OMELO
NAMAMBOZI
CHINGOMBE
**Kapila (Rhodes Park)**
KATEMO

Namibian Embassy

MUSHEMI
KASISI

**Chachacha**

MALASHA
MAKANTA
MULOMBWE
PARIRENYETWA
KATEMO

TITO
KABANGA

CHILEKWE
MWAMBA

Longacres Hostel

KALUNDWE

**Maluba (Fairview)**
Democratic Republic of the Congo Embassy

PROTEA

ANDREW MWENYA
BEIT
CHIPOMA
LOS ANGELES BOULEVARD

HAILE SELASSIE AVE

Market

CHIPARAMBA

CAIRO

CHURCH

LUANO

LUBWA
MWAIMWENA

Lusaka Girls Primary School

Zimbabwean Embassy

Lusaka Club

DAR ES SALAAM

Police

NYAKASEYA

CHIKWA
BIRDCAGE

Lusaka Boys Primary School

LOS ANGELES BOULEVARD

Cinema
NKWAZI
HEROES

CHILUBI

CHURCH

Pamodzi

Inter-Continental
Tanzanian Embassy

Lusaka
Library

AA

ITUNA
MUCHISHA

Theatre Club
SUEZ

Church
High Court
CHILUFYA
MULENGA

Botswanan Embassy

FREEDOM WAY
KATONDO

DEDAN KIMATHI

Lusaka Railway Station

DUSHAMBE

KAYOMBO

Holiday Inn Garden Court
Lusaka Ridgeway
CHIMANGA

Canadian Embassy

Inter-Continental Ndeke
MPANGWE

Synagogue

BUTEKO
SAPELE

Intercity Bus Terminal

KAYOMBO

INDEPENDENCE AVE

Civic Centre

MOGADISHU

Kenyan Embassy

UNITED NATIONS

KATUNJILA

Australian Embassy
CHAINDA

KWAME
NKRUMAH

MBOYA

Freedom Statue

RAPHAEL KOMBE

NSUNZE

**Cathedral Hill**

Dutch Embassy

MZEE KENYATTA

CHISIDZA

Kulima Towers
City Bus Station

Cinema
Buses

CHANGA

Cenotaph

FAIRLEY

British & American Embassies

NGUMBO

BEN BELLA

Comesa Building

CHAKWU

Hindu Temple
ISUNGA

Lotus Primary School

Edwin Imboela Stadium

**Luburma (Madras)**

GOVERNMENT

**Ridgeway**

INDEPENDENCE AVEN

Market
SIND
DELHI

MUKUPE
OBOTE
GANDHI

Police

National Archives

University of Zambia Ridgeway Campus

NSUMBU

BOMBAY

Palace Cinema

KARACHI

Metropolitan Sports Club

BURMA

Burma Road Primary School

JACARANDA

JOHN MBITA

NGULUBE

Kamwala Clinic

Lotus Sports Club

MOPANI

Mumuni Primary School

NKAN DABWE
SEKOU TOURE

PAUL BANDE

NATIONALIST

LUANGWA
LUENA

Lusaka City Tennis Club

INDUS
LUCHELE

ZIMBA
OBOTE

Kabwata Cultural Centre

CHAKUNKULE
ZINNIA

Nationalist Stadium

MANENEKELA
KAPUMI

CHONGWE
CIP
DONGWE
KALUNGWISHI
LUTEMPWE
MANSHYA
KWANDO
LUMEZI
KAKUZI
LUKULU
MKUSHI
CHILIMBULU
MALATA
MIBYA
MBOYA

HIBISCUS

University Teaching Hospital

CHITE

BEN BELLA

LUAPULA
MUSI
MACHI

NANGOMBE
MWAMBWA

Kamwala Secondary School

St Patrick's Primary School

**Kabwata**

LIVINGSTONE
UFULU

Police

CHIPEMBELE
KANGO

David Kaunda Technical Scho

LUAMBA
MUSANYA
LII
LUNU
LUSITU

DR AGGREY
KANSOKOMA
CHITE
MATALA
SEVENTH
NKATENGA

Kabwata Clinic

MASA

NINTH
BURMA

Waddington Centre

**Missi**

**M** 0 — 600
**Yd** 0 — 600

**Kamwala**

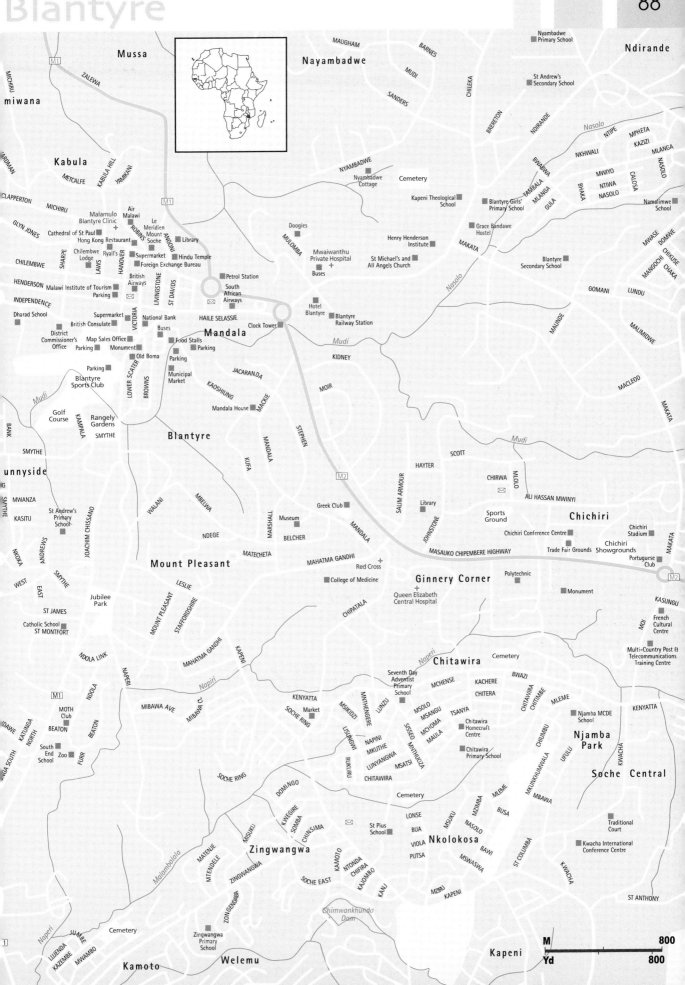

Mussa
miwana
Kabula
MICHIRU
ZALEWA
M1

Nayambadwe
MAUGHAM
BARNES
MUDI
SANDERS
CHILEKA
BRERETON

Nyambadwe Primary School
St Andrew's Secondary School
Ndirande

Nyambadwe Cottage
Cemetery
Kapeni Theological School
NDIRANDE
BWABWA
Nasolo
NTIPE
MPHETA
KAZIZI
MLANGA
NKHWALI
MWIYO
NTIWA
NASOLO
BHAKA
CALOSA
NASOLO
GULA
MLANGA
TAMBALA

MICHRU
MALAMULO Blantyre Clinic
Air Malawi
Le Meridien Mount Soche
ROBINS
Library
Cathedral of St Paul
Hong Kong Restaurant
Chilembwe Lodge
Ryall's
Supermarket
Foreign Exchange Bureau
Hindu Temple
British Airways
Malawi Institute of Tourism
Parking
Dharad School
Supermarket
National Bank
British Consulate
Buses
District Commissioner's Office
Map Sales Office
Parking
Monument
Old Boma
Parking
Blantyre Sports Club
Municipal Market

Blantyre Girls' Primary School
Grace Bandawe Hostel
Blantyre Secondary School
Henry Henderson Institute
St Michael's and All Angels Church
MAKATA
Doogles
MULOMBA
Mwaiwanthu Private Hospital
Buses
Petrol Station
South African Airways
Hotel Blantyre
Blantyre Railway Station
Clock Tower
Food Stalls
Parking
Mandala
HAILE SELASSIE
Mudi
KIDNEY
Nasolo
MWASE
DOMWE
CHIKUSE
CHAKA
MANGOCHI
GOMANI
LUNDU
MAUNDE
MACLEOD
MALIMIDWE

Mussa
Kabula
Golf Course
Mudi
Rangely Gardens
SMYTHE
KAMPALA
Blantyre
KAOSHIUNG
MACKIE
Mandala House
JACARANDA
STEPHEN
MOIR
Mudi
SCOTT
HAYTER
CHIRWA
MLOLO
ALI HASSAN MWINYI
Chichiri
MAKATA
Chichiri Stadium
Chichiri Showgrounds
Portuguese Club

unnyside
MWANZA
KASITU
St Andrew's Primary School
JOACHIM CHISSANO
KUFA
MBELWA
WALANI
NDEGE
MARSHALL
Museum
BELCHER
Greek Club
MANDALA
Library
Sports Ground
Chichiri Conference Centre
Trade Fair Grounds
JOHNSTONE
SALIM ARMOUR
M2

BANK
SMYTHE
ANDREWS
SMYTHE
WEST
EAST
ST JAMES
Catholic School
ST MONTFORT
Jubilee Park
LESLIE
MOUNT PLEASANT
STAFFORDSHIRE
Mount Pleasant
MATECHETA
MAHATMA GANDHI
Red Cross
College of Medicine
Ginnery Corner
Queen Elizabeth Central Hospital
Polytechnic
Monument
MOI
French Cultural Centre
KASUNGU
Multi-Country Post & Telecommunications Training Centre

NKOKA
NDOLA LINK
NDOLA
NAPERI
MAHATMA GANDHI
KAPENI
Napiri
M1
MOTH Club
BEATON
MIBAWA AVE
MIBAWA CT
Napiri
KENYATTA
Market
SOCHE RING
CHIPATALA
Seventh Day Adventist Primary School
Chitawira
MCHENSE
KACHERE
CHITERA
BWAZI
Cemetery
CHITAWIRA
CHITIMBE
MLEME
Njamba MCDE School
KENYATTA

IDAWE
KATUNGA NORTH
South End School
Zoo
FURR
BEATON
MSIKIDZI
LUNZU
MSOLO
MSANGU
MCHOMA
MAULA
TSANYA
Chitawira Homecraft Centre
Chitawira Primary School
CHIDMBU
UFULU
Njamba Park
Soche Central

SOCHE RING
MISUKU
DOMINGO
KWEGIRE
SOMBA
CHINSIMA
LISUNGWI
NAPINI
MKUTHE
LUNYANGWA
RUKIURU
CHITAWIRA
Cemetery
LONSE
MZIMBA
MSUKU
BUA
VIOLA
Nkolokosa
NASOLO
BUSA
MLEME
MBAWA
MKUNKHUMWALA
Traditional Court
Kwacha International Conference Centre

Zingwangwa
MATENJE
MTENDELE
ZINGWANGWA
St Pius School
KAMOTO
NTONDA
CHIFIRA
KAJOMBO
KANJ
PUTSA
BAWI
MSWASIWA
ST COLUMBA
KWACHA
Malombolola
ZON GENDABA
Zingwangwa Primary School
Welemu
SOCHE EAST
MZIRU
Chimwankhunda Dam
Kapeni
ST ANTHONY
Cemetery
Napiri
LUJENDA
JUMBE
KAZEMBE
MWAMBO
Kamoto

M
Yd
800
800

# Dar es Salaam

INDIAN

OCEAN

*Msimbazi Bay*

SELANDER BRIDGE

Police

Church

MINDU

URAMBO

Palm Beach

Sea View

UPANGA

Etienne's

LUGALO

OCEAN

ISIMANI

MITTU

LONGIDO

MAGORE

KITONGA

Aga Khan

KALENGA

MINDU

MALIK

NKOMO

+ Muhimbili

MALI

NYANGORO

UNDALI

MAWENI

ALYKHAN

ALI HASSAN MWINYI

Golf Course

UNITED NATIONS

ISEYA

KIBASILA

Upanga

OCEAN

MATHURADAS KAPIDAS

MAZENGO

MFAUME

OLYMPIO

ALYKHAN

MAGORE

Gymkhana Club

CHIMARA

MATAKA

Sheraton

Ocean Road Hospital

SENEGAL

Court

OHIO

GHANA

MIRAMBO

Botanical Gardens

Karimjee Hall

Library

SHAABANI ROBERT

FIRE STATION

Kisutu

UWT

YMCA

St Alban's Church

GARDEN

National Museum

MOROGORO

NYATI

FARU

KIPANDE

KISUTU

YWCA

KIBO

OHIO

SAMORA MACHEL

TWIGA

LIVINGSTONE

Embassy

PAMBA

NDOVU

UDOWE

MAKTABA

Parliament

LUTHULI

State House

RUFIJI

KARIAKOO

M.TENDENI

Mchafukoge

SIMU

MKWEPU

OCEAN

WANYAMWEZI

MSIMBAZI

NYASA

Morogoro

AFRICA

CHUSI

Askari Monument

Starlight

MADARAKA

MAGOGONI

AMANI

SIKUKUU

UKAMI

Buses

JAMHURI

ASTA

SEWA

ZANAKI

Agip

Kilimanjaro

High Court

MAFIA

MKUNGUNI

CHAGA

MALI

INDIRA GANDHI

New Africa

Lutheran Centre

SIKUMA

MKUNGUNI

BAND

Motel Afrique

BRIDGE

SAMORA MACHEL

Cenotaph

KIVUKONI FRONT

MAFIA

TANDAMUTI

LUMUMBA

MSHIHIRI

INDIA

MALUTA

MANSFIELD

SOKOINE DRIVE

Buses

PEMBA

NARUNG

OMBE

MAHIWA

Mosque

JANAT

MORDGORO

Twiga

Kariakoo Market

MCHIKICHI

MARKET

Mosque

St Joseph's Cathedral

Kariakoo

+ Clinic

MISSION

City Hall

MUHONDA

AGGREY

Mosque

ALGERIA

UHURU

Clock Tower

Police

LINDI

RAILWAY

Buses

KIPATA

NKRUMAH

Railway Station

*Harbour*

LINDI

LIBYA

+ ID Clinic

SOMALI

Police

M          500

KIUNGANI

*Malindi Wharf*

Yd          500

MBARUKU

KISARAWE

KONGO

VIWANDA

*Kigamboni*

Buses

LUGODA

PUGU

GEREZANI

GEREZANI

Keko

BANDARI

*Main Quay*

KILWA

Police

# Nairobi

PARKLANDS ■ Esperia

MASARI

SECOND PARKLANDS

BATU BATU GDNS

Aga Khan Hospital ✛

C62

Cemetery

CITY PARK

Holiday Inn Nairobi Mayfair Court ■

MSAPO CL

MSAPO LA

FIRST PARKLANDS

MAJATHA

BHANDARI

THIRD PARKLANDS

LIMURU

City Park

WAIYAKI WAY

MPESI

MPAKA

CRESCENT LA

THE CRESCENT

MP Shah Hospital ✛

Shopping Centre ■

Police ■

PARKLANDS

WAMBUGU GR

WAMBUGU LA

WAMBUGU GDNS

WAMBUGU RD

FIRST PARKLANDS

Premier Club ■

Shimba Union Club ■

Shopping Centre ■

West View

KASKAZI

MUTHITHI

MUKINDURI

OJIJO CL

Parklands Club

TAARIFO

MADAME CURIE

MUHUGU LA

MUHUGU RD

FOREST RD

MSHALE

CROSSWAY

HIMALAYA

MOGOTIO

NOSHABA

Shopping Centre

SPORTS

MUKUI

FOREST LANE

SOIT OLOLOL

WOODVALE

Westlands

WESTLANDS

CHIROMO LA.

PLUMS

CORK

OJIJO RD

WINDSOR Golf

MUNAE

KOLOBOT

POKOT

LIMURU

Kenya Institute of Education ■

NDEGE

MURANGA

DESAI

MADRAS

Nairobi

RIVERSIDE DRIVE

CHIROMO ROAD

A104

MUTHITHI

KEIYO

GALLA

SAMBURU

KIPKOBUS

CHEMILIL

SHILLINGI

KEEKU

TIWI

KIVULI

MURANGA LANE

BUJUNI

NAHAR SINGH

KINSHASA

SIMBI

RING ROAD RIVERSIDE

Kirichwa Kubwa

ARBORETUM DRIVE

International Casino

MUSEUM HILL

NGARA

National Museum ■

Game Park Car Passes Office

A2

MBOGO

CHAMBERS

MBUYU

Maternity Hospital ✛

NGARA LA

NGARA

IRUNGU RIIKA RD

RUNGU RIIKA LA.

DESAI

BORAN

THINGIRA

LOME

Chiromo

Snake Park ■

MBUYU

Fig Tree ■

RAMESH GAUTAMA

Shan Cinema ■

MUSINDI LA

MUSINDI RD

JODONGO LA

JODONGO RD

Nairobi Arboretum

Art Gallery ■

ARBORETUM RD

KOLOBOT

Masonga Wai

University Sports Grounds

Boulevard ■

Voice of Kenya Studios ■

Nairobi

KIJABE

KIPANDE

Kenya International ■

Market

Kenya Arts Society ■

STATE HOUSE RD

UHURU

Norfolk ■

HARRY THUKU

Kenya National Theatre ■

Police ■

Globe Cinema ■

New Parkside ■

KIRINYAGA

NGIRIAM RD

KEEKOROK

NGARIAMA LA.

RIVER

KILOME

NGARIAMA

CROSS RD

KIRINYAGA

Casino ■

KUMASI

CROSS LA

KIVEMA

MAMLAKA

Centre YMCA ■

Kenya Cultural Centre ■

Synagogue ■

UNIVERSITY

Jevanjee Gardens

MURANGA

MOI

Meridian Court ■

NDUMBERI

Parking ■

Fire Station ■

LAGOS

New Kenya Lodge ■

DUBOIS

DURUMA

RIVER

DOROBO

United Kenya Club ■

MONROVIA

Nairobi Safari Club Terminal ■

NJUGU

BIASHARA

MUINDI MBINGU

TUBMAN

Library ■

Cinema ■

LATEMA

Iqbal ■

TSAVO

TIMBOROA

ACCRA

LUTHUDI

Gardens

Goethe Institute ■

French Cultural Centre ■

M DADDAH

Embassy ■

Library ■

Nation Centre ■

Cinema ■

TOM MBOYA

GABORONE

SHEIKH KARUME

Sports Ground

NYERERE

KOINANGE

LOITA

Parking ■

MARKET

Jamia Mosque ■

BANDA

KIMATHI

KENYATTA

Cinema ■

Oakwood ■

New Stanley ■

Gallery ■

Watatu ■

National Archives ■

Dolat ■

RONALD NGALA

TEMPLE LA

UDOMA

YMCA ■

MAM LAKA

Central Park

STANDARD

WABERA

KAUNDA

MAMA NGINA

Hilton ■

Gloria ■

Florida Night Club ■

Ambassadeur ■

Library ■

Bus Terminal ■

MFANGANO ST

Nairobi Serena ■

POSTA ✉

Holy Family Cathedral ■

CInema ■

CITY HALL

City Hall ■

Cinema ■

NKRUMAH AVE

GEDI

Cinema ■

Princess ■

HAKATI

HAILE SELASSIE

WERUGA

STATE HOUSE RD

STATE HOUSE AVE

STATE HOUSE CRESCENT

Nairobi Hill

KENYATTA

Nairobi Province HQ Immigration Department ■

Intercontinental ■

City Square

Inoculation Centre ✛

Office of the President ■

Kenyatta Conference Centre ■

Parking ■

TAIFA

Parking ■

Parking ■

Cinema ■

NKRUMAH LA

Hermes ■

EXCHANGE

RAILWAY

MILIMANI RD

RALPH BUNCHE

MILIMANI LANE

Milimani ■

Heron Court ■

MILIMANI RD

All Saints Cathedral ■

PROCESSIONAL

Jomo Kenyatta's Mausoleum ■

HARAMBEE

Police HQ ■

TUMBO

Railways Clinic ✛

HAILE SELASSIE

MOI

Sagret ■

Police ■

Panafric ■

CATHEDRAL

Uhuru Fountain

Parliament Buildings ■

PARLIAMENT

✉

NGAIRA

Nairobi Railway Station ■

LENANA

WATO

VALLEY

Fairview ■

Uhuru Park

Phoenix Players ■

Donovan Maule Theatre ■

PATE BAY

STATION

PEDESTRIAN BRIDGE

Grosvenor ■

BISHOPS

FIRST NGONG

SECOND NGONG

UPPER HILL

Railway Sports Club ■

WORKSHOP

WOODLANDS RD

Hurlingham Shopping Centre ■

Reservoir

Silver Springs ■

Nairobi Youth Hostel ■

THIRD NGONG

FOURTH NGONG

RAGATI

HAILE SELASSIE

Railway Golf Club ■

FACTORY

ISEBANIA

ARGWINGS KODHEK

FIFTH NGONG

RALPH BUNCHE

National Library ■

Jex Blake Gardens

Railway Museum ■

COMMERCIAL

Shopping Centre ■

VALLEY

Nairobi Hospital ✛

Nairobi Club ■

KIBO

RAGATI

CHIYULU

HILL

MARA

Golf Course

LOWER HILL

A104

BUNYALA

DUNGA

NGONG

Ngong

Sports Ground

Parking ■

Teaching Hospital ✛

KIBO

MARA

MENENGAI

Nairobi Hill

KILIMANJARO

KENYA

UPPER HILL

Cemetery

MUCAI RD

MICAL DR

MBAGATHI

Public Service Club ■

Parking ■

Kenyatta National Hospital ✛

Police ■

HOSPITAL

LONGONOT

ELGON

M

Yd

600

600

AERODROME

UHURU

MASABA

SOLAI

BARICHO

CHEKORIO

LUSAKA

Golf Course Estate

MBAGATHI WAY

Industrial

# Kampala, Bujumbura & Kigali

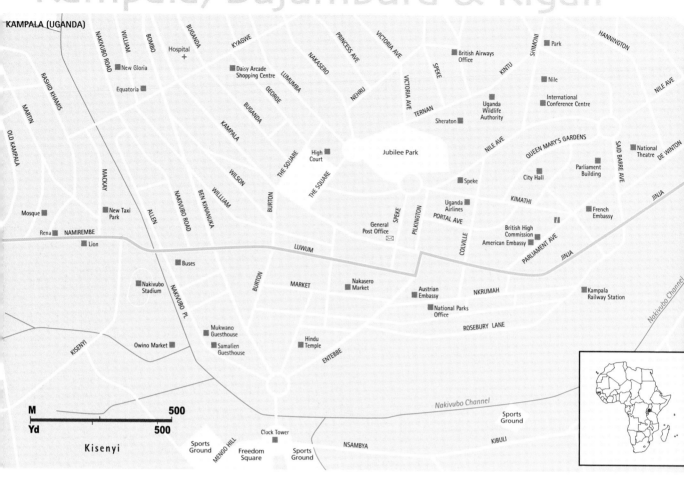

## KAMPALA (UGANDA)

RASHID KHAMIS
NAKIVUBO ROAD
WILLIAM
BOMBO
BUGANDA
KYAGWE
NAKASERO
PRINCESS AVE.
VICTORIA AVE.
HANNINGTON
SHIMONI
Park
British Airways Office
Hospital +
New Gloria
Daisy Arcade Shopping Centre
LUMUMBA
GEORGE
NEHRU
VICTORIA AVE.
SPEKE
TERNAN
KINTU
Nile
International Conference Centre
Equatoria
BUGANDA
Uganda Wildlife Authority
NILE AVE.
Sheraton
MARTIN
OLD KAMPALA
KAMPALA
Jubilee Park
QUEEN MARY'S GARDENS
National Theatre
DE WINTON
MACKAY
WILSON
THE SQUARE
High Court
NILE AVE.
Speke
City Hall
Parliament Building
SAID BARRE AVE.
ALLEN
NAKIVUBO ROAD
BEN KIWANUKA
WILLIAM
BURTON
THE SQUARE
KIMATHI
Mosque
New Taxi Park
SPEKE
PILKINGTON
Uganda Airlines
PORTAL AVE.
COLVILLE
British High Commission
French Embassy
JINJA
Rena
NAMIREMBE
Lion
General Post Office
American Embassy
PARLIAMENT AVE.
JINJA
Buses
LUWUM
Austrian Embassy
NKRUMAH
Kampala Railway Station
BURTON
MARKET
Nakasero Market
National Parks Office
Nakivubo Stadium
NAKIVUBO PL.
ROSEBURY LANE
Nakivubo Channel
KISENYI
Mukwano Guesthouse
Hindu Temple
Owino Market
Samalien Guesthouse
ENTEBBE
M 500
Yd 500
Nakivubo Channel
Sports Ground
Kisenyi
Clock Tower
Sports Ground
MENGO HILL
Freedom Square
Sports Ground
NSAMBYA
KIBULI

## BUJUMBURA (BURUNDI)

Imprimerie Nationale
Kwijabe
AVE DE LA JEUNESSE
BOULEVARD DU PORT
CHAUSSÉE DU PEUPLE MURUNDI
Bwiza
AVE DU STADE
Mosque
Cercle Hippique
Golf Course
Paroisse St-Michel
Rohero II
BOULEVARD DE L'INDÉPENDENCE
Stadium
Sources du Nil
North Korean Embassy
Russian Embassy
BOULEVARD DU 1ER NOVEMBRE
Libyan Embassy
Mosque
BOULEVARD DE L'UPRONA
Burundi Palace
Dutch Embassy
French Embassy
Présidence
BOULEVARD DE L'INDÉPENDENCE
Quartier Asiatique
Italian Embassy
Air Burundi
Rwandan Embassy
AVE DE LA NTAHANGWA
L'IMBO
Tanzanian Embassy
Stadium
AVE URB
DES SWAHILIS
German Embassy
Market
American Embassy
CHAUSSÉE PRINCE LOUIS RWAGASORE
Rohero I
Cuban Embassy
DE LA SCIENCE
AVE DE L'ENSEIGNEMENT
Musée Vivant
AVE DE LA POSTE
Rwagasore Hospital
AVE DU 13 OCTOBRE
PLACE DE LA RÉVOLUTION
Institut Géographique du Burundi
AVE PIERRE NGENDANDUMWE
AVE DES NON ALIGNÉS
AVE DU 18 SEPTEMBRE
BLVD DE LA LIBERTÉ
CHAUSSÉE DU GITEGA
AVE DE NGOZI
Kabondo
Cathedral
BOULEVARD DU 28 NOVEMBRE
M 500
Yd 500
Athénée

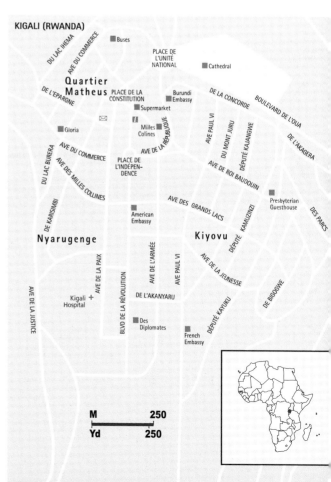

## KIGALI (RWANDA)

Buses
DU LAC IHEMA
AVE DU COMMERCE
PLACE DE L'UNITÉ NATIONAL
Cathedral
Quartier Matheus
DE L'EPARGNE
PLACE DE LA CONSTITUTION
Burundi Embassy
DE LA CONCORDE
BOULEVARD DE L'OUA
Supermarket
Gloria
Milles Colines
AVE DE LA RÉPUBLIQUE
AVE PAUL VI
DU MONT JURU
DÉPUTÉ KAJANGWE
DE L'AKAGERA
DU LAC BURERA
AVE DU COMMERCE
PLACE DE L'INDÉPEN-DENCE
AVE DE ROI BAUDOUIN
DES PARCS
DE KARISIMBI
AVE DES MILLES COLINES
AVE DES GRANDS LACS
Presbyterian Guesthouse
American Embassy
Kiyovu
DÉPUTÉ KAMUZINZI
DE BIGOGWE
Nyarugenge
AVE DE L'ARMÉE
AVE PAUL VI
AVE DE LA JEUNESSE
AVE DE LA PAIX
Kigali Hospital
DE L'AKANYARU
AVE VI
DÉPUTÉ KAYUKU
AVE DE LA JUSTICE
BLVD DE LA RÉVOLUTION
Des Diplomates
French Embassy
M 250
Yd 250

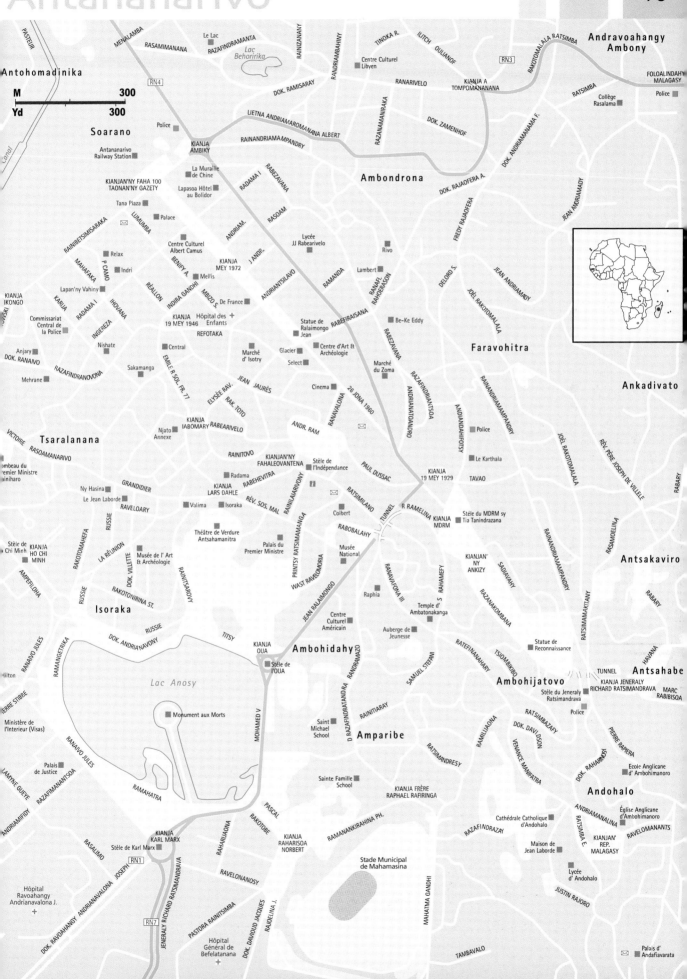

Antohomadinika

**M** 300
**Yd** 300

Soarano

Le Lac
RASAMIMANANA
RAZAFINDRAMANTA
Lac
Behoririka

RAINIZANANY
RANDRIAMBAHINY
TINOKA R.
IUTCH OULIANOF
RAKOTOMALALA RATSIMBA

**Andravoahangy
Ambony**

RN3

FOLOALINDAHY
MALAGASY

Police

RN4

Police

Antananarivo
Railway Station

KIANJA
AMBIKY

La Muraille
de Chine

KIANJAN'NY FAHA 100
TAONAN'NY GAZETY

Lapasoa Hôtel
au Bolidor

Tana Plaza

LUMUMBA

Palace

RAIN/BETSIMISARAKA

Relax

Indri

Mellis

RADAMA I

RABEZAVANA

RASOAM

RADAM.

J. ANDR.

ANDRIANTSILAVO

Lycée
JJ Rabearivelo

Rivo

Lambert

RANAFI.
RAHDERASON

RAMANDA

Be-Ke Eddy

Centre Culturel
Libyen

Centre Culturel
Libyen

DOK. RAMISARAY

RANARIVELO

LIETNA ANDRIAMAROMANANA ALBERT

RAINANDRIAMAMPANDRY

RAZANAMANIRAKA

DOK. ZAMENHOF

**Ambondrona**

KIANJA A
TOMPOMANANANA

Collège
Rasalama

RATSIMBA

DOK. ANDRIAMANAMA F.

JEAN ANDRIAMADY

FREDY RAJAOFERA

DOK. RAJAOFERA A.

JOËL RAKOTOMALALA

JEAN ANDRIAMADY

DELORD S.

**Faravohitra**

**Ankadivato**

Centre Culturel
Albert Camus

KIANJA
MEY 1972

Hôpital des
Enfants

REFOTAKA

Central

Marché
d' Isotry

Glacier

Select

Statue de
Ralaimongo
Jean

Centre d'Art &
Archéologie

Marché
du Zoma

Cinema

26 JONA 1960

RABEFIRAISANA

RABEZAVANA

RAZAFINDRIANTSOA

ANDRIANATOANDRO

Police

Le Karthala

KIANJA
19 MEY 1929

TAVAO

RAINANDRIAMAMPANDRY

JOËL RAKOTOMALALA

RÉV. PÈRE JOSEPH DE VILLELE

RABARY

RASAMOELINA

**Antsakaviro**

**Tsaralanana**

VICTOIRE

RASOAMANARIVO

KIANJA
IABOMARY

RABEARIVELO

Njato
Annexe

Radama

KIANJAN'NY
FAHALEOVANTENA

Stèle de
l'Indépendance

PAUL DUSSAC

ANDIANDAHIFOTSY

RAINANDRIAMAMPANDRY

Ny Hasina

Le Jean Laborde

GRANDIDIER

RAVELOARY

Valima

Isoraka

KIANJA
LARS DAHLE

RABEHEVITRA

RÉV. SOS. MAL.

RAINILAIARIVONY

RATSIMILANO

Colbert

RABOBALAHY

R RAMELINA

KIANJA
MDRM

Stèle du MDRM sy
Tia Tanindrazana

KIANJAN'
NY
ANKIZY

SADAVAHY

RAINANDRIAMAMPANDRY

RATSIMAMAKITANY

HAVANA

**Antsahabe**

Stèle de
Chi Minh

KIANJA
HO CHI
MINH

RAKOTOMAHEFA

RUSSIE

LA RÉUNION

Théâtre de Verdure
Antsahamanitra

Palais du
Premier Ministre

Musée
National

Raphia

Centre
Culturel
Américain

Auberge de
Jeunesse

RAZANAKOMBANA

Statue de
Reconnaissance

TSIOMBIKIBO

TUNNEL

KIANJA JENERALY
RICHARD RATSIMANDRAVA

MARC
RABIBISOA

**Ambohijatovo**

**Isoraka**

AMPEFILOHA

RUSSIE

RUSSIE

RAKOTONIRINA ST.

RANITSAROVY

TITSY

DOK. ANDRIANAVONY

Musée de l' Art
& Archéologie

WAST RAVEOMORIA

JEAN RALAIMONGO

RANAVALONA III

S. RAHAMEFY

Temple d'
Ambatonakanga

RATEFINANAHARY

SAMUEL STEFANI

Stèle du Jeneraly
Ratsimandrava

Police

RATSIMBAZAFY

DOK. DAVIDSON

VENANCE MANIFATRA

PIERRE RAPIERA

DOK. RAHARIMPY

Ecole Anglicane
d' Ambohimanoro

**Tombeau du
Premier Ministre
Rainiharo**

EMILE R. SOL. FR. 77

ELYSÉE RAV.

RAK. TOTO

JEAN JAURÈS

ANDR. RAM

RANAVALONA

Palais du
Premier Ministre

**Ambohidahy**

KIANJA
OUA

Stèle de
l'OUA

**Amparibe**

RANDRAMPAZO

RAINITIARAY

Saint
Michael
School

RAMILIJAONA

D RAZAFINDRATANDRA

**Andohalo**

**Ambohimanoro**

Hilton

Ministère de
l'Interieur (Visas)

RANANO JULES

Palais
de Justice

RAMANGETRIKA

RAMAHATRA

RANAVO JULES

RAZAFIMANANTSOA

Lac Anosy

Monument aux Morts

MOHAMED V

Sainte Famille
School

KIANJA FRÈRE
RAPHAEL RAFIRINGA

Cathédrale Catholique
d'Andohalo

ANDRIAMANALINA

Église Anglicane
d'Ambohimanoro

RAVELOMANANTS

Maison de
Jean Laborde

KIANJAN'
REP.
MALAGASY

RATSIMBA E.

RAMONJISOA

IERE STIBBE

ANDRIAMIFIDY

LAMYNE GUEYE

KIANJA
KARL MARX

Stèle de Karl Marx

RASALIMO

RN1

RAHARIBAONA

RAKOTORE

PASCAL

KIANJA
RAHARISOA
NORBERT

RAMANANKIRAHINA PH.

Lycée
d' Andohalo

RAZAFINDRAZAY

JUSTIN RAJORO

Hôpital
Ravoahangy
Andrianavalona J.

DOK. RAVOAHANGY ANDRIANAVALONA JOSEPH

JENERALY RICHARD RATSIMANDRAVA

RN7

PASTORA RAINITSIMBA

RAVELONANOSY

DOK. DAVIOUD JACQUES

RAJOELINA J.

Stade Municipal
de Mahamasina

MAHAMA GANDHI

MAHATMA GANDHI

TAMBAVALO

Hôpital
Général de
Befelatanana

Palais d'
Andafiavarata

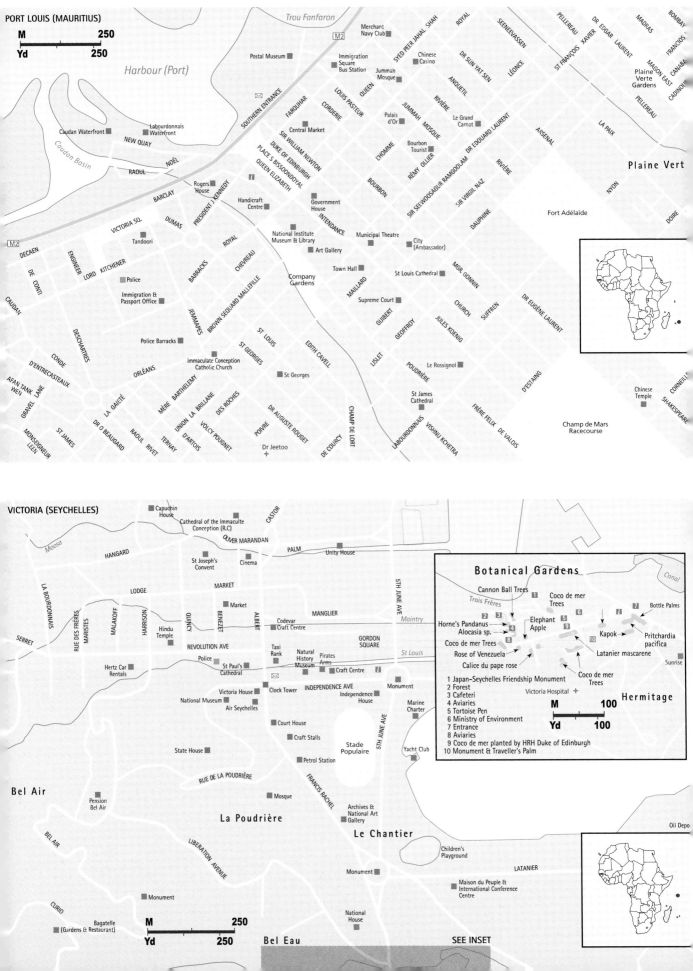

Port Louis & Victoria

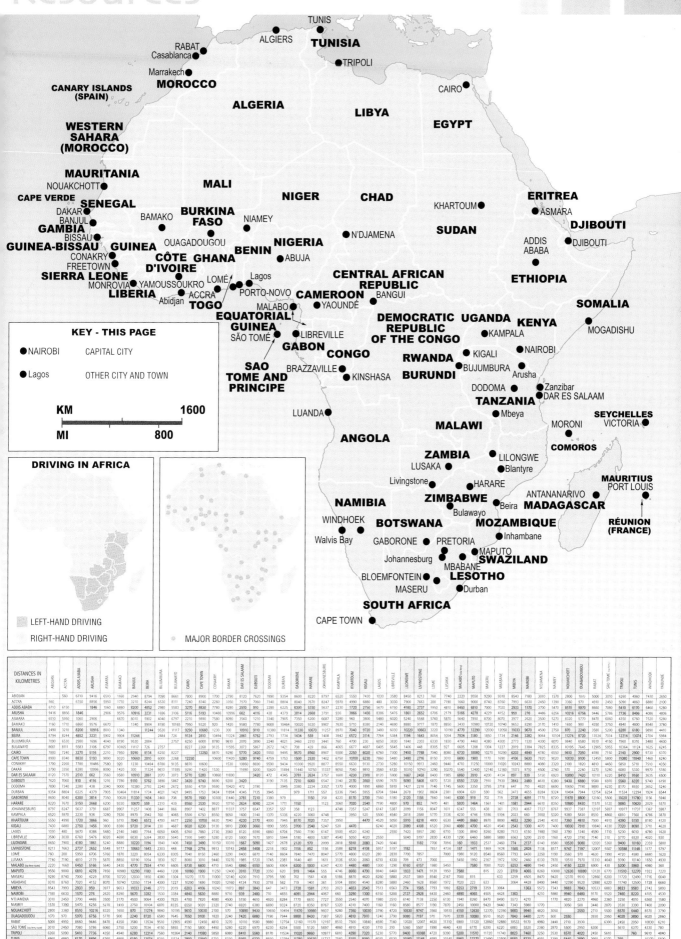

KEY - THIS PAGE

● NAIROBI — CAPITAL CITY

• Lagos — OTHER CITY AND TOWN

KM 1600
MI 800

DRIVING IN AFRICA

▨ LEFT-HAND DRIVING
RIGHT-HAND DRIVING

• MAJOR BORDER CROSSINGS

## SOUTH AFRICA

### SOUTH AFRICA MULTIPLE LISTINGS

**Sabie Extreme Adventures**
013 764 2118 ww.satic.co.za
**Jacana Marketing and Reservations**
012 346 3550 ww.jacanacollection.co.za
**SANParks** 012 428 9111 ww.parks-sa.co.za
**Cape Nature Conservation**
021 426 0723 ww.cnc.org.za
**Bass Lake Adventures**
016 366 1127 ww.basslake.co.za
**Day Trippers**
021 511 4766 ww.daytrippers.co.za
**Wild Coast Trails**
039 305 6455 ww.wild-coast.co.za
**Active Africa**
021 788 8750 ww.activeafrica.co.za
**Aloe Afrika Adventures**
042 293 3871 aloe@agnet.co.za
**Wildthing Adventures** 021 423 5804
ww.wildthing.co.za
**Living on the Edge Adventures**
011 954 5584 ww.livingontheedge.co.za
**Emvelo KZN Wildlife**
033 845 1000 ww.kznwildlife.com
**Stormsriver Adventures**
042 281 1836 ww.stormsriver.com
**Garden Route Eco Adventure Tours**
044 691 2128 ww.great.co.za
**Bokpoort Horseback Adventures & Game Ranch** 058 256 1181 ww.bokpoort.co.za
**Safcol** 012 481 3615 ww.safcoltourism.co.za
**Downhill Adventures** 021 422 0388
**Cape Sports Center**
022 772 1114 ww.capesport.co.za
**Golden Monkey Reservations**
013 737 8191 ww.big5country.com
**SA Tourism 011 895 3000**
**ww.southafrica.net**

### ABSEILING / RAPP JUMPING

**Table Mountain, W.Cape**•Abseil Africa
021 424 4760 ww.abseilafrica.co.za
**Knysna and Robberg, W.Cape**•SEAL Advent.
ww.sealadventures.co.za 044 382 5599
•Adventure Centre Knysna Heads
044 384 0831 ww.headsadventurecentre.co.za
**Gauteng and nationwide**•Pure Rush
Adventures 082 605 1150 ww.purerush.co.za
**Mpumalanga**•Sabie Extreme Adventures
**Free State**•Bergwoning 058 256 1124
ww.bergwoning.co.za
**Howick Falls, KwaZulu-Natal**•Over the Top
Advent. 033 344 3044 ww.overthetop.co.za
**Eastern Cape**•Oribi Xtreme
039 687 0253 ww.oribigorge.co.za

## ROCK CLIMBING & MOUNTAINEERING

•Mountain Club of South Africa
021 465 3412 ww.mcsa.org.za
**Table Mountain & Cederberg, W.Cape**
•Blue Mountain Adventures
021 439 8199 tonyblue@iafrica.com
•Guided Ascents in Africa 021 788 3894
ww.southscape.co.za •Active Africa
•Cape Town School of Mountaineering
021 531 4290 ww.ctsm.co.za
**Free State**•Clarens Adventure
058 256 1358 ww.cranford.co.za
**Waterval Boven, Mpumalanga**•Roc & Rope
Adventures 013 257 0363 ww.rocrope.com
**Drakensberg and KwaZulu-Natal**•Peak High
Mountaineering ww.peakhigh.co.za
033 343 3168 •Wildways Mountaineering
031 767 2160 ww.wildways.za.net•Little
Switzerland Res. 036 438 6222 ww.lsh.co.za

### KLOOFING

**Eastern Cape**•Stormsriver Adventures
**Western Cape**•Venture Forth Excursions
021 424 0116 ww.ventureforth.co.za
•Day Trippers•Quantum Adventures
083 727 7055 ww.quantumadventures.co.za
•180 Degree Adv. 021 462 0992 ww.180.co.za
**Mpumalanga** •Sabie Extreme Adventures

### HIKING

**Gauteng, Mpumalanga, Free State, Limpopo,
North West**•Hiking Africa Safaris & Tours 082
854 5853 ww.hikingafrica.co.za
•Jacana Marketing and Reservations
•Safcol •Anvie Ventures 012 662 1140
ww.anvieventures.co.za
**Western Cape**
•Cape Nature Conservation•Active Africa
•Cape of Good Hope & Hoerikwaggo Trails
SANParks 012 428 9111 ww.parks-sa.co.za
•Whale trail, De Hoop Reserve
028 425 5020 dehoopinfo@sdm.dorea.co.za
•Oystercatcher Trail, Mossel Bay
082 550 4788 forban@mweb.co.za
**KwaZulu-Natal** •Emvelo KZN Wildlife
**Mpumalanga**•Golden Monkey Reservations
**Eastern Cape & Wild Coast** •Wild Coast
Trails•Wild Coast Holiday Reservations
+27 43 743 6181 ww.wildcoast.co.za
**Dolphin Trail, Tsitsikamma** Stormsriver
Advent.•Amatola Trail 043 642 2571
amatolhk@dwaf.gov.za

## HORSERIDING

**Limpopo**•Wait a Little Horse and Game Ranch
083 273 9788 ww.waitalittle.co.za
•Jacana Marketing and Reservations
**Eastern Cape** •Wild Coast Trails
**Waterberg North West**•Equus Horse Safaris
014 721 0063 / 11 721 0062 ww.equus.co.za
•Horizon Horseback Adventures
+27 83 236 8500 horizonranch@yebo.net
**Free State and Mpumalanga**
•Bokpoort Horseback Adventures & GR
**KwaZulu-Natal**•Biggarsberg Horse Trails
034 651 1378 ww.horseadventures.co.za
•Maputaland Horse Safaris
035 574 8825 ww.maputaland.net
**Winelands, W.Cape**•Spier 021 809 1908
reservations@spier.co.za•Wine Valley Horse
Trails 021 869 8687 ww.horsetrails.co.za
**Cederberg & West Coast**•Excelsior Farm
022 914 5853 ww.picketberg.com
•Karukareb 027 482 1675 ww.karukareb.co.za
**Garden Route, W.Cape**
•Garden Route Eco Adventure Tours

### CAMEL RIDING

**Cape Town** •Cape Camel Rides
021 789 1711 ww.naturefarm.co.za

### CAVING

**Gauteng**•Wild Cave Adventures
011 956 6197 ww.wildcaves.co.za
**Western Cape**•Cango Caves
044 272 7410 ww.cangocaves.co.za

### SANDBOARDING

**Gauteng**•Pure Rush Industries
ww.purerush.co.za 082 605 1150
**Jeffrey's Bay, E.Cape**•Aloe Afrika Advent.
**Cape Town**•Downhill Advent. 021 422 0388

### SNOW SKIING / SNOWBOARDING

**Rhodes, E.Cape**•Tiffindell Ski & Alpine Resort
011 787 9090 ww.snow.co.za

### GAME VIEWING

•SANParks•Emvelo KZN Wildlife
•CC Africa 011 809 4300 ww.ccafrica.com
•Shamwari Game Reserve 042 203 1111
ww.shamwari.com

### HISTORICAL TOURS

•Fugitives Drift Lodge 034 642 1843
ww.fugitives-drift-lodge.com•Isibindi Eco
Reserve 011 467 1886 ww.zulunet.co.za
•Dundee 034 212 1347 ww.tourdundee.co.za

All telephone numbers listed with the South African dialling codes (if the numbers are located in South Africa), and all numbers outside of South Africa are given the standard international dialling codes (ie +260 3 for the Victoria Falls area in Zimbabwe). Please note that there is a high turnover of tourism and activity-based operations within Southern Africa, so the numbers listed in this section might change without notice. For space purposes, all website addresses listed are prefixed with "ww." instead of the standard "www.".

## 92

## BIRDING

•Birding Africa ww.birdingafrica.com
021 683 1898•Birdlife South Africa 035 753 5644
ww.birdlife.org.za•Lawsons Bird Watching
Tours +27 13 741 2458 www.lawsons.co.za

## MOUNTAINBIKING

**W.Cape**•Cape Nature Conservation
•Downhill Adventures•Day Trippers
**Garden Route**•Knysna Cycleworks
044 382 5153 ww.knysnacyles.co.za
•Mountain Biking Africa 082 783 8392
ww.mountainbikingafrica.co.za
**Northern Cape**•Kalahari Adventure Centre
ww.kalahari.co.za 054 451 0177
**Mpumalanga, North West, Limpopo**
•Jacana Marketing and Reservations
•Safcol•Dome Highland Trails
018 294 8572 domeavnt@iafrica.com
**Free State**•Bokpoort Horseback Adventures

## 4X4 TRAILS

•Continental Off-Road Academy
011 467 4040 ww.conti4x4academy.com
•Four Wheel Drive Club of SA 057 357 1605
•SANParks•Safcol•All Fours 4x4
014 743 1665 ww.serendipitytrails.co.za
**Gauteng and Mpumalanga**•Jacana Marketing
& Res.•Bass Lake Adventures
**Limpopo**•Jacana Marketing and Res.
•African Ivory Route 015 295 2829
ww.africanivoryroute.co.za•Taggallongg
011 975 3293 ww.tagalong.co.za
**Eastern Cape**•Off Road Adventures
082 783 1288 ww.off-road-adventures.co.za
**Free State**•Moolmanshoek Advent. Farm
051 933 2220 www.moolmanshoek.co.za
**KwaZulu-Natal**•Beach & Bush Advent.
031 569 1397 www.beachandbush.co.za
**W. Cape**•Cape Nature Conservation
•Cederberg Guided 4x4,  021 975 6531
ww.cederberg4x4.co.za •Klipbokkop Mtn
Resort Trail 023 340 4183 ww.klipbokkop.co.za
**Northern Cape**•Kalahari 4x4 Adventures
054 332 3098 www.kalahari4x4hire.co.za
•Khamkirri 082 821 6649 ww.khamkirri.co.za

## QUADBIKING

**Western Cape**•Adventure Village
021 424 1580 ww.adventure-village.co.za
**Gauteng, North West**•Bush bandits
011 768 2040 www.bushbandits.co.za
•Living on the Edge Adventures
**Mpumalanga**•Golden Monkey Reserv.
**KwaZulu-Natal**•Four Rivers Rafting
& Advent. ww.fourriversadventures.co.za
036 468 1693

## TRAIN RIDES

**Garden Route** •Outeniqua Choo-Tjoe
+27 44 801 8289 ww.onlinesources.co.za

## SCUBA DIVING

**Sodwana Bay, KZ-Natal**•Adventure Mania
082 653 7824 ww.adventuremania.co.za
•Coral Divers ww.coraldivers.co.za
035 571 0050•Sodwana Bay School of Diving
035 571 0117 ww.sodwanadiving.co.za
**Aliwal Shoal, KZ-Natal**•African Watersports
039 973 2505 ww.africanwatersports.com
**Cape Town, W.Cape** •Bubble Blowers
021 554 3817 info@bubbleblowers.co.za
•Dusky Diving School 021 426 1622
dusky@icon.co.za•Enviro Divers
021 715 3915 enviro@fre.absa.co.za
•Orca Industries 021 671 9673
ww.orca-industries.co.za •Scuba Shack
021 782 7358 info@scuba-shack.co.za

## SHARK CAGE DIVING

**Gansbaai, W.Cape**•Adventure Diving Safaris
012 991 3134 www.adventuredivingsafaris.com
•White Shark Adventures 028 384 1380
ww.whitesharkdiving.com
•White Shark Ecoventures 021 532 0470
ww.white-shark-diving.co.za•White Shark
Expeditions 028 312 3287 ww.sharklady.co.za
**Mossel Bay**•Shark Africa 044 691 3796
ww.sharkafrica.co.za

## SHARK DIVING

**False Bay, W.Cape**•African Shark Eco-
Charters 082 553 2945 sharky1@mweb.co.za

## SARDINE RUN

**Wild Coast and KZN South Coast**
•Blue Wilderness Safaris 039 973 2348
blue.wild@sco.eastcoast.co.za

## INLAND DIVING

**Gauteng, North West, Mpumalanga**
•Bass Lake Adventures •Komati Springs
082 650 2279 ww.technicaldivingafrica.com

## SEA KAYAKING

**West Coast, Langebaan, Cape Colombine &
Berg River** •Cape Sports Centre•West Coast
Guided Trails / The Beach Camp
082 926 2267 ww.ratrace.co.za
**Cape Peninsula** •Real Cape Adventures
082 556 2520 ww.seakayak.co.za
•Coastal Kayak Trails 021 439 1134
ww.kayak.co.za •Mikes Ocean Kayaks
021 790 2359 ww.mikesoceankayaks.co.za
**Wilderness Lagoon** •Eden Adventures
044 877 0179 ww.eden.co.za
**Plettenberg Bay/Knysna** •Kayak Ocean Blue
044 533 5083 ww.oceanadventures.co.za

•Dolphin Adventures 083 590 3405
ww.dolphinkayak.com
**Seal Island, Mossel Bay**
•Garden Route Eco Adventure Tours
**St Lucia & Umfolozi, KZN**•St Lucia Kayak
Safaris 035 550 5036 dandy@telkomsa.net

## WHITEWATER RAFTING & KAYAKING

**Mpumalanga**•Hardy Ventures 013 751 1693
ww.hardyventure.co.za•Otter's Den & White-
water 015 795 5488 ww.ottersden.co.za
**Gauteng, Free State, NW**•Whitewater Training
056 811 2597 www.whitewatertraining.co.za
•Living on the Edge Adventures•Splash
Whitewater Kayak School 011 475 0707
ww.splashwhitewater.co.za
**Tugela & Buffalo rivers, KwaZulu-Natal**
•Isibindi River Explorers 034 218 2460/
011 467 1886 ww.paddlesa.com•Zingela River
Tours and Safaris 036 354 1962
ww.zingelasafaris.co.za•River Tours and
Safaris 011 803 9775 ww.rafting.co.za
**Orange & Doring rivers, N. & W.Cape**
•Wildthing Adventures•Felix Unite (& Breede
R.) 021 683 6433 ww.felixunite.com •Intrapid
Rafting 021 461 4918 raftsa@iafrica.com
•Aquatrails 021 762 7916
ww.aquatrails.co.za •Kalahari Adventure
Centre (Orange River only) 054 451 0177
ww.augrabies.co.za •Bushwhacked
027 761 8953 ww.bushwhacked.co.za
•Gravity Adventure Group (also Palmiet
River) 021 683 3698 ww.gravity.co.za

## WHALE / DOLPHIN WATCHING

**KZN** •Adventures Extreme Ocean Safaris
082 960 7682 ww.oceansafaris.co.za
**Garden Route, W.Cape** •Ocean Blue
044 533 5083 ww.oceanadventures.co.za•Ocean
Safaris 044 533 4963 ww.oceansafaris.co.za
**Gansbaai** •Dyer Island Cruises
028 384 0406 ww.dyer-island-cruises.co.za

## FISHING (ALL SORTS!!)

•Charles Norman Safaris 011 888 3591
ww.sportfishafrica.co.za

## FLYFISHING

**Mpumalanga**•Belfast Fly Fishing Assoc.
belfast_fly_fish_ass@mweb.co.za
013 253 0748•Dullstroom Flyfishers
011 887 8787 razorspike@mweb.co.za
**W.Cape**•Cape Piscatorial Society
021 424 7725 ww.piscator.co.za

## BIG GAME FISHING

**W.Cape**•Big Game Fishing Saf. 021 674 2203

## KITEBOARDING / WINDSURFING

**Langebaan, W.Cape**•Cape Sports Centre
**Cape Town**•Windswept 082 961 3070
ww.windswept.co.za
**Port Elizabeth, E.Cape**•The Kite Store
041 585 1918 ww.kites.co.za
**Durban, KZN**•Ocean to Air 031 301 1110
ww.ocean2air.co.za
**Gauteng** •Xtreme Sports 083 501 4575
ww.xtremesports.co.za

## SAILING

•Sailing SA 021 511 0929 ww.sailing.org.za
•Ocean Leisure Co. 031 301 9660
ww.oceanleisureco.com•Ocean Sailing
Academy 031 301 5726 ww.oceansailing.co.za

## HOBIE SAILING

**W.Cape**•Drum Africa 021 785 5201
ww.drumafrica.co.za

## SURFING

**Durban** •Kevin Olsen's School of Surfing
082 530 3785 ww.surfweb.co.za
**Cape Town**•Downhill Adventures•Gary's
Surf School 021 788 9839 ww.garysurf.co.za
**Plettenberg Bay, Garden Route**•International
Surf School fun@surfschool.za.net
**Jeffreys Bay, E.Cape**•Jeffreys Bay Surf School
042 293 1625 ww.islandvibebackpackers.com
•Aloe Afrika Adventures

## WATERSKIING

**Gauteng**•Leisure Lakes 011 314 3589
ww.leisurelakes.co.za
**Cape Town**•Blue Rock Cable Waterski
021 858 1330 ww.cablewaterski.co.za

## FLYING

•Aero Club of SA ww.aeroclub.org.za
011 805 0366•Flight Training College of Africa
011 315 3992 ww.ftcafrica.com•43 Air School
046 624 2433 ww.43airschool.com

## SCENIC FLIGHTS

**Garden Route** •African Ramble 044 533 9006
ww.aframble.co.za

## AEROBATIC FLYING

•Yakattack Promotions 083 462 0570
ww.yakaa.co.za

## BUNGEE JUMPING

**Bloukrans & Gouritz, E. & W.Cape**
•Face Adrenalin 042 281 1458
ww.faceadrenalin.com

## BRIDGE SWING

**Gouritz, W.Cape**•Wildthing Adventures
**Graskop, Mpumalanga**•Big Swing Int.
013 767 1621 bigswing@mweb.co.za
**Gauteng**•Living on the Edge Adventures

## TREETOP CANOPY TOURS

**Tsitsikamma, E.Cape**•Stormsriver Advent.
**Natal Midlands**•Karkloof Canopy Tour
033 330 3415 ww.karkloofcanopytour.co.za

## PARAGLIDING

•SAHPA 012 668 1219 ww.sahpa.co.za
**Gauteng**•Paragliding Adventures
011 907 7968 ww.flysa.co.za
•Paragliding Afrika 011 880 9229
ww.adventuresportscompany.co.za
**W.Cape** •Airborne Paragliding 021 434 2011
ww.airborne-africa.com•Para-pax 082 881 4724
ww.parapax.com•Parapente Cape
021 762 2441 ww.wallendair.co.za

## BALLOONING

**Gauteng & North West**•Airtrack Adventures
011 957 2322 ww.hotairballoons.co.za•Bill
Harrop's Original Balloon Safaris 011 705 3201
ww.balloon.co.za
**Winelands, W.Cape**•Wineland Ballooning
021 863 3192 balloon@kapinfo.com
**Garden Route** •Balloon Drifters
044 279 4045 ww.balloondrifters.co.za
**Mpumalanga**•Balloons Over Africa
013 741 1247 ww.balloonsoverafrica.co.za
•Life Ballooning 013 665 3265
bookings@lifeballooning.co.za

## SKYDIVING

•Parachute Association of South Africa
ww.para.co.za 021 553 3398
**Gauteng**•Icarus Skydiving School
011 452 8858 ww.icarus.co.za
•Skydive Extreme 083 242 2813
ww.skydiveextreme.co.za
**Eastern Cape**•E.P Skydive
082 800 9263 ww.epskydivers.com
**Cape Town/Citrusdal, Western Cape**
•Skydive Cape Town 082 800 6290
ww.skydivecapetown.za.com
•Skydive Citrusdal 021 462 5666
ww.skydive.co.za
**Garden Route / Mossel Bay**•Outeniqua
Skydivers 082 824 8599 ww.altitude.co.za

## SWAZILAND

### SWAZILAND MULTIPLE LISTINGS
**Big Game Parks**
+268 528 3943 ww.biggameparks.org
**Swazi Trails** +268 416 2180 or
011 704 1975 ww.swazitrails.co.sz
**Swaziland Tourism +268 404 9693**

## HIKING

•Big Game Parks •Swazi Trails

## HORSERIDING

•Big Game Parks •Hawane Horse Trails
hawane@realnet.co.sz +268 603 0435

## GAME VIEWING

•Big Game Parks •Nisela Safaris
+268 303 0318 ww.niselasafaris.co.za

## CAVING

•Swazi Trails

## 4X4 TRAILS

•Asambeni Bo +268 604 6238
asambenibooking@yahoo.co.uk

## MOUNTAINBIKING

•Swazi Trails

## QUADBIKING

•Bush bandits +27 11 768 2040
ww.bushbandits.co.za

## WHITEWATER RAFTING

**Great Usutu River**•Swazi Trails

## PARAGLIDING

•Emoyeni Paragliding School
+268 505 7405 airsports@realnet.co.sz

## LESOTHO

### LESOTHO MULTIPLE LISTINGS
**Trading Post**
+266 223 40202 tradingpost@leo.co.ls
ww.africandream.org // malotiroute // Lesotho
**Lesotho Tourist Board +266 31 3760**

## HIKING, HORSERIDING, FISHING

•Malealea Lodge & Pony Trek Centre
051 447 3200 ww.malealea.co.ls
•Semonkong Lodge 051 933 3106
ww.placeofsmoke.co.ls
•Hotel Mount Maluti mmh@leo.co.ls
+266 222 78 5224•Sani Top Chalet
033 702 1158 sanitop@futurenet.co.za

## 4X4 TRAILS

•The Trading Post•Sani Tours 033 701 1064
ww.sanitours.co.za•Major Adventures
033 701 1628 ww.majoradventures.co.za

## MOUNTAINBIKING & QUADBIKING

•The Trading Post

## SNOW SKIING

•Hotel Mount Maluti +266 222 78 5224
mmh@leo.co.ls

## NAMIBIA

### NAMIBIA'S MULTIPLE LISTINGS
**Namibia Wildlife Resorts**
+264 61 236975 reservations@nwr.com.na
**Reit Safari Namibia**
+264 61 250764 ww.reitsafari.com
**Namibia Tourism Board +264 61 290 6000**
**www.namibiatourism.com**

## ROCK CLIMBING / ABSEILING

**Spitzkoppe, Brandberg**
•Walkers Rock and Rope Adventures
walker@iafrica.com +264 64 40 3122
•Guided Ascents in Africa
021 788 3894 ww.southscape.co.za
•Blue Mountain Adventures
021 439 8199 tonyblue@iafrica.com

## HORSE TRAILS

**Windhoek, Lüderitz and Namib**
•Reit Safari Namibia•Klein Aus Vista
+264 63 258021 ww.namibhorses.com
•The Desert Homestead +264 63 293243
ww.deserthomestead-namibia.com
**Swakopmund** •Okakambe Trails
+264 64 402799 ww.okakambe.de
**Etosha**•Epacha Horse Trails
+264 67 697047 ww.epacha.com

## CAMEL RIDING

**Windhoek and Namib**
•Reit Safari Namibia

## HIKING

**Namib Naukluft & Fish River Canyon**
•Namibia Wildlife Resorts•Tok Tokkie Trails
+264 63 693011 toktokki@iway.na
•Canyon Adventure Trail +264 63 693007
www.canyonnaturepark.com•Klein Aus Vista
+264 63 258021 ww.namibhorses.com

## GAME VIEWING

**Windhoek** •Harnas Wildlife Foundation
+264 61 237304 ww.harnas.org
**Etosha** •Namibia Wildlife Resorts

## 4X4 TRAILS

•JJ 4x4 Adventures 044 2724576
ww.jj4x4adventures.co.za
**Kalahari** •Kalahari–Namib Eco 4x4 Route
+264 63 281218 ww.kalahari-namib.co.za
**Lüderitz** •Coastway Tours
+264 63 202002 ww.coastways.com.na
**Windhoek**•Windhoek-Okahandja 4x4 Trail
+264 61 234607•Uri Adventures +264 61
231246 ww.uriadventures.com

## QUADBIKING

**Swakopmund / Walvis Bay**•Dare Devil
Advent. +264 64 401183 ww.namplaces.com
•Namibia Quadbike Advent. +264 64 462686
bpwcsc@mweb.com.na
•Outback Orange +264 64 406096
ww.outbackorange.com
**Sossusvlei**•Sossusvlei Eco Quad
+264 63 293293 ww.sossusvlei-mirage.com

## MOUNTAINBIKING

•Outside Adventures +264 61 251586
ww.namibia.adventures.com
•Boundless Adventures 021 843 3142
ww.boundlessadventures.co.za

## OVERLAND SAFARIS

•Chameleon Safaris +264 61 247668
ww.chameleonsafaris.com

## ANGLING

**Swakopmund**•Laramon Tours +264 64 402359
laramontours@mweb.com.na
•Henry's Fishing +264 64 404828
boatfish@iafrica.com.na•Ocean Adventures &
Angling Tours +264 64 404281
oceanadv@iway.na•Sunrise Fishing
+264 64 404561 ww.sunrisetours.com.na
**Upper Zambezi River, Caprivi Strip**
•Kalizo Lodge +264 66 252802
ww.natron.net/kalizo

## SEAL & DOLPHIN CRUISES

**Swakopmund**•Mola Mola +264 64 205511
ww.mola-mola.com.na•Levo Tours
+264 64 207555 ww.levotours.com•Laramon
Tours laramontours@mweb.com.na
+264 64 402359•Ocean Adventures
+264 64 404281 oceanadv@iway.na

## CANOEING AND RAFTING

**Orange River**•Wildthing Adventures
021 423 5804 ww.wildthing.co.za•Felix Unite
021 683 6433 www.felixunite.com
•Kalahari Adventure Centre 054 451 0177
ww.augrabies.co.za•Bushwhacked
027 761 8953 ww.bushwhacked.co.za
**Kunene River**•Gravity Adventure Group
021 683 3698 ww.gravity.co.za•Epupa Camp
+264 61 232740 ww.epupa.com.na
•Kunene River Lodge +264 65 274300
info@kuneneriverlodge.com

## SEA KAYAKING

**Walvis Bay**
•Eco-Marine Kayak Tours +264 64 203144
ww.gateway-africa.com/kayak/index.html

## HOT-AIR BALLOONING

•Namib Sky Adventures +264 63 293233
namibsky@mweb.com.na•Francolino Flyins
+264 67 697041 francolino-flyins@iway.na

## SKYDIVING / SOARING

**Swakopmund**•Skydive Swakopmund
+264 64 402841 ww.skydiveswakop.com.na
**Namib**•Bitterwasser Lodge & Flying Centre
+264 63 265300 ww.bitterwasser.com

## SCENIC FLIGHTS &
## HELICOPTER RIDES

•Pleasure Flights and Safaris
+264 64 40 4500 ww.pleasureflights.com.na

## FLYING FOX (FOEFIE SLIDE), RÖSSING

•Dare Devil Adventures +264 64 401183
ww.namplaces.com

*Information supplied by Namibia Tourism Board*
*(021 419 3190) ww.namibiatourism.com.na*

## BOTSWANA

BOTSWANA'S MULTIPLE LISTINGS
**Uncharted Africa Safaris**
+267 212 277 unchart.res@info.bw
**Abercrombie & Kent** 011 781 0740 /
+267 662 688 ww.akdmc.com
**Moremi Safaris and Tours**
011 465 3842 ww.moremi-safaris.com
**Department of Tourism +267 353 024
ww.gov.bw/tourism**

## GAME VIEWING

**Chobe National Park, Okavango Delta**
•Adventure Safaris +267 370 0166
ww.adventure-safaris.com•Uncharted Africa
Safaris•Abercrombie & Kent
•Moremi Safaris and Tours
**Mashatu** •Mashatu Game Reserve
031 716 3500 ww.malamala.com

## ELEPHANT SAFARIS

**Okavango Delta**•Moremi Safaris & Tours
011 465 3842 ww.moremi-safaris.com
•Elephant Back Safaris +267 661 260
ebs@info.cbw

## WALKS WITH BUSHMEN

**Chobe NP**•Moremi Safaris and Tours

## HORSERIDING

**Okavango Delta**•Okavango Horse Safaris
+267 686 1671 ww.okavangohorse.com
•African Horseback Safaris +267 686 3154
ww.africanhorseback.com
**Tuli Block** •Limpopo Valley Horse Safaris
031 716 3500 ww.lhvsafari.com

## BIRDING

•Moremi Bird Safaris mk.birdsaf@info.bw

## GAME TRACKING ON FOOT

**Moremi** •Department of Wildlife & National
Parks +267 371 405
ww.game-reserve.com/botswana

## CAVING

**Gcwihaba Caverns**•Department of Tourism
+267 353 024 ww.gov.bw/tourism

## 4X4 TRAILS

**From Maun through Okavango Delta, and
Chobe National Park to Vic Falls**
•Botswana Parks and Reserves +267 580 774

## MOUNTAINBIKING

**Mashatu**•Mashatu Game Reserve
ww.malamala.com 031 716 3500
•180 degree adventures 021 462 0992
ww.180.co.za

## QUADBIKING

**Makgadikgadi Pans**•Bush bandits
+27 11 768 2040 ww.bushbandits.co.za
•Jacks Camp ww.wilderness-safaris.com

**GAME VIEWING IN *MOKOROS***
**Okavango Delta**
•ww.game-reserve.com/Botswana
+267 371 405
•Uncharted Africa Safaris•Abercrombie &
Kent•Moremi Safaris and Tours

**MOTORBOAT SAFARIS**
**Okavango Delta**•ww.game-reserve.com/
botswana +267 371 405•Uncharted Africa
Safaris•Abercrombie & Kent
•Moremi Safaris and Tours

**AERIAL GAME VIEWING**
**& SCENIC FLIGHTS**
**Okavango Delta & Chobe National Park**
•Moremi Air Services  moremi.air@info.bw
+267 686 3632•Moremi Safaris and Tours

## ZAMBIA

**ZAMBIA'S MULTIPLE LISTINGS**
**Shearwater Adventures** +263 13 444 71
ww.shearwateradventures.com
**Safari Par Excellence** 011 781 3851 or
+260 332 0606 ww.safparx.com
**Mvuu Lodge** 016 987 1837 ww.mvuulodge
**Chiawa Camp** +260 1 261588
ww.chiawa.com
**Bundu Adventures** +260 3 324 407
ww.bundu-adventures.com
**Changa Changa Adventures** +260 3 324407
ww.zambiatourism.com/changachanga
**Zambia Tourism www.zambiatourism.com**

### HIKING
**Batoka Gorge** •Taita Falcon Lodge +260 3
321850 ww.zambiatourism.com/taita
**Lower Luangwa River**
•Changa Changa Adventures

### ABSEIL
**Batoka Gorge**•Abseil Zambia +260 3 321188 or
+263 11 213825 ww.thezambeziswing.com

### HORSERIDING
**Livingstone**•Chundukwa Adventure Trails
+260 3 324006 chunduka@zamnet.zm
**Lusaka**•Chaminuka Private Game Reserve
+260 1 222694 ww.chaminuka.com or
ww.maplanga.co.za

### ELEPHANTBACK SAFARIS
•Maplanga Africa 011 794 1446
ww.maplanga.co.za

### GAME VIEWING / WALKING SAFARIS
**South Luangwa / Kafue**
•The Bushcamp Company Ltd.
+260 62 45051 ww.bushcampcompany.com
•Robin Pope Safaris +260 6 246090
ww.robinpopesafaris.net•Wilderness Safaris
+263 70 7660 ww.wilderness-safaris.com
•Remote Africa Safaris ww.remoteafrica.com

•Land & Lake Safaris +265 1 757 120
ww.landlakemalawi.com
•Barefoot Safaris +265 1 707 346
ww.barefootsafarismalawi.com
**North Luangwa**•Shiwa Safaris
+260 1 229261 ww.shiwasafaris.com
**Lower Zambezi** •Chiawa Camp
+260 1 261588 ww.chiawa.com
**Lusaka**•Chaminuka Private Game Reserve
+260 1 222694 ww.chaminuka.com
**Livingstone**•Wilderness Safaris
+263 70 7660 ww.wilderness-safaris.com

### PHOTOGRAPHIC / BIRDING SAFARIS
**South Luangwa**•Robin Pope Safaris
+260 6 246090 ww.robinpopesafaris.net

### QUADBIKING
**Batoka Gorge**•The Livingstone Quad
Company +260 332 0058 ww.batokasky.com

### MOUNTAINBIKE SAFARIS
**Countrywide**•Boundless Adventures
021 843 3142 ww.boundlessadventures.co.za

### WHITEWATER RAFTING
**Batoka Gorge, Zambezi River**
• Adrift +263 13 43589 ww.adrift.co.uk
• Frontiers Rafting +263 134 1092
ww.africanadrenalin.co.za/frontiers
•Bundu Adventures•Safari Par Excellence

### JETBOATING
**Zambezi River, Livingstone**•Jet Extreme
ww.jetextreme.com +263 11 208 386
•Shearwater Adventures •Safari Par Excellence

### RIVER BOARDING, WHITEWATER
### KAYAKING (AND TANDEM KAYAKING)
**Batoka Gorge, Zambezi River**
•Bundu Adventures •Safari Par Excellence

### HOUSEBOATING
**Kariba** •Gwembe Safaris
+260 3 32 4024 ww.gwembesafaris.com

### CANOE SAFARIS
**Livingstone/Vic Falls**
•Safari Par Excellence•Bundu Adventures
•Chundukwa Adventure Trails
•Lower Zambezi/Mana Pools
•Cansaf Adventures and Canoeing Safaris
011 803 5928 ww.cansaf.com
•Karibu Safaris +27 31 563 9774
ww.karibu.co.za
•Chiawa Camp •Mvuu Lodge
**Lower Luangwa River**
•Changa Changa Adventures

### RIVER CRUISES
**Zambezi river, Livingstone**
•The African Queen 084 505 2052
ww.theafricanqueen.co.za
•Victoria Falls River Safaris
+260 3 324024 riversafaris@zamnet.zm

### FISHING
**Lower Zambezi**
•Chiawa Camp •Mvuu Lodge
•Zambezi Royal Chundu Fishing and
Safari Lodge 011 953 3224
ww.icon.co.za/~chundu/
**Upper Zambezi**  •Tiger Camp
+260 1 262810 tiger@zamnet.zm
**Lake Tanganyika**  •Nkamba Bay Lodge
+260 288884 nkamba@zamnet.zm

### SCUBA DIVING
**Lake Tanganyika**  •Tanganyika Lodge
+260 224616 atd@zamnet.zm

### MICROLIGHT AND HELICOPTER FLIPS,
### 'FLIGHT OF ANGELS'
**Livingstone/Vic Falls**
•Batoka Sky +260 332 0058
ww.batokasky.com•Safari Par Excellence
**South Luanwa**•Remote Africa Safaris
ww.remoteafrica.com

### BUNGEE JUMPING
**Victoria Falls Bridge**
•Shearwater Adventures

### FLYING FOX / GORGE SWING
**Batoka Gorge**
•The Zambezi Swing +260 3 321188 or
+263 11 213825 ww.thezambeziswing.com

### FLY-IN SAFARIS
•Ulendo Safaris +265 1 754 950
ww.ulendosafaris.com
*NB Many activities around Vic Falls / Livingstone
can be organized from Zimbabwea or Zambia.*

## ZIMBABWE

ZIMBABWE MULTIPLE LISTINGS
**Zimbabwe National Parks and Wildlife**
+263 4 706 077 natparks@africaonline.co.zw
**Natureways**
+263 4 861 766 ww.natureways.co.zw
**Wilderness Safaris**
+263 70 7660 ww.wilderness-safaris.com
**Safari Par Excellence** 011 781 3851 or
+260 332 0606 ww.safparx.com
**Shearwater Adventures** +263 13 44471
ww.shearwateradventures.com
**Batoka Sky** +260 332 0058
ww.batokasky.com
**Wild Horizons** ww.wildhorizons.co.zw
**Zimbabwe Tourist Office**
**011 616 9534 www.zimbabwe.co.zw**

### HIKING, CLIMBING
•Zimbabwe Tourist Office
**Chimanimani National Park**
•Zimbabwe National Parks and Wildlife

## 94

## GAME VIEWING / WALKING SAFARIS
**Gonarezhou Park, Chiredzi**
•Zimbabwe National Parks and Wildlife
**Zambezi Escarpment, above Mana Pools**
•Chipembere Safaris +263 61 2946
chipsaf@zol.co.za
**Mana Pools National Park**
•Natureways •Wilderness Safaris
**Hwange, Matusadona**
•Wilderness Safaris •Wild Horizons

### HORSE TRAILS
**Mavuradona Wilderness** •Natureways
**Vic Falls** •Zambezi Horse Trails
ww.horsesafari.co.zw +263 11 20 9115
•Safari Par Excellence
•Shearwater Adventures
**Matopos National Park**
•Zimbabwe National Parks and Wildlife

### ELEPHANTBACK SAFARIS
•Wild Horizons
**Nakavango Estate, Vic Falls**
•Shearwater Adventures
**Matopos Hills, Bulawayo**
•Camp Amalinda +263 9 24 3954
ww.amalinda.co.za

### 4X4 TRAILS
•Taggallongg 011 975 3293
ww.tagalong.co.za
**DIY trails through Kariba, Mana Pools,
Hwange National Park**
•Zimbabwe National Parks and Wildlife

### WHITEWATER RAFTING
**Batoka Gorge, Zambezi River**
•Adrift +263 13 43589 ww.adrift.co.uk
•Frontiers Rafting +263 134 1092
africanadrenalin.co.za/frontiers/index.htm
•Shearwater Adventures
•Safari Par Excellence

### RIVER SPEEDBOAT TRIPS
**Zambezi River / Vic Falls**
•Jet Extreme +263 11 208 386
ww.jetextreme.com
•Shearwater Adventures
•Safari Par Excellence

### RIVER BOARDING, WHITEWATER (AND TANDEM) KAYAKING
**Batoka Gorge, Zambezi River**
•Safari Par Excellence

### CANOE SAFARIS
**Lower Zambezi/Mana Pools**
•Cansaf Adventures and Canoeing Safaris
ww.cansaf.com 011 803 5928
•Karibu Safaris ww.karibu.co.za
•Natureways •Safari Par Excellence

### TIGER FISHING & HOUSEBOATING
**Lake Kariba** •Sengwa Safaris
+263 61 2281 ww.sengwa.com
•River Horse Safaris +263 61 2422
ww.riverhorsesafaris.com
•Taga Safaris 011 465 5678 tagasafaris.co.za
•Zimbabwe National Parks and Wildlife

### INLAND SCUBA DIVING
•Chinhoyi Caves Pro Divers
kynic@mweb.co.zw +263 4 336307

### BUNGEE JUMPING
**Victoria Falls Bridge**
•Shearwater Adventures

### GORGE SWING & FLYING FOX
**Rapid 4, Batoka Gorge**
•Adrift +263 13 43589 ww.adrift.co.uk

### HELICOPTER FLIPS / 'FLIGHT OF ANGELS'
**Vic Falls** •Shearwater Adventures
•Safari Par Excellence •Batoka Sky

### MICROLIGHT FLIGHTS
**Vic Falls** •Batoka Sky

## MOZAMBIQUE

MOZAMBIQUE MULTIPLE LISTINGS
**Indigo Bay** 011 465 6904 or
+258 23 82340 ww.indigobayonline.com
**Mozambique Connection**
011 803 4185 ww.mozcon.com
**Barra Lodge** 011 314 3355
ww.barralodge.co.za
**Guinjata Bay** 013 741 2795 ww.guinjata.com
**Classic Sailing Adventures** 042 294 1550
ww.classic-sailing-adventures.com
**Island Quest Sailing and Diving**
011 802 5695 ww.islandquest.co.za
**Hartley's Safaris** 011 467 4704
ww.hartleys.co.za
**Wildlife Adventures** 021 422 2017
ww.wildlifeadventures.co.za
**Marlin Lodge** +27 12 543 2134
ww.marlinlodge.co.za
**Praia do Sol** 082 570 4300 ww.pdsol.coza

### HORSERIDING
**Bazaruto** •Indigo Bay •Barra Lodge

### GAME VIEWING/SAFARIS
•Barefoot Safaris +265 1 707 346 ww.barefoot-safarismalawi.com•Hartley's Safaris
**Maputo Elephant Reserve**
•Mozambique Connection

### DUNEBOARDING
•Indigo Bay

### QUADBIKING
•Barra Lodge•Guinjata Bay

### 4X4 TRAILS
•Mozambique 4x4 trails 012 665 4230
ww.landrovercenturionadventures.com
**Pofuri Trail, Imhambane Prov. & Maputo
Elephant Res.**•Mozambique Connection

### OFFROAD BIKING
•Extreme Biking Safaris 015 516 4037
antman@northnet.co.za

### SCUBA DIVING
**Ponto do Ouro/Ponta Malongane**
•Devocean Diving ww.devoceandiving.com
082 332 9029 •Simply Scuba 011 678 0972
ww.simplyscuba.co.za•Hartley's Oceans and
Islands 011 467 4704 ww.hartleys.co.za
•Adventure Diving Safaris 012 991 3134
ww.adventuredivingsafaris.com
**Central Mozambique**
•Barra Lodge•Guinjata Bay
**Bazaruto Archipelago**•Classic Sailing
Adventures•Island Quest Sailing & Diving
•Marlin Lodge•Indigo Bay•Hartley's Safaris
**Northern Mozambique Archipelago**
•Pemba Beach Hotel 011 465 6904 or
+258 72 21 770 ww.pembabeach.com
•Wildlife Adventures

### SAILING
**Central Mozambique**
•Barra Lodge•Praia do Sol
**Bazaruto Archipelago**•Classic Sailing
Adventures•Island Quest Sailing and
Diving•Indigo Bay
**Pemba / Northern Mozambique Archi-
pelago**•Wildlife Adventures•Pemba Beach
Resort 011 467 1277 ww.raniafrica.com
**Inhaca Island**•Mozambique Connection

### SEA KAYAKING
**Inhaca Island**•Hardy Ventures
013 751 1693 ww.hardyventure.co.za

### GAME FISHING
•CharlesNormanSaf.ww.sportfishafrica.co.za
011 888 3591•Classic Sailing Advent.
•Marlin Lodge•Indigo Bay•Safaris Unlimited +254 289 1168 ww.safarisunlimited.com

### WATERSKIING
•Praia do Sol 082 570 4300 ww.pdsol.coza
•Indigo Bay•Classic Sailing Adventures

### DOLPHIN SAFARIS
**Ponta Do Ouro**•Dolphin Encountours
011 462 4551 ww.dolphin-encountours.co.za

### DHOW TRIPS
**Inhaca Island**•Mozambique Connection

### MICROLIGHTING
**Zongoene Lodge**•Mozambique Connection

### PARASAILING
•Praia do Sol

## MALAWI

### MALAWI MULTIPLE LISTINGS
**Mulanje Mountain Conservation Trust**
+265 1 466 282 ww.mountmulanje.net
**Nyika Safaris** +265 133 0180
ww.nyika.com
**Central African Wilderness Safaris**
+265 177 1153
ww.wilderness-safarismalawi.com
**Land & Lake Safaris** +265 1 757 120
ww.landlakemalawi.com
**Barefoot Safaris** +265 1 707 346
ww.barefootsafarismalawi.com
**Kayak Africa** 021 783 1955
ww.kayakafrica.co.za
**Danforth Yachting** +265 996 0077
ww.danforthyachting.com
**Jambo Africa Tours** +265 1 635 356
ww.jamboafricatoursmalawi.com
**Malawi Tourism**
**ww.tourismmalawi.com**

### HIKING
**Countrywide**•Land & Lake Safaris
**Mulanje Mountains**
•Mulanje Mountain Conservation Trust
**Nyika Plateau**•Nyika Safaris
**Liwonde National Park**
•Central African Wilderness Safaris
**Lengwe National Park, Nyala Park, Zomba**
**Plateau**•Jambo Africa Tours

### CLIMBING
**Mulanje Mountains**
•Mulanje Mountain Conservation Trust

### GAME VIEWING
**Lengwe National Park, Nyala Park, Zomba**
**Plateau**•Jambo Africa Tours
**Shire River and Liwonde National Park**
•Central African Wilderness Safaris
•River Safaris ww.riversafarimalawi.com
+265 1 542 552•Land & Lake Safaris
**Nyika Plateau and Vwaza Marsh**
•Nyika Safaris

### HORSERIDING
•Nyika Safaris•Barefoot Safaris

### SCUBA DIVING / SNORKELLING
**Lake Malawi**•Scuba Shack +265 9 93 4220
doogles@africa-online.net •Club Makokola
+265 1 594 244 ww.clubmak.com
•Kayak Africa •Kaya Mawa
+871 76 168 4670 ww.kayamawa.com

### KAYAKING
•Kayak Africa

### SAILING
•Danforth Yachting•Barefoot Safaris
•Lake Malawi Marathon
ww.yachtingmarathon.com

### FISHING
**Lake Malawi**
•Danforth Yachting•Land & Lake Safaris

### RIVERBOAT SAFARIS
**Shire River, Liwonde National Park**
•Central African Wilderness Safaris
•Riverboat Safaris +265 1 542 552
ww.riversafarimalawi.com

### MOUNTAINBIKING
•Boundless Adventures 021 843 3142
ww.boundlessadventures.co.za
•Land & Lake Safaris

### FLY-IN SAFARIS
•Ulendo Safaris +265 1 754 950
ww.ulendosafaris.com

## KENYA

### KENYA MULTIPLE LISTINGS
**Savage Wilderness Safaris**
+254 252 1590 ww.whitewaterkenya.com
**Serena Active** +255 27 2 504158
ww.serenahotels.com
**Active Kenya** +254 2 4446371
ww.activekenya.com
**Safaris Unlimited** +254 289 1168
ww.safarisunlimited.com

### GAME VIEWING & WALKING SAFARIS
•Savage Wilderness Safaris•Hartley's Safaris
011 467 4704 ww.hartleys.co.za
•Serena Active•Active Kenya•Safaris
Unlimited•Lets Go Travel +254 2 444 7151
ww.lets-go-travel.net

### HORSERIDING
•Offbeat Safaris +254 2 571 649
ww.offbeatsafaris.co.za
**Masai Mara and Chyulu Hills**
•Safaris Unlimited

### CAMEL SAFARIS
**Great Rift Valley**
•African Frontiers +254 62 32766

### MOUNTAINEERING
**Mount Kenya**•Savage Wilderness Safaris
•Blue Mountain Adventures
021 439 8199 tonyblue@iafrica.com
•Guided Ascents in Africa 021 788 3894
www.southscape.co.za

### PHOTOGRAPHIC SAFARIS
**Masai Mara**•Safaris Unlimited

### 4X4 TRAILS
**Rift Valley** •Mountain Rock Hotel +254 062
62099 baserock@africaonline.country.ke

### MOUNTAINBIKING
**Rift Valley, Masai Mara**•Bike Treks
+254 20 444 637 ww.biketreks.co.ke

Laikipia Plateau•Black Mamba Safaris
ww.bicycleafrica.com
**Amboseli & Masai Mara National Parks**
•Serena Active

### SAND YACHTING
•Active Kenya

### WHITEWATER RAFTING
**Tana and Athi Rivers**
•Savage Wilderness Safaris

### SCUBA DIVING
**Mombasa**•Diani Marine +254 1272367
Dimarine@africaonline.co.ke•Buccaneer Dive
Centre +254 11485163
info@buccaneerdiving.com •Hartley's Oceans
and Islands
ww.hartleys.co.za  011 467 4704

### SAILING
•Savage Wilderness Safaris

### KITESURFING
•Active Kenya

### BALLOONING
•Balloon Safaris +254 20 605003
info@balloonsafaris.co.ke •Bungiwalla
+254 20 523 094 reblin@mitsuminet.co.ke
•Adventures Aloft +254 20 214 168

## TANZANIA

### TANZANIA MULTIPLE LISTINGS
**Serena Active** +255 27 2 504158
ww.serenahotels.com
**Wild Frontiers** 011 702 2035
www.wildfrontiers.com
**Hartleys Safaris** 011 467 4704
ww.hartleys.co.za
**Zanzibar Beach Resort and Dive Centre**
+27 31 301 9660 ww.zanzibarbeachresort.com

### SAFARIS
**Serengeti, Ngorongoro & Lake Manyara**
•Serena Active•Wild Frontiers•Hartley's
Safaris•Adventure Dynamics International
011 447 7013 ww.adventuredynamics.co.za
**Selous, Ruaha NP, Mufinidi and the northern**
**parks**•Ruaha Ruaha River Lodge
ww. ruahariverlodge.com +255 741 327706
•Hartley's Safaris

### BIRDING
**Selous, Lake Manyara & all major parks**
•Birding & Beyond Safaris +255 744 286058
ww.tanzaniabirding.com

### HIKING
**Countrywide**•Serena Active
**Ngorongoro area**•Wild Frontiers

### MOUNTAINEERING
**Mount Kilimanjaro and Mount Meru**
•Savage Wilderness Safaris +254 252 1590

ww.whitewaterkenya.com•Wild Frontiers

•Guided Ascents in Africa 021 788 3894

ww.southscape.co.za•Blue Mountain Advent.

021 439 8199 tonyblue@iafrica.com

## MARATHON RUNNING

•Kilimanjaro Marathon 011 702 2035

ww.kilimanjaromarathon.com

## MOUNTAINBIKING

**Ngorongoro, Serengeti, Lake Manyara**

•Serena Active

**Dar es Salaam and Zanzibar**

•Boundless Adventures 021 843 3142

ww.boundlessadventures.co.za

## SCUBA DIVING

**Zanzibar**•East Africa Diving & Watersport

+255 747 420588 EADC@zitec.org

•One Ocean The Zanzibar Dive Centre

+255 242 238374 ww.zanzibaroneocean.com

•Zanzibar Beach Resort & Dive Centre

•Hartley's Oceans and Islands

011 467 4704 ww.hartleys.co.za

## CANOEING

**Lake Manyara**•Serena Active

## SAILING

**Zanzibar**•Zanzibar Beach Resort

& Dive Centre

## BOATING

**Lake Tanganyika**•Barefoot Safaris

+265 1 707 346 ww.barefootsafarismalawi.com

## SEA KAYAKING

**Zanzibar**•180 Degree Adventures 021 462 0992

ww.180.co.za•Zanzibar Beach Resort

## BALLOONING

**Serengeti National Park**•Serengeti Balloon

Safaris ww.balloon safaris.com

## PARAGLIDING TOURS

**Rift Valley** •Wild Frontiers

## MADAGASCAR

MADAGASCAR MULTIPLE LISTINGS

**Animaltracks Islandventures**

011 454 0543 www.animaltracks.co.za

**Classic Sailing Adventures** 042 294 1550

ww.classic-sailing-adventures.com

**Sakatia Passions** +261 20 866 1462

ww.sakartia-passions.com

**Island Quest Sailing and Diving**

011 802 5695 www.islandquest.co.za

## HIKING

**Isalo, Ankarana & Andringitra NP**

•Animaltracks Islandventures

## GAME VIEWING & LEMUR TRACKING

•Animaltracks Islandventures

## 4X4 TRAILS

•Animaltracks Islandventures

## SAILING

•Classic Sailing Adventures

•Island Quest Sailing and Diving

## SEA KAYAKING

•Kayak Africa 021 783 1955

ww.kayakafrica.co.za

## SCUBA DIVING

•Sakatia Passions

•Animaltracks Islandventures

•Island Quest Sailing and Diving

•Classic Sailing Adventures

## BIG GAME FISHING

•Sakatia Passions

•Animaltracks Islandventures

## SALTWATER FLYFISHING

•Uncharted Safaris 047 564 1057

ww.wildcoast.com/outspan

## SEYCHELLES

SEYCHELLES MULTIPLE LISTINGS

**Island Charters** +248 32 4056

ww.seychelles.net/islandcharters

**Seychelles Underwater Centre**

+248 247 357 ww.diveseychelles.com.sc

**Seychelles Tourism 011 791 0300**

**sto.seychelles@intekom.co.za**

**www.aspureasitgets.com**

## HIKING

•Morne Seychellois National Park

+248 22 46 44 forestry@seychelles.net

## CANYONING

•Ducrot Daniel + 262 6 92 659067

ww.canyoning-cilaos.com

## SAILING

•Dream Yacht Seychelles +248 23 2681

ww.dream-yacht-seychelles.com

•Island Charters

## SCUBA DIVING

**Mahe**•Seychelles Underwater Centre

**Praslin**•Octopus Dive Centre

+248 23 2350 octopus@seychelles.net

## BIG GAME FISHING

•Island Charters•Marlin Charters

+248 51 11 70 ww.seychelles.net/marlin

## SNORKELLING WITH WHALE SHARKS

•Seychelles Underwater Centre

## MAURITIUS

MAURITIUS MULTIPLE LISTINGS

**Yemaya Adventures** +230 283 8187

ww.yemayaadventures.com

**Mauritius Tourism 031 562 1320**

**mauritius@ie.co.za www.mauritius.net**

## MOUNTAINEERING

•Vertical World +230 395 3207

verticalworld@usa.net

## HIKING

**Black River Gorges National Park**

•Reservations +230 464 4016

## BIRDING

•Casela Bird Park + 230 452 0693

## MOUNTAINBIKING

•Yemaya Adventures

## 4X4 TRAILS

•Espace Adventure +230 670 4301

ww.mttb-mautourco.com

## SAILING

•Terres Oceanes +230 262 7188

ww.terresoceans.com

## SEA KAYAKING

•Yemaya Adventures

## CANOEING

•Mad'Cameleon +261 20 226 3086

madcam@dts.mg

## SCUBA DIVING

•Sinbad Diving +230 262 7913

ww.kuxville.de•Sea Fan Diving Centre

+230 415 1544 explorer@intnet.mu

•Centre De Plongée, Rodrigues

+230 831 6000 cottonb@intnet.mu

## SUBMARINE TOURS

•Blue Safari Submarine

+230 263 3333 ww.blue-safari.com

## BIG GAME FISHING

•Professional Big Game Fishing Charter Assoc.

+230 483 5051 moana@intnet.mu

•Morne Anglers Club +230 483 5801

## KITESURFING

•Kuxville Kitesurfing +230 262 7913

ww.kuxville.de

## RÉUNION (France)

**RÉUNION MULTIPLE LISTINGS**
**Aquaventure** + 262 692 70 1335
http://monsite.wanadoo.fr/AQUAVENTURE
**Austral Aventure**
ww.creole.org/austral-aventure
**Réunion Tourism** 011 268 0498
**ww.la-reunion-tourisme.com**

### MOUNTAINEERING
•Maison de la Montagne de la Réunion
+ 262 262 907 878 ww.reunion-nature.com
•Aquaventure•Alpanes + 262 262 44 7629
ww.perso.wanadoo.fr/alpines

### HIKING
**GR1 & GR2, and hikes in the cirques de**
**Mafate, Salazie and Cilaos**
•Department of Nature (Central Reserv.)
+ 262 262 907 878 ww.reunion-nature.com
•Cilaos Aventure + 262 2 62 316185
ww.cilaosaventure.com
•Réunion Sensations + 262 262 31 8484
reunionsensations.com•Austral Aventure

### HORSERIDING
•Equi Montagne + 262 262 23 62 51
ww.equimontagne.com

### MOUNTAINBIKING
•Ducrot Daniel + 262 6 92 659067
ww.canyoning-cilaos.com
•Austral Aventure

### 4X4 TRAILS
•Kreolie 4x4 + 262 262 39 5087
ww.kreolie4x4.com

### SAILING
•Blue Sail +262 262 33 1739
ww.bluesail-reunion.com

### SCUBA DIVING
•Abyss Plongée + 262 262 34 7979
ww.abyss-plongee.com•Bleu Ocean
+ 262 262 34 9749 ww.bleuocean.fr

### BIG GAME FISHING
•Réunion Fishing Club +262 262 24 3610
ww.reunionfishingclub.com

### SURFING/BODY BOARDING
•Billabong Surf School +262 692 31 5316
billabong.surfschool@wanadoo.fr
•Ecole de Surf et Body Board des Roches
Noires +262 262 246328
ww.web-soleil.com/ecolesurf

### WHITEWATER RAFTING & KAYAKING
•Aquaventure

### PARAGLIDING & HANG-GLIDING
•Air Lagon Parapente 262 34 9114
ww.betemps.fr.fm•Parapente Réunion
262 24 87 84 ww.parapente-reunion.fr
•ww.azurtech.com 34 91 89

## GREAT LAKES –
## RWANDA, BURUNDI & UGANDA

**GREAT LAKES MULTIPLE LISTINGS**
**Wild Frontiers** 011 702 2035 or
+256 41 321479 ww.wildfrontiers.com
**Uganda Wildlife Authority**
+256 41 346287 ww.uwa.or.ug
**Birding & Beyond Safaris**
+255 744 286058 ww.tanzaniabirding.com
**Nile River Explorers**
+256 43 12 0236 ww.raftingafrica.com
**Adrift** +265 77 454 206
ww.surfthesource.com

### CLIMBING / TREKKING
**Ruwenzori Mountains**
•Ruwenzori Mountaineering Services
+256 75 59 8461
ww.uwa.or.ug/RM_Guidlines.htm
•Wild Frontiers
•Guided Ascents in Africa
ww.southscape.co.za 021 788 3894
**Mount Elgon, Lake Mburo National Park**
**and Kibale Forest**
•Uganda Wildlife Authority
•Wild Frontiers

### GORILLA TRACKING
**Mgahinga and Bwindi National Parks**
•Mgahinga Gorilla National Park
+256 41 346287 ww.uwa.or.ug
ww.aaa-agency.com/gorilla-permits.htm
•Bwindi +256 41 346287
ww.uwa.or.ug/bwindi.html

### GAME & CHIMPANZEE VIEWING
•Uganda Wildlife Authority
•Birding & Beyond Safaris
+255 744 286058 ww.tanzaniabirding.com

### BIRDING
•Birding & Beyond Safaris
•Tropical Birding 021 556 4124
ww.tropicalbirding.com
**Queen Elizabeth National Park**
•Uganda Wildlife Authority
ww.uwa.or.ug/bird.html +256 41 346287

### MOUNTAINBIKING & QUADBIKING
**Jinja**•Nile River Explorers•Adrift

### RAFTING / KAYAKING /
### RIVERBOARDING
**River Nile, Jinja**
•Nile River Explorers•Adrift

### FISHING
**Lake Victoria** •GC Tours +256 41 321479
ww.wildfrontiers.com
**Queen Elizabeth & Murchison Falls NP**
•Uganda Wildlife Authority
+256 41 346287 ww.uwa.or.ug/bird.html

### SAILING
Lake Victoria •Wild Frontiers

### BOATING
**Queen Elizabeth National Park**
•ww.uwa.or.ug/queen.html
**Murchison Falls National Park**
•ww.uwa.or.ug/Murchison.html
+256 41 346287

### BUNGEE JUMPING
Jinja •Adrift

### SCENIC FLIGHTS
•Aero Club ww.kaftc.com
•Wild Frontiers

### GORILLA TREKKING
**Volcano NP or Nyungwe Forest**
•ORTPN +250 576514
ww.rwandatourism.com
•Wild Frontiers

### GAME VIEWING AND BIRDING
**Akagera National Park**
•margie@gbdhospitality.co.za

### CULTURAL / GENOCIDE SITES VISITS
•ORTPN +250 576514
ww.rwandatourism.com

### SAILING / BOATING
**Lake Kivu, Gisenyi**
•kivusun@southernsun.com

### PHOTOGRAPHIC CREDITS
The spread number is followed by a letter in
order of appearance on the spread.

*Fiona McIntosh* 56c, 77, 79-80.
*Jean du Plessis* 26c, 27b, 29a.
*Jeremy Jowell* 81ac.

### IMAGES OF AFRICA
*Ariadne van Zandbergen* 20bcd, 23ac, 39a, 41b,
42acd, 49; 51a, 52-55, 56b, 57ab, 58; 60c, 64d,
69a, 72; 74a, 75a, 76, 81bd. *Alain Proust* 82abc.
*Andrew Bannister* 6c, 31, 67, 68bc, 69c, 70a,
71abd. *Colour Library* 16c 36a.
*Chanan Weiss* 10c, 16a, 28ab, 29c, 30a, 56a,
61bc, 69bd, 71c.
*Hein von Horsten* 6d, 14ad, 17a.
*Daryl & Sharna Balfour* 4b, 65a, 68a, 70bc.
*Erhardt Thiel* 9a. *Gerhard Dreyer* 13bd.
*Ian Michler* 4a, 26a, 33a, 34abd, spreads 43-48,
51bcd. *Jacques Marais* 7b.
*Keith Begg* 38, 40c, 41ad. *Keith Young* 9c, 13c.
*Lanz von Horsten* 6a, 22ad, 23d.
*Leonard Hoffmann* 10b, 14b, 20a.
*Mark Skinner* 3a; 37.
*Martin Harvey* 5a&b, 6b, 9b, 24; 26d, 27a&c,
28c, 29b, 30bc, 31, 32bcd, 33bc, 34c, 35, 78.
*Nigel J Dennis* 14c, 16b, 22bce, 36bd, 92.
*Peter Blackwell* 5c, 50, 60ab, 61a, 62d, 63abcd,
64ab, 65d, 73, 74c, 75bc. *Rod Haestier* 18a.
*Peter Pickford* 15ab, 26b, 32a.
*Peter Ribton* 4c, 57c, 62abc, 64c, 65bc.
*Roger de la Harpe* 5d, 19bc, 39bcde, 40abd, 41c,
42b. *Ryno* 12c.
*Shaen Adey* 3b, 7a, 10a, 11, 12abd, 15c, 17bcd,
18bc, 21a, 23b. *Tony Camacho* 36c, 74b.
*Walter Knirr* 13a, 19d, 21bcd.